STRAPAROLA.

Volume I.

British Library Cataloguing-in-Publication Data
A catalogue record for this book is available from
the British Library

THE NIGHTS

OF

STRAPAROLA

BY

GIOVANNI FRANCESCO STRAPAROLA

NOW FIRST TRANSLATED INTO ENGLISH BY

W. G. WATERS

ILLUSTRATED BY E. R. HUGHES, A.R.W.S

VOLUME I

Contents.

ILLUSTRATIONS TO VOL. I.

Introduction.

HE name of Giovanni Francesco Straparola has been handed down to later ages as the author of the "Piacevoli Notti," and on no other account, for the reason that he is one of those fortunate men of letters concerning whom next to nothing is known. He writes himself down as "da Caravaggio;" so it may be reasonably assumed that he first saw the light in that town, but no investigator has yet succeeded in indicating the year of his birth, or in bringing to light any circumstances of his life, other than certain facts connected with the authorship and publication of his works. The ground has been closely searched more than once, and in every case the seekers have come back compelled to admit that they have no story to tell or new fact to add to the scanty stock which has been already garnered. Straparola as a personage still remains the shadow he was when La Monnoie summed up the little that was known about him in the preface to the edition, published in 1725, of the French translation of the "Notti."

He was doubtless baptized by the Christian names given above, but it is scarcely probable that Straparola can ever have been the surname or style of any family in Caravaggio or elsewhere. More likely than not it is an instance of the Italian predilection for nicknaming—a coined word designed to exhibit and perhaps to hold up to ridicule his undue loquacity; just as the familiar names of Masaccio, and Ghirlandaio, and Guercino, were tacked on to their illustrious wearers on account of some personal peculiarity or former calling. Caravaggio is a small town lying near to Crema, and about half way between Cremona and Bergamo. It enjoyed in the Middle Ages some fame as a place of pilgrimage on account of a spring of healing water which gushed forth on a certain occasion when the Virgin Mary manifested herself. Polidoro Caldara and Michael Angelo Caravaggio were amongst its famous men, and of these it keeps the memory, but Straparola is entirely forgotten. Fontanini, in the "Biblioteca dell' eloquenza Italiana," does not name him at all. Quadrio, "Storia e ragione d'ogni poesia," mentions him as the author of the "Piacevoli Notti," and remarks on his borrowings from Morlini. Tiraboschi, in the index to the "Storia della letteratura Italiana," does not even give his name, and Crescimbeni [1] concerns himself only with the enigmas which are to be found at the end of the fables. It is indeed a strange freak of chance that such complete oblivion should have fallen over the individuality of a writer so widely read and appreciated.

The first edition of the first part of the "Piacevoli Notti" was published at Venice in 1550, and of the second part in 1553. It would appear that the author must have been alive in 1557, because, at the end of the second part of the edition of that year,[2] there is a paragraph setting forth the fact that the work was printed and issued "ad instanza dell' autore." Some time before 1553 he seems to have been stung sharply on account of some charges of plagiarism which were brought against him by certain detractors, for in all the unmutilated editions of the "Notti" published after that date there is to be found a short introduction to the second part, in which he somewhat acrimoniously throws back these accusations, and calls upon all "gratiose et amorevole donne" to accept his explanations thereof, admitting at the same time that these stories are not his own, but a faithful transcript of what he heard told by the ten damsels in their pleasant assembly. La Monnoie, in his preface to the French translation (ed. 1726), maintains that this juggling with words can only be held to be an excuse on his part for having borrowed the subject-matter for his fables and worked it into shape after his own taste. "Il declare qu'il ne se les est jamais attribuées, et se contente du mérite de les avoir fidèlement rapportées d'après les dix damoiselles. Cela, comme tout bon entendeur le comprend, ne signifie autre chose sinon qu'il avoit tiré d'ailleurs la matière de ces Fables, mais qu'il leur avoit donné la forme."

---

[1] "Istoria della volgar poesia" (Ven. 1731).

[2] In 1556 the two parts were first issued bearing the same date, but with a different title-page.

This contention of La Monnoie seems reasonable enough, but Grimm, in the notes to "Kinder und Hausmärchen," has fallen into the strange error of treating Straparola's apology as something grave and seriously meant, and in the same sentence improves on his mistake by asserting that Straparola took all the fairy tales from the mouths of the ten ladies. "Von jenem Schmutz sind die Märchen[1] ziemlich frei, wie sie ohnehin den besten Theil des ganzen Werkes ausmachen. Straparola hat sie, wie es in der Vorrede zum zweiten Bande (vor der sechsten Nacht) heisst, aus dem Munde zehn junger Fräulein aufgenommen und ausdrücklich erklärt, dass sie nicht sein Eigenthum seien."

The most reasonable explanation of this mistake lies in the assumption that Grimm never saw the introduction to the second part at all. Indeed, the fact that he often uses French spelling of the proper names suggests that he may have worked from the French translation. Straparola makes no distinction between fairy tales and others. His words are, "che le piacevoli favole da me scritte, et in questo, et nell' altro volumetto raccolte non siano mie, ma da questo, et quello ladronescamente rubbate. Io a dir il vero, il confesso, che non sono mie, e se altrimente dicessi, me ne mentirei, ma ben holle fedelmente scritte secondo il modo che furono da dieci damigelle nel concistorio raccontate."

Besides the "Notti" only one other work of Straparola's is known to exist—a collection of sonnets and other poems published at Venice in 1508, and (according to a citation of Zanetti in the "Novelliero Italiano," t. iii., p. xv, Ven. 1754, Bindoni) in 1515 as well.[2] A comparison of these dates will serve to show that, as he had already brought out a volume in the first decade of the century, the "Piacevoli Notti" must have been the work of his maturity or even of his old age. With this fact the brief catalogue of the known circumstances of his life comes to an end.

Judging from the rapidity with which the successive editions of

---

[1] To add to the confusion, the English translator of Grimm gives "stories" as the equivalent for "Märchen."

[2] M. Jannet in his preface to the "Facétieuses Nuits de Straparole" (Paris, 1857), says he has not been able to find a copy of this work in any library. There is one in the British Museum, under the title, "Opera nova da Zoan Francesco Streparola da Caravazo novamēte stampata Sonetti CXV., Strabotti XXXV., Epistole VII., Capitoli XII." (Ven. 1508, per Georgio de Ruschoni).

the "Notti" were brought forth from the press after the first issue —sixteen appeared in the twenty years between 1550 and 1570—we may with reason assume that it soon took hold of the public favour.[1] Its fame spread early into France, where in 1560 an edition of the first part, translated into French by Jean Louveau, appeared at Lyons, to be followed some thirteen years later by a translation of the second part by Pierre de la Rivey, who thus completed the book. He likewise revised and re-wrote certain portions of Louveau's translation, and in 1725 an edition was produced at Amsterdam, enriched by a preface by La Monnoie, and notes by Lainez. There are evidences that a German translation of the "Notti" was in existence at the beginning of the seventeenth century, for in the introduction to Fischart's "Gargantua" (1608) there is an allusion to the tales of Straparola, brought in by way of an apology for the appearance of the work, the writer maintaining that, if the ears of the ladies are not offended by Boccaccio, Straparola, and other writers of a similar character, there is no reason why they should be offended by Rabelais. The author of the introduction to a fresh edition of the same work (1775) remarks that he knows the tales of Straparola from a later edition published in 1699. Of this translation no copy is known to exist.

In the "Palace of Pleasure" Painter has given only one of the fables, the second Fable[2] of the second Night; and in Roscoe's "Italian Novelists" another one appears, the fourth Fable of the tenth Night. At the end of the last century the first Fable of the first Night was printed separately in London under the title, "Novella cioe copia d'un Caso notabile intervenuto a un gran gentiluomo Genovese."[3] A translation of twenty-four of the fables, prefaced by a lengthy and verbose disquisition on the author, reputed to be from the pen of Mazzuchelli, appeared at Vienna in 1791;[4] but Brackel-

---

[1] The "Decameron" did not reach its sixteenth edition till fifty years after its first publication.

[2] In his introduction to the recent edition of Painter, Mr. Joseph Jacobs cites the presence of this fable as an argument that Painter must occasionally have translated directly from the Italian. There is no reason, however, why he should not have used Louveau's work.

[3] It was published with seven other stories in a volume, "Novelle otto rarissime stampate a spese de Signor Giacomo conte de Clambrassil, J. Stanley, et Wogan Browne. Londra, Giacomo Edwards, 1790."

[4] Brackelmann says that it was a selection from the first six nights, while Grimm

mann, in his "Inaugural Dissertation" (Gottingen, 1867), has an examination of the introduction above named, which goes far to prove that Mazzuchelli had little or nothing to do with it. In 1817 Dr. F. W. V. Schmidt published at Berlin a translation into German of eighteen fables selected from the "Notti," to which he gave the title "Die Märchen des Straparola." To his work Dr. Schmidt affixed copious notes, compiled with the greatest care and learning, thus opening to his successors a rich and valuable storehouse both of suggestion and of accumulated facts. It is almost certain that he must have worked from one of the many mutilated or expurgated editions of the book, for in the complete work there are several stories unnoticed by him which he would assuredly have included in his volume had he been aware of their existence.

One of the chief claims of the "Notti" on the consideration of later times lies in the fact that Straparola was the first writer who gathered together into one collection the stray fairy tales, for the most part brought from the East, which had been made known in the Italian cities—and in Venice more especially—by the mouth of the itinerant story-teller. These tales, incorporated in the "Notti" with others of a widely different character, were without doubt the principal source of the numerous French "Contes des Fées" published in the seventeenth and eighteenth centuries. Perrault, Madame D'Aulnoy, and Gueulette took from them many of their best fables; and these, having spread in various forms through Northern and Western Europe, helped to tinge with a hue of Orientalism the popular tales of all countries—tales which had hitherto been largely the evolution of local myths and traditions.

Four of Straparola's fables are slightly altered versions of four of the stories in the "Thousand and One Nights,"[1] which, as it will scarcely be necessary to remark, were not translated into any European language till Galland brought out his work at the beginning of the eighteenth century. One of these, the third Fable of the fourth Night, is substantially the same as the story of the Princess Parizade

maintains that it contains the whole of these, and Grimm's English translator says that it "only contains six stories." In fact, it is made up chiefly of the contents of the first six nights, but in addition to these it contains fables from Nights VII., VIII., and XIII. It would appear that neither Dunlop nor Schmidt knew of the existence of this work.

[1] Night IV., Fable I.; Night IV., Fable III.; Night V., Fable III., and Night XII., Fable III.

and her envious sisters, given in Galland's translation. To account
for this close resemblance we may either assume that Galland may
have looked at Straparola's fable, or that Straparola may have listened
to it from the mouth of some wandering oriental or of some Venetian
traveller recently come back from the East—the tale, as he heard it,
having been faithfully taken from the same written page which
Galland afterwards translated. Another one, the story of the Three
Hunchbacks—the third Fable of the fifth Night—has less likeness to the original, and has been imitated by Gueulette in his
"Contes Tartares." The treatment of the story of the Princess
Parizade by Straparola furnishes an illustration to prove that, bad as
his style was, he was by no means deficient in literary skill and taste.
He brings into due prominence the wicked midwife, who is *particeps
criminis* with the queen-mother and the sisters in the attempted
murder of the children, and who has on this account full and valid
motive for acting as she did, seeing that interest and self-preservation
as well would have prompted her to compass their destruction. On
the other hand, in the Arabian tale it is hard to understand why the
female fakir should have been led to persuade the princess to send
her brothers off on their quest. Again, in the fable of Prince
Guerrino[1] Straparola has displayed great ingenuity in weaving
together a good story out of some half dozen of the widely-known
fairy motives, any one of which might well have been fashioned into
a story by itself.

After reading the "Notti" through one can hardly fail to be struck
by the amazing variety of the themes therein handled. Besides the fairy
tales—many of them classic—to which allusion has already been made,
there is the world-famous story of Puss in Boots, an original product
of Straparola's brain. There are others which may rather be classed as
romances of chivalry, in the elaboration of which a generous amount of
magic and mystery is employed. The residue is made up of stories of intrigue and buffo tales of popular Italian life, some of which—not a large
number, when one takes into consideration the contemporary standard
of decency in such matters—are certainly unpleasant in subject and
coarse in treatment, but with regard to the majority of these one is
disposed to be lenient, inasmuch as the fun, though somewhat in-
delicate, is real fun. When the duped husband, a figure almost as

---

[1] Night V., Fable I.

inevitable in the Italian Novella as in the modern French novel, is brought forward, he is not always exhibited as the contemptible creature who seems to have sat for the part in the stories of the better known writers. Indeed, it sometimes happens that he turns the tables on his betrayers ; and, although Straparola is laudably free from the vice of preaching, he now and then indulges in a brief homily by way of pointing out the fact that violators of the Decalogue generally come to a bad end, and that his own sympathies are all on the side of good manners. It is true that one misses in the "Notti" those delicious invocations of Boccaccio, commonly to be found at the end of the more piquant stories, in which he piously calls on Heaven to grant to himself and to all Christian men *bonnes fortunes* equal to those which he has just chronicled.

The scheme of the "Notti" resembles in character that of the Decameron, of Le Cene, and of other collections of a similar kind. In the Proem to the work it is set forth how Ottaviano Maria Sforza, the bishop-elect of Lodi—the same probably who died in 1540, after a life full of vicissitude—together with his daughter Lucretia, is compelled by the stress of political events to quit Milan. The Signora Lucretia is described as the wife of Giovanni Francesco Gonzaga, cousin of Federico, Marquis of Mantua, but as no mention of this prince is made it may be assumed that she was already a widow. Seeing that her husband died in 1523, an approximate date may be fixed for the "Piacevoli Notti," but historical accuracy in cases of this sort is not to be expected or desired. After divers wanderings the bishop-elect and his daughter find a pleasant refuge on the island of Murano, where they gather around them a company of congenial spirits, consisting of a group of lovely and accomplished damsels, and divers cavaliers of note. Chief amongst the latter is the learned Pietro Bembo, the renowned humanist and the most distinguished man of letters Venice ever produced. With him came his friend Gregorio Casali, who is described as "Casal Bolognese, a bishop, and likewise ambassador of the King of England." Both Gregorio Casali and his brother Battista were entrusted by Henry VIII. with the conduct of affairs of state pending between him and the Pope, and the former certainly visited England more than once. The king showed him many signs of favour during his stay, and when in 1527 Casali found himself shut up in Rome by the beleaguering army of the Constable of Bourbon, he was allowed free exit on the ground of his ambassa-

c

dorial rank. Bernardo Cappello, another friend of Bembo, is also of the company, and a certain Antonio Molino, a poet of repute, who subsequently tells a fable in the dialect of Bergamo—a feat which leads to a similar display of local knowledge on the part of Signor Benedetto Trivigiano, who discourses in Trevisan. It may be remarked, however, that by far the greater number of the fables are told by the ladies.

But the joyous company assembled in the palace at Murano find divers other forms of recreation beside story-telling. They dance and they sing ballads, which are for the most part in praise of the gracious Signora Lucretia, but the chief byplay of the entertainment consists in the setting and solving of riddles. As soon as a fable is brought to an end the narrator is always called upon by the Signora to complete the task by propounding an enigma. This is then duly set forth in puzzling verses, put together as a rule in terms obscure enough to baffle solution, often entirely senseless, and now and again of a character indecent enough to call down upon the propounder the Signora's rebuke on account of the seeming impropriety of the subject. In fact, a certain number of these enigmas are broad examples of the *double entendre*. The first reading of them makes one wonder how such matter could ever have been put in print, and agree fully with the anger of the Signora, but when the graceful and modest damsel, who may have been the author, proceeds to give the true explanation of her riddle she never fails to demonstrate clearly to the gentle company that her enigma, from beginning to end, is entirely free from all that is unseemly. In " French and English " Mr. Philip Gilbert Hamerton tells a story illustrating the late survival of this sort of witticism in France. In the early days of Louis Philippe, on one occasion when the court was at Eu, the mayor of the town and certain other local notables were bidden to *déjeuner* at the chateau, and after the banquet the mayor, in accordance with an old French fashion, asked leave to sing a song of his own making. This composition had two meanings, one lying on the surface and perfectly innocent, and the other, slightly veiled, which, though not immoral, was prodigiously indecent. When the true nature of the song was realized, there was for a second or two silence and confusion amongst the company, but at last, by good luck, someone laughed. The dangerous point was safely rounded, and the mayor brought his song to an end amidst loud applause.

When he published his translation into French of the second

part of the "Notti," Pierre de la Rivey made alterations in almost all
the enigmas therein contained, and re-wrote many of those which had
already been translated by Louveau, but in neither case did his work
tend to make them more decent. In reading over the enigmas as
Straparola left them one often feels that the line of reticence, recognized by contemporary decorum, has been crossed, otherwise there
would be no need for the ladies to hide their faces, or for the Signora
to visit the culprit for the time being with her well-deserved rebuke.
But Straparola's untouched work is almost decent compared with De
la Rivey's emendations.

In spite of the blots above designated, there will be found in the
"Notti" a smaller proportion of stories calculated to outrage modern
canons of taste than in any of the better known collections of Italian
novelle. The judgments which have been dealt out to Straparola on
the score of indecency by Landau ("Beiträge," p. 130), by the writer
of the article in the "Biographie Universelle," and by Grimm in his
notes to "Kinder und Hausmärchen," seem to be unduly severe.
In certain places he is no doubt brutally coarse, but the number of
fables defaced in this manner is not large. If one were to take the
trouble to compare the rendering given by Basile in the "Pentame-
rone," of stories told also by Straparola, with the rendering of the
same in the "Notti," the award for propriety of language would
assuredly not always be given to the Neapolitan, who, it should be
remembered, was writing a book for young children. In few of
the collections of a similar character is there to be found so genuine
a vein of comedy, and for the sake of this one may perhaps be permitted to beg indulgence for occasional lapses—lapses which are
assuredly fewer in number and probably not more heinous in character
than those of novelists of greater fame. Straparola turns naturally
towards the cheerful side of things, the lives of the men and women
he deals with seem to be less oppressed with the *tædium vitæ* than
are the creatures of the Florentine and Sienese and Neapolitan novel-
writers, and the reason of this is not far to seek. Life in Venice,
when once the political constitution was firmly and finally fixed on an
oligarchic basis, was more stable, more secure, more luxurious than
in any of the other ruling cities of Italy. Social and political con-
vulsion of the sort which vexed the neighbouring states was almost
unknown, and, though the forces of the Republic might occasionally
suffer defeat and disaster in distant seas and in the Levant, life went

on peacefully and pleasantly within the shelter of the Lagunes. The
religious conscience of the people was easy-going, orthodox, and
laudably inclined to listen to the voice of authority; neither disposed
to nourish within the hidden canker of heresy, nor to let itself be
worked up into ecstatic fever by any sudden conviction of ungodli-
ness such as led to the lighting of the Bonfire of Vanities in Florence.
In a society thus constituted it was inevitable that life should be
easier, more gladsome, and more secure than in Milan, with the constant struggle of Pope against Emperor, and later on under the
turbulent despotism of the Viscontis and Sforzas; or than in
Florence, with its constant civil broils and licentious public life, which
not even the craft and power of the leaders of the Medici could dis-
cipline into public order; or than in Naples, dominated by the
Aragonese kings and harried by the greedy mercenaries in the royal
employ; or than in Rome itself, vexed continually by intrigue, political and religious, and by the tumults generated by the violence and
ambition of the ruling families.

A reflection of the gracious and placid life the Venetians led will
be apparent to all who may observe and compare the art of Venice
with the art of Milan, or Florence, or Naples. What a contrast is
there between that charming idyll which Titian has made of the
marriage of St. Catherine,[1] a group full of joy, and beauty, and sun-
light, and set in the midst of one of those delightful sub-alpine
landscapes which he painted with such rare skill and insight, and the
many other renderings of the same subject by Lombard or Tuscan
masters, who, almost invariably, put on the canvas some foreshadow-
ing of the coming tragedy in the shape of the boding horror of the
toothed wheel! The Madonnas of Carpaccio and Bellini are stately
ladies, well nourished, and having about them that unmistakable
air of distinction which grows up with the daily use and neighbour-
hood of splendid and luxurious modes of life. There is no doubt a
look of gravity and holiness upon their handsome faces, but there is
no sign, either in the pose or in the glance of them, that they are
conscious of any embarrassment, and it would take a very keen eye
to discern a trace of quasi-divinity, or of any trouble aroused by the
caress of the mysterious child, or of the burden of that " intolerable
honour " which has been thrust upon them unsought—a mood which

---

[1] In the National Gallery.

latter-day preachers have detected in renderings of the same theme conceived and executed in the more emotional atmosphere of the Val d'Arno. Take these Venetian Madonnas out of their pictured environment, and put on them a gala dress and sumptuous jewels, and one will find a bevy of comely dames who might well have kept company with the Signora Lucretia of the " Notti " in the fair garden at Murano, and listened to some sprightly story from Messer Pietro Bembo or from Messer Antonio Molino; or they might have gone out with the youths and damsels of whom Browning sings,

> "Did young people take their pleasure when the sea was warm in May ?
> Balls and masks begun at midnight, burning ever to mid-day,
> When they made up fresh adventures for the morrow, do you say ?"

In the pictures he draws Straparola illustrates a life like this, with now and then a touch of pathos, perhaps undesigned, as in the prologue to the second Night, where he tells of the laughter of the blithe company, ringing so loud and so hearty that it seemed to him as if the sound of their merriment yet lingered in his ears.[1] There was, therefore, good reason why Straparola's imaginary exiles from the turbulent court of Milan should have sought at Murano, under the sheltering wings of St. Mark's lion, that ease and gaiety which they would have looked for in vain at home ; there were also reasons equally valid why he should make the genius of the place inspire with its jocund spirit the stories with which the gentle company gathered around the Signora Lucretia wiled away the nights of carnival. In the whole of the seventy-four fables there are hardly half-a-dozen which can be classed as tragic in tone, but of these one—the story of Malgherita Spolatina[2]—is the finest of the whole collection. It is rarely one meets with anything told with such force and sincerity ; yet, in placing before his readers this vivid picture of volcanic passion and studied ruthless revenge, Straparola uses the simplest treatment and succeeds à merveille. The fact that this fable and certain others of more than average merit belong to the category of stories to which no source or origin in other writings has been assigned, raises a regret that Straparola did not trust more to his own inventive powers and draw less freely upon Ser Giovanni and Morlini. Of these creations of his own the story of Flamminio Veraldo[3] is admirably

---

[1] *Di che le donne, et parimente gli huomini fecero si gran risa che ancora ridono.*
[2] Night VII., Fable II.   [3] Night IV., Fable V.

told and strikingly original and dramatic in subject; so is that of Maestro Lattantio,[1] and, for a display of savage cynicism and withering rage, it would be hard to find anything more powerfully portrayed than the death of Andrigetto.[2]

In the fables of adventure, and in every other case where such treatment is possible, Straparola deals largely with the supernatural. All the western versions, except Straparola's, of the story best known to us as " Giletta of Narbonne " and as " All's Well that Ends Well," are worked out without calling in auxiliaries of an unearthly character. Boccaccio and Shakespeare bring together the husband and the forsaken wife by methods which, if somewhat strained, are quite natural; but Straparola at once calls for the witch and the magic horse, and whisks Isabella off to Flanders forthwith.[3] The interest of the reader is kept alive by accounts of the trials and dangers—a trifle bizarre now and again—which heroes and heroines are called to undergo, the taste of the age preferring apparently this stimulant to the intense dramatic power exhibited in the story of Malgherita, and demanding that the ending should be a happy one, for the pair of lovers nearly always marry in the end, and live long and blissful years. In the tales of country life and character the fun is boisterous and even broad, but it is always real fun, and the laugh rings true. Straparola is often as coarse as Bandello, but, unlike Bandello, he never smirches his pages merely for the sake of setting forth some story of simple brutality, or of leading up to a climax which is at the same time painfully shocking and purposeless. Il Lasca in " Le Cene " makes as free use of the *beffe* and the *burle* as Straparola, but the last-named showed in the " Notti " that he was incomparably the better hand in dealing with his material. Il Lasca as a rule sets out his subject on the lines of the broadest farce, but he cannot keep to genuine farce, his natural bent of mind leading him always to elaborate his theme in some unseemly and offensive fashion. Very often he is obscene and savage at the same time, and the abominable practical jokes he makes his characters play the one on the other must surely have outraged even the coarse feeding taste of the age in which he wrote. He delights in working up long stories of lust, and of infidelity, and of vengeance worked on account of these, in a spirit of heartless cruelty which, more often than not, is horrible without being in the least impressive, for the

---

[1] Night VIII., Fable V.   [2] Night X., Fable IV.
[3] Night VII., Fable I.

reason that, fine stylist as he was, he lacked the touch of the artist. Masuccio, though his savage indignation against the vices of the priests and monks occasionally became mere brutality, sounded now and then the note of real tragedy, and, inferior as he was to Il Lasca in style, was by far the better story-teller of the two. Both of these would be commonly set down as abler writers than Straparola, yet, by some means or other, the latter could put a touch upon his work which was beyond the power of the others—something which enables one to read the "Notti" without being conscious of that unpleasant aftertaste which one almost always feels on laying down either "Le Cene" or "Il Novellino."

No other of the Italian novelists used a style as bad as Straparola's. Errors in grammar abound, and his bald meagre periods often fail to express adequately the sense of the idea he manifestly wishes to portray. His faulty prose did not escape the censure of his contemporaries, for Messer Orfeo dalla Carta, in his introduction to the first part of the "Notti" (edition 1554), makes allusion to it, begging the reader at the same time not to be repelled by what he calls "il basso et rimesso stilo dello autore;" and La Monnoie, in the preface to the French translation (edition 1726) writes in a similar strain. Dalla Carta, probably by way of banter, advances an apology for Straparola's slovenly work in terms taken from that introduction to the second part which has already been cited, explaining that the author did not write his fables as he would have done, but as they had been told to him by the ten damsels who were the narrators.

Straparola's Italian is much more like the Italian of the present day than the English of Sidney or the German of Hans Sachs is like modern English or German, but this is not remarkable, considering how much earlier prose writing as an art came to perfection in Italy than in the rest of Europe. The impression gained by reading his prose is that he cared vastly more for subject than for treatment. He laid hold of whatever themes promised to suit his purpose best as a story-teller, careless as to whether other craftsmen had used them before or not, and these he set forth in the simplest manner possible, taking little heed of his style or even of his grammar. He hardly ever indulges in a metaphor. One never feels that he has gone searching about fastidiously for some particular turn of phrase or neatly-fitting adjective; on the other hand, one is often obliged to pause in the middle of some long sentence and search for his meaning in the strange mixture of phrases strung together. Perhaps this spontaneity, this absence of studied design, may have helped to win for him the wide popularity he enjoyed. His aim was to lead his readers into some enchanted garden of fairyland; to thrill them with the woes and perils of his heroes and heroines; to shake their sides with laughter over the misadventures of some too amorous monk or lovesick cavalier, rather than to send them into ecstasy over the measured elegance of his phrases. In many of the later editions of the " Notti," the meaning has been further obscured, and the style rendered more rugged than ever, owing to the frequent and clumsy excisions made by the censors of morals. The early exclusion of the fourth Fable of the ninth Night shows that the eye of authority was soon attracted towards the popular novelist of the age. The motive for this activity was nominally the care of public morals, and one of the few extant references to Straparola is with regard to the expurgation of his works. In " Cremona Illustrata," by Franciscus Arisius (Cremona, 1741), we read concerning Caravaggio : " In hoc enim oppido inclytæ stirpis Sfortiadum antiquo feudo ortum habuit Io. Franciscus Straparola cujus liber sæpe editus circumfertur italice hoc programmate : 'Le tredici piacevolissime notti overo favole ed enimmi.' Liber vetitus a sacra indicis congregatione et jure quidem merito cum obscenitates sordidas contineat moribus plerumque obnoxias et pluribi vulgatas. Optime quippe animadvertit Possevinus S. J. de cultura ingeniorum cap. 52, quod expediens esset homines potius nasci mutos et rationis expertes, quam in propriam et aliorum perniciam divinæ providentiæ dona convertere, imo ante eum ejusdem sententiæ fuisse M. F. Quintilianum licet gentilem, ipse Possevinus confirmat."

On reading even the most severely castrated edition of the "Notti," one may be at first a little surprised to find that some of the most indecent stories (in spite of the care of public morals) have been left almost untouched, and it is not until one realizes the fact that expurgation has been held to mean the cutting out of every word concerning religion and its professors, that one fully under-stands the principle upon which " Possevinus S. J." and his colleagues worked. The presence of matter injurious to public morals had evidently less to do with the action of these reformers than certain anecdotes describing the presence of priests and nuns in certain places where, by every rule of good manners, they ought not to have been found. In plain words, the book was prohibited and castrated on

account of the ugly picture of clerical morals which was exhibited in
its pages.[1]   A glance at any of the editions issued " con licenza de'
superiori" will show that the revisers went to their work with set
purpose, caring nought as to the mangled mass of letterpress they
might leave behind them.   In some fables bits are cut out so
clumsily that the point of the story is entirely lost; in others the
feelings of orthodoxy are spared by changing the hero of amorous
intrigue from a *Prete* to a *Giovene*.   In one a pope is reduced to a
mere initial (of course standing for a layman), and the famous story
of Belphegor is left out altogether.   It was surely little short of im-
pertinent to ask for a condemnation of the " Notti " on the ground
of offence to public decency from a generation which read such
books as " Les facétieuses journées" of Chapuys and " Les contes
aux heures perdues;" which witnessed the issue of Morlini's novels
and of Cinthio degli Fabritii's book, " Dell' origine delli volgari
proverbii," printed "cum privilegio summi pontificis et sacræ
Cæsareæ majestatis;" a generation for which Poggio's obscene fables
were favourite reading, and which remembered that Pietro Bembo
had been a cardinal and Giovanni di Medici a pope.

It is impossible to indicate precisely the sources of the fables
seriatim, seeing that in many cases there was available for Straparola
a choice of origins.   An approximate reckoning would give fifteen
fables to the novelists who preceded him, twenty-two to Morlini,
four to mediæval and seven to oriental legends, thus leaving twenty-
eight to be classed as original.   Towards the close of his work
it would appear that his imagination must have been stricken with
sterility, or that he became indolent, for of the concluding twenty
fables nineteen are mere translations from Morlini.   It is not impro-
bable that such wholesale borrowing as this may have been the
cause of the charges of plagiary to which allusion has already been
made.   From beginning to end he certainly made free use of all the
storehouses of materials which were available, selecting therefrom
whatever subjects pleased him, and working them up to the best of

---

[1] " Die XIII. nächtlichen Erzählungen sammt den Logogryphen welche Argellati,
'ingeniosissime conflata quamvis parum pudice,' nennt wurden zu Rom durch das
Decret vom 16ten Dec. 1605, einigen darin enthaltenen unzüchtigen Stellen wegen
verbothen" (preface to Vienna translation, 1791).   The book must have been condemned by the index some time before this, as the issue of 1604, Ven., "con licenza
de' Superiori " is rigorously castrated.

d

his skill. It was unreasonable to censure him on this score, seeing that in what he did he merely followed the fashion of the age. If he borrowed from Ser Giovanni, had not Ser Giovanni borrowed also from the " Directorium " and the " Gesta Romanorum "? Folk-lorists have discovered for us the fact that all the stories the world ever listened to may, by proper classification, be shown to be derived from some half-dozen sources. As the sorting and searching goes on, new facts constantly come to light, the drift of which tends to prove that the charge of plagiarism is now almost meaningless. It is hard to say what new and strange fruits may not be gathered from the wide field now covered by the folk-lorist. Formerly he hunted only in the East; now we find him amongst the Lapps and the Zulus—in Labrador, and in the South Pacific as well. A still more extended search will very likely find a fresh source for those of the fables in the " Notti " which have heretofore been classed as the original work of Straparola, and will discover for us a new and genuine author of " Puss in Boots."

Orfeo dalla Carta to all delightful and
lovesome ladies, greeting.

CONSIDERING in my mind, kindly ladies, how many
in number and how high in excellence are those heaven-
born and lofty spirits who, in ancient and in modern
times as well, have written down those various fables
which, when you read them, give you no small
pleasure, I understand—and you in like manner will
understand—that they were moved thus to write for no other reason
than to give you solace and entertainment. Since I opine, or rather
since I am certain that this is the case, you, delightful and lovesome
ladies as you are, will not be wroth if I, your good servant, shall publish
in your name the Fables and the Enigmas of the ingenious Messer
Gioanfrancesco Straparola da Caravaggio, set forth by him with no
less elegance than learning. And even if the substance of these should
not furnish for your hearing the same pleasure and delight as you are
accustomed to find in certain other writers, do not on this account
contemn him by thrusting him aside and rejecting him altogether, but
rather with joyful faces take him to you as you are accustomed to take
the others; because if you, as you read his pages, will bear in mind
the diversity of events and the subtle wit contained therein, you will
at least derive from them no small instruction.

Besides this, you must not remark too narrowly the poor and
negligent style of the author, for the reason that he wrote his fables,
not as he wished to write them, but as he heard them from the ladies

who related them,[1] adding nought thereunto and taking nought there-from.   And if you shall find him in any respect wanting, blame not him, who did his work to the best of his power and knowledge, but blame me who have published it against his wish.   Accept, therefore, with gladsome looks this little gift from me your servant; who, if it be shown to him (as he hopes it may) that his offering is pleasing to you, will in the future do his best to lay before you other things which may prove to be still more to your pleasure and contentment.   Be happy and remember me!

From Venice on the XI. day of January, MDLIIII.

[1] " Ma ben holle fedelmente scritte secondo il modo, che furono da dieci damigelle nel concistorio raccontate."—STRAPAROLA, *Introduction to Book II.*

Proem.

The Fables and Enigmas of Messer Giovanni Francesco Straparola da Caravaggio.

Book the First.

PROEM.

IN Milan, the capital of Lombardy, an ancient city abounding in graceful ladies, adorned with sumptuous palaces, and rich in all those things which are fitted to so magnificent a town, there resided Ottaviano Maria Sforza, Bishop-elect of Lodi, to whom by claim of heredity (Francesco Sforza, Duke of Milan, being dead) the sovereignty of the state rightfully belonged. But through the falling in of evil times, through bitter hatreds, through bloody battles, and through the never-ending vicissitudes of state affairs, he departed thence and betook himself secretly to Lodi with his daughter Lucretia, the wife of Giovanni Francesco Gonzaga, cousin of Federico, Marquis of Mantua, and there they abode some months. Long time had not passed before his kinsmen discovered his whereabouts, and began forthwith to annoy him; so the unhappy prince, finding himself still the object of their ill will, took with him what jewels and money he had about him, and withdrew with his daughter, who was already a widow, to Venice, where they found friendly reception from Ferier Beltramo, a noble gentleman of most benevolent nature, amiable and graceful, who with great courtesy gave them pressing invitation to take up their abode in his own house. But to share the home of another generally begets restraint, so the duke, after mature deliberation, resolved to depart and to find elsewhere a dwelling of his own. Wherefore, embarking one day with his daughter in a small vessel, he went to Morano, and having come there his eyes fell upon a marvellously beautiful palace which at that time stood empty. He entered it, and having taken note of its lovely position, its lofty halls, its superb loggias, its pleasant gardens filled with smiling flowers and rich in all sorts of fruit and blooming herbs, he found them all highly to his taste. Then he mounted the marble staircase and surveyed the magnificent hall, the exquisite chambers, and the balcony built over the water, which commanded a view of the whole place. The princess, captivated by the charm of the pleasant spot, besought her father so strongly with soft and tender speeches, that he to please her fancy hired the palace for their home. Over this she rejoiced greatly, for morning and evening she would go upon the balcony to watch the scaly fish which swam about in numerous shoals through the clear salt water, and in seeing them dart about now here now there she took the greatest delight. And because she was now forsaken by the ladies who had formerly been about her court, she chose in their places ten others as beautiful as they were good; indeed, time would fail wherein to describe their virtues and their graces. Of these the first was Lodovica, who had lovely eyes sparkling like the brightest stars, and everyone who looked upon her could not but admire her greatly. The next was Vicenza, of excellent carriage, of fine figure, and of polished manners, whose lovely and delicate face shone with refreshing beauty upon all who beheld it. The third was Lionora, who, although by the natural fashion of her beauty she seemed somewhat haughty, was withal as kindly and courteous as any lady to be found in all the world. The fourth was Alteria, with lovely fair hair, who held her womanly devotion ever at the service of the Signora. The fifth was Lauretta, lovely in person, but somewhat disdainful, whose clear and languishing glances surely enslaved any lover who ventured to court them. The sixth was Eritrea, who, though she was small of stature, yielded to none of the others in beauty and grace, seeing that she had two brilliant eyes, sparkling even brighter than the sun's rays, a small mouth, and a rounded bosom, nor was there to be found in her anything at all which was not worthy of the highest praise. The seventh was Cateruzza, surnamed Brunetta, who, all graceful and amorous as she was, with her sweet and loving words entangled not only men in her snares, but could even have made descend from heaven the mighty Jove himself. The eighth was Arianna, who, though young in years, was grave and sedate in her seeming, gifted with a fluent tongue, and encompassed with divine virtues, worthy of the highest praise, which shone like the stars scattered about the heavens. The ninth was Isabella, a highly-gifted damsel, and one who, on account of her wit and skilful fence of tongue, commanded the admiration of the whole company. The last was Fiordiana, a prudent damsel, with a mind stored with worthy thoughts, and a hand ever prompt to virtuous deeds beyond any other lady in all the world. These ten charming damsels gave service to their Lady Lucretia both in a bevy and singly. The Signora, in addition to these, chose two matrons reverend of aspect, of noble blood, of mature age, and of sterling worth, to assist her with their wise counsels, the one to stand at her right hand and the other at her left. Of these one was the Signora Chiara, wife of Girolamo Guidiccione, a gentleman of Ferrara; and the other the Signora Veronica, the widow of Santo Orbat, of one of the oldest houses of Crema. To join this gentle and honourable company there came many nobles and men of learning, amongst whom were Casal Bolognese, a bishop, and likewise ambassador of the King of England, and the learned Pietro Bembo, knight of Rhodes and preacher to the citizens of Milan, a man of distinguished parts and standing highest in the Signora's favour. After these came Bernardo Capello, counted one of the chief poets of the time, the amiable Antonio Bembo, Benedetto Trivigiano, a man of jovial easy manners, and Antonio Molino, surnamed Burchiella, with his pretty wit, Ferier Beltramo, a courteous gentleman, and many others whom it would be tedious to name in turn. It was the custom of these, or at any rate of the greater part of them, to assemble every evening at the palace of the Signora Lucretia, and to entertain her with graceful dances, and playful discourse, and music and song, thus graciously beguiling the fleeting hours. Sometimes, too, certain problems would be propounded, to which the Signora alone could find solution; but as the days of Carnival drew nigh, days always vowed to playfulness and riot, the Signora bade them, under pain of her displeasure, to assemble next evening on purpose to arrange what manner of feast they themselves should keep. At the dusk of the next evening they all duly appeared in obedience to her behest, and, having seated themselves according to their rank, the Signora thus addressed them: "Honourable gentlemen and you gracious ladies, now that we are come together according to our wont, it seems well to me that we should order these pleasant and gentle diversions of ours so as to furnish us with some jovial pastime for the days of Carnival which are yet to run. Each one of you therefore will propose what may seem most acceptable, and the form of diversion which proves to be to the taste of the greatest number shall— if it be seemly and decorous—be adopted."

The ladies, and the gentlemen as well, declared with one voice that everything should be left to the Signora's decision; and she, when she perceived their will, turned towards the noble company and said: "Since it pleases you that I should settle the order of our entertainment, I, for my part, would counsel that every evening, as long as Carnival lasts, we should begin with a dance; then that five ladies should sing some song of their own choosing, and this finished, that these five ladies, in order to be determined by lot, should tell some story, ending with an enigma which we will solve, if our wit be sufficient therefor. At the end of the story-telling we will disperse to our homes for the night. But if these propositions of mine be not acceptable to you, I will readily bow to any other which may please you, and now I invite you to make your wishes known."

The project set forth by the Signora won the favour of all; wherefore she commanded a golden vase to be brought forthwith, and into this were cast papers bearing the names of five of the damsels present. The first to be drawn forth was that of the fair Lauretta, who, bashful as she was, blushed softly as the early hues of dawn. Next came the name of Alteria, then Cateruzza, then Eritrea, and then Arianna. The drawing over, the Signora caused to be brought in the musical instruments, and set on the head of Lauretta a wreath of laurel in token that she should make beginning of their entertainment on the evening following.

It now pleased the Signora that the company should fall to dancing, and almost before she had signified this wish to Signor Antonio Bembo, that gallant gentleman took by the hand Fiordiana, with whom he was somewhat enamoured, and the others of the company followed this example straightway, and kept up the measure merrily. Loath to forego such pleasure, they gave over reluctantly, and bandying many soft speeches, the young men and the damsels withdrew to another apartment, in which were laid out tables with sweetmeats and rare wines, and there they spent a pleasant time in jesting one with another. When their merriment was over, they took leave of the Signora, who gracefully dismissed them all.

As soon as the company had come together the next evening in the beautiful palace of the Signora, she signed to the fair Lauretta to begin her singing, and Lauretta without waiting for farther command stood up, and, after respectfully saluting the Signora, went up on a raised platform, upon which was placed a beautiful chair covered with draperies of rich silk. Then having called her four chosen companions, they sang in tender angelic cadence the following song in praise of the Signora:

SONG.

Lady, by your kindly hand,
Which ever waits on love's behest;
By your voice of sweet command,
That bids us in your presence rest;
You hold in fee your servants' love,
And rank with spirits blest above.

You quit the city's din and heat,
And let us in your smile rejoice;
You call us willing to your feet,
To listen to our lady's voice;
Then let us loudly celebrate
Your dignity and queenly state.

And though upon our charmed sight
Earth's fairest visions soft may fall;
Your grace, your wit, your beauty bright,
Will blur them and outshine them all.
To laud another should we seek,
Our tongues your praise alone would speak.

When the five damsels gave over singing, in token that their song had come to an end, the instruments began to sound, and the graceful Lauretta, upon whom the lot had fallen to tell the first story of the evening, gave the following fable without waiting for further sign from the Signora.

Night the First.

Night the First.

THE FIRST FABLE.

Salardo, son of Rainaldo Scaglia, quits Genoa and goes to Montferrat, where he disobeys certain injunctions laid upon him by his father's testament, and is condemned to death therefor; but, being delivered, he returns to his own country.

N every work, let it be good or bad, which we undertake, or propose to undertake, we ought first to consider the issue thereof. Wherefore, as we are now about to make beginning of our sportive and pleasant entertainment, I will protest that it would have been vastly more agreeable to me, had the lot willed it that some other lady should begin the story-telling; because I do not feel myself in any wise competent for the undertaking; because I am wanting in that fluency of speech which is so highly necessary in discourse of this kind, seeing that I have had scanter usage in the art of elocution than the charming ladies I see around me. But, since it pleases you, and has been decided by lot that I should be the first, I will begin—so as not to cause any inconvenience to this worshipful assemblage—my task of story-telling with the best of the faculties granted to me by divine providence. I will moreover leave open for those of my companions who shall come after me a wide and spacious field so that they may be able to relate their fables in an easier and more graceful style than I have at command.

Blessed, nay most blessed that son must be held to be who obeys his father with all due reverence, forasmuch as he thereby carries out the commands of the Eternal God, and lives long in the land, and prospers in all his works. And on the other hand he who is disobedient may be reckoned unhappy, nay most unhappy, seeing that all his undertakings come to a wretched and ill-starred end, as you will easily understand from the fable I am about to relate to you.

You must know then, gentle ladies, that at Genoa (a very ancient city, and as pleasant a one as there is in the world) there lived, not long ago, a gentleman named Rainaldo Scaglia, a man of great wealth, and endowed no less generously with wit and knowledge. He had a son called Salardo, whom he loved beyond all his other possessions, and this youth he had caused to be educated in every worthy and liberal art, letting him want nothing which might serve for his training and advancement. It happened that in his old age a heavy sickness came upon Rainaldo, who, seeing that his end was near, called for a notary, and made his will, which gave to Salardo all his goods. Beyond this he begged his son to honour his memory by keeping certain precepts ever in his mind, and never to act counter thereto. The first precept was that, no matter how great might be the love he had for his wife, he should never trust her with any important secret. The second was that he should never adopt another man's child as his own, supposing his marriage to be a fruitless one. The third was that he should never abide in a state, of which the chief magistrate wielded powers of life and death unchecked. Having given to his son these precepts, Rainaldo turned his face to the wall, and breathed his last.

After his father's death, Salardo, a young, rich, well-born gallant, grieved but moderately; and, in lieu of troubling about the administration of his estates or taking to heart his father's precepts, was in hot haste to find a wife, and began to search for one of sufficiently good descent, and with a person to his taste. Before his father had been a year dead, he married Theodora, the daughter of Messer Odescalco Doria, a Genoese noble of the first rank. She was very beautiful and of virtuous mind, though somewhat haughty, and Salardo was so deeply enamoured of her that he could not bear, night or day, to let her go out of his sight. For several years they lived together without a child being born to them; and then Salardo, yearning for an heir and disregarding the counsel of his father, determined to adopt a child and to bring him up as his heir. Having gained his wife's consent, he lost no time in carrying out his purpose, and adopted the son of a poor widow, calling the boy by the name of Postumius, and educating him with the utmost care.

In the course of time it happened that Salardo grew weary of
Genoa, and determined to seek a home elsewhere, not because he did
not find the city all that was fair and pleasant, but simply because he
was infected with that desire for change which, not seldom, seizes
upon those who live for pleasure alone. Therefore, with great store
of money and jewels, and with sumptuous equipage, he left Genoa
with Theodora his beloved wife, and his adopted son Postumius, and
having traversed Piamonte, made a halt at Montferrat. Here he
soon began to make the acquaintance of divers of the citizens, through
going with them to the chase, and in other social gatherings in which
he took great delight; and, in consequence of his wealth and gene-
rosity, he soon achieved a position of honour and repute.

The rumour of Salardo's splendid hospitality came before long to
the ears of the ruling prince, the Marquis of Montferrat, who, when
he saw that the newcomer was a handsome young man, well born,
rich, of courtly manners, and ready for any gallant enterprise, took him
into high favour and would seldom let a day pass without seeing
him. At last, so great was the influence of Salardo over the marquis,
it fell out that anyone who wanted a favour done to him by the
latter would always manage to let his petition pass through Salardo's
hands. Wherefore Salardo, mindful of the favour he enjoyed, was
ever eager to devise some new pleasure for his patron, who, as
became a young man, was much given to field sports, and kept a
great number of falcons and hounds for the chase, and all appurte-
nances of venery, worthy of his high estate. But he would never go
hunting or hawking save in the company of Salardo.

One day Salardo, being alone, began to consider the great fortune
which had befallen him through the favour of the prince, and by-and-
by his thoughts turned to his son Postumius, how discreet, and
dutiful, and upright, and graceful he was. 'Ah!' he said to himself, 'my poor old father was indeed sorely in error about these
precepts of his. He must, like many old men, have become imbecile
with age; either this cause, or some frenzy, must have urged him to
command me so particularly not to adopt a strange child as my own,
or to become the subject of an absolute prince. I now see the folly
of his precepts, for what son born to a father could be more sober,
courteous, gentle, and obedient, than Postumius, whom I have
adopted, and where should I find greater affection and more honourable treatment than is given to me by the marquis, an absolute prince

and one knowing no superior? And, exalted as he is, he pays me so much worship and love that it seems sometimes as if I stood in the highest place, and he in one beneath me. Of a truth I know not what to think of it; of a truth it is a common trick of old people to forget the tastes and inclinations of their youth, and to lay down for their children rules and regulations, imposing thereby burdens which they themselves would not touch with the tips of their fingers. And this they do, moved not by love, but by the craving to keep their offspring longer in subjection. Now, because I have disburdened myself of two of the pledges imposed upon me by my father without any evil consequence, I will quickly get rid of the third; for I am assured that when I shall be free from it my dear wife will only love me the more. And she herself, whom I love more than the light of my eyes, will give ample proof of the imbecility, or even madness, of wretched old age, which finds its chief joy in imposing, with its dead hand, intolerable restrictions on the living. Truly my father must have been insane when he made his will, for to whom is my trust due if not to her who has left her home and kinsfolk and become of one heart and soul with me. Surely I may confide to her any secret, however important it may be; so I will put her fidelity to the test, not on my own account, for I doubt it not, but to prove her strength, and to give an example to those foolish ones who rate disobedience to the wishes of dead and gone dotards as an unpardonable sin.'

In these terms Salardo girded at his father's wise injunctions, and deliberated how he might best rid himself of them entirely. After a little he left his house and went over to the mews at the palace, where the falcons of the marquis were kept, and of these he took one which was a great favourite of its owner, and secretly conveyed it to the house of a friend of his whose name was Francesco. He handed over the bird to his friend, and begged him, for the sake of the love there was between them, to hold it for him till the time should come when he might disclose the object of his request. Then, when he had returned to his home, he took a falcon of his own, and, having privily killed it, he bore it to his wife, saying: 'Theodora, my beloved wife, I, as you well know, find it hard to get a moment's rest on account of the many hours I am compelled to spend in attendance on the marquis, hunting, or fowling, or jousting, or in some other sport; and sometimes I hardly know whether I am dead or alive. Wherefore, to keep him from spending all his time over the chase, I have played him a trick he will relish but little. However, it may perhaps keep him at home, and give us and others some repose.' To this his wife said : 'And what have you done?' 'I have killed his best falcon,' Salardo replied, 'the favourite of all; and when he looks for it in vain I believe he will die of rage.' And here he lifted his cloak and took out the falcon which he had killed, and, having handed it over to his wife, directed her to have it cooked for supper. When Theodora heard this speech, and saw the dead falcon, she was deeply moved to grief, and, turning to Salardo, reproached him severely for his foolish jest. 'For what reason have you committed such a grave offence,' she said, 'and put such an insult on the marquis, who holds you so dear, and heaps such high favour upon you, and sets you above all others? Alas ! Salardo, I fear our ruin is near. If, peradventure, the marquis should come to know what you have done, you would assuredly be in great danger of death.' Salardo answered : ' But how can he ever know this ? The secret is yours and mine alone, and, by the love you have borne and still bear me, I pray you be careful not to reveal it, for if he should learn it our ruin would be complete.' 'Have no fear of this,' said Theodora, ' I would rather die than disclose it.'

The falcon was cooked and served at supper, and Salardo and his wife took their seats, but the lady refused to eat of the bird, though Salardo, with gentle words, enticed her thereto. At last, as she remained obstinate, he gave her such a buffet on the face that her cheek became scarlet from the blow. Wherefore she began to weep and lament bitterly that he should thus misuse her, and at last rose from the table, muttering beneath her breath that she would bear in mind that blow as long as she might live, and that in due time she would repay him. When morning was come, she stole early from her bed, and hastened to tell the marquis of the falcon's death, which news so fired him with rage that he ordered Salardo to be seized forthwith, and to be hanged without trial, and all his goods to be divided into three parts, of which one should be given to his wife as accuser, another to his son, and the remaining one to the man who should act as hangman.

Now Postumius, who was now a lusty well-grown youth, when he heard his father's doom and the disposition of his goods ordered by the marquis, ran quickly to Theodora and said to her : 'Mother, would it not be wiser for me to hang my father myself, thus gaining the third of his goods which would otherwise pass to a stranger.' And to this Theodora replied: 'Truly, my son, you speak well, for if you do this, your father's riches will remain with us intact.' So Postumius went straightway to the marquis to ask leave to hang his father, and thus earn the hangman's share, which boon the marquis graciously allowed.

Now Salardo had confided the whole of his secret to his faithful friend Francesco, and at the same time had begged him, when the hangman should be ready to do his work, to go to the marquis and beg him to let Salardo be brought before him, and graciously to listen to what he might have to say in his defence, and Francesco was loyal in carrying out this request. Meantime, the wretched Salardo, loaded with fetters, was awaiting in prison the hour which should see him led to a disgraceful death on the scaffold. 'Now I know,' he cried, with bitter weeping, 'that my good old father in his wisdom gave me those precepts for my profit. He gave me sage counsel, and I, senseless ribald as I am, cast it aside. He, mindful of my safety, warned me against my domestic enemies, and I have delivered myself into their hands, and handed over to them my riches to enjoy. He, well skilled in the disposition of despots, who in the space of an hour will love and hate, exalt and abase, counselled me to shun them; but I, as if eager to sacrifice at once my substance, my honour, and my life, thrust my head into the jaws of this marquis, and put my faithless wife to the proof. Ah, Salardo, better had it been for you to follow in your father's footsteps, and let others seek the company of princes! Now I see into what strait my foolish confidence in myself, in my wife, in my wicked son, and, above all, in this ungrateful marquis, has led me. Now I see the value of the love of this prince for me. How could he deal more cruelly with me than by robbing me of my goods, my life, and my honour in one blow, showing thus how his love has turned to hate? I recognize now the truth of the proverb which says that a prince is like wine in a flagon, sweet in the morning and sour at eve. Where is now my nobility and my kinsmen? Is this the end of my loyalty, uprightness, and courtesy? O my father, I believe that, dead though you be, when you gaze into the mirror of eternal goodness, and see me about to be hanged, because, forsooth, I disbelieved and disregarded your wise and loving counsel, you will pray to God to have compassion on my youthful errors, and I, your disobedient and ungrateful son, pray to you also for pardon.'

While the unhappy Salardo was thus communing with himself, Postumius, with the air of a practised hangman, went with a body of police to the prison, and, arrogantly presenting himself to Salardo, spake thus: 'My father, forasmuch as you are bound to be hanged by the order of the marquis, and as the third part of your goods is to go to him who ties the noose, I am sure, for the love you bear me, you will not be wroth at the part I have chosen to play, seeing that thereby your goods, in lieu of passing to strangers, will remain with your own family.'

Salardo, after listening attentively to this speech, replied: 'God bless you, my son; the course you have chosen pleases me much, and if at first the thought of death terrified me, I am now content to die after listening to your words. Do your office, therefore, quickly.' Postumius first implored his father's pardon, and then, having kissed him, put the halter about his neck, and exhorted him to meet death with patience. Salardo, when he saw the turn things were taking, stood astonished, and, after a little, was led out of prison with his arms bound and a halter round his neck, and, accompanied by the hangman and the officers, was hurried towards the place of execution. Arrived there, he turned his back towards the ladder which stood against the gibbet, and in this attitude he mounted step by step. When he had reached the top he looked down courageously upon the assembly, and told them at full length the cause which had brought him there, and with gentle words he implored pardon for any affront he might have given, and exhorted all young people to be obedient to their fathers. When the people heard for what cause Salardo was condemned, there was not one who did not lament his unhappy fate and pray he might yet be pardoned.

While the events above named were taking place, Francesco betook himself to the palace, and, having been introduced, thus addressed the marquis: 'Most worshipful sir, if ever you have been prompted to show pity towards anyone, you are now doubly bound to deal mercifully with the case of this friend of yours who is now, for no fault of his, led out to suffer a shameful death. Consider, my lord, for what reason you condemned Salardo, who loved you so dearly, and never by thought or deed wrought an offence against you. Most gracious prince, only suffer your faithful friend to be brought into your presence, and I will clearly demonstrate to you his innocence.' The marquis, with his eyes aflame with rage at

Francesco's petition, made an effort to thrust him out of his presence, but the suppliant threw himself down at the feet of the marquis, and, embracing his knees, cried out with tears: ' As you are a just prince, have pity, O noble marquis! and let not the guiltless Salardo die because of your anger. Calm yourself, and I will prove his innocence; stay your hand but one hour, for the sake of that justice which you and your fathers have always reverenced, lest it be said of you that you put your friend to death without cause.'

The marquis, violently angered against Francesco, now broke silence: ' I see you wish to go the way of Salardo. If you go on enraging me thus I will assuredly have you set by his side.' ' My lord,' Francesco replied, ' I ask for no greater boon than to be hanged alongside Salardo, if, after having made inquiry, you do not find him innocent.' This last speech moved the marquis somewhat, for he reasoned that Francesco would never have spoken thus without being assured of Salardo's innocence, seeing that he thereby ran the risk of the halter himself. Wherefore he accorded the hour's delay, and, having warned Francesco that he must look to be hanged if he should fail to prove his friend's innocence, he sent a messenger straightway to the place of justice with an order to delay the execution, and to bring Salardo, bound as he was and with the rope about his neck, and the hangman and officers as well, into his presence without delay.

Salardo, on being brought before the marquis, noted that his face was still clouded with anger, and outspake at once with clear voice and undaunted carriage: ' My lord, the service I freely gave you, and the love I bore you, scarcely deserved such a reward as the shame and indignity you have put upon me in thus condemning me to a disgraceful death. I admit that my folly, so to call it, deserved your anger; but I was guilty of no crime heinous enough to warrant you in condemning me thus hastily and unheard. The falcon, on account of which your anger was kindled, lives safe and sound. It was never in my mind to kill it or to insult you. I wanted to use it as a means of trying an experiment, the nature of which I will now disclose to you.' Having thus spoken, Salardo bade Francesco go fetch the falcon and return it to its master; and then he told the marquis the whole story of the precepts he had received from his father, and how he had disregarded every one. The marquis, when he listened to this frank and candid speech, and saw his falcon, handsome and well nourished as ever, was, for the moment, struck dumb; but when he had fully realized his error of having condemned a guiltless man to death unheard, he raised his eyes, which were full of tears, and turned them on Salardo, saying: ' Salardo, if you could clearly realize all I feel at this moment, you would know that the pain you have suffered from the halter round your neck and the bonds about your arms is as nought compared with the anguish which now torments me. I can hardly hope ever to be happy again after having done so grievous an injury to you, who loved and served me so faithfully. If it were possible that all should be undone, how gladly would I undo it; but, since this is out of the question, I will do my utmost to wipe out my offence, and to give you all the reparation I can.'

Having thus spoken, the marquis with his own hands unfastened the halter from Salardo's neck, and loosened his bonds, embracing him the while with the greatest tenderness; and, having taken him by the right hand and led him to a seat by his own, he ordered the halter to be put round the neck of Postumius, and the youth to be led away to execution, because of his wicked conduct; but this Salardo would not permit. ' Postumius,' he said to the wretched youth, ' what shall I now do with you, whom, for the love of God, I have nurtured from childhood, only to be so cruelly deceived? On one side is my past love for you; on the other, the contempt I feel for the wicked deed you planned to do. One calls upon my fatherly kindness to forgive you, the other bids me harden my heart against you. What then shall I do? If I pardon you, men will jeer at my weakness; if I punish you as you deserve, I shall go counter to the divine exhortation to forgiveness. But that men may not tax me either with too great leniency, or too great severity, I will neither make you suffer in your person, nor will I myself endure the sight of you any more; and in place of my wealth, which you so greedily desired, you shall have the halter which you knotted round my neck, and keep it always as a remembrance of your wicked deed. Now begone, and let me never see you or hear of you again.'

With these words he drove out the wretched Postumius, of whom nothing more was ever heard. Theodora, as soon as she was told of Salardo's liberation, fled to a certain convent, where she soon ended her days miserably, and Salardo, when he heard the news of her death, took leave of the marquis and returned to Genoa, where, after having given away all the wealth he did not want for his own use, he lived long and happily.

During the telling of Lauretta's story divers of the hearers were moved to tears, but when they heard that Salardo had been delivered from the gibbet, and Postumius ignominiously expelled, and of Theodora's flight and ill-starred end, they were heartily glad. The Signora gave the word to Lauretta to propound her enigma, so that the order of entertainment agreed upon the previous evening might be observed, and the damsel with a smiling face gave it in these words:

> In a prison pent forlorn,
> A tiny son to me was born.
> Ah, cruel fate! The savage elf,
> Scarce bigger than a mite himself,
> Devoured me in his ravenous lust,
> And changed me into sordid dust.
> A mother fond I was of late,
> Now worse e'en than a slave's my fate.

The fair Lauretta, when she saw that no one was likely to solve her riddle, said, "This enigma of mine concerns the dry bean which is imprisoned between two husks; where, later on, she engenders a worm no bigger than a mite. This worm feeds upon her, and finally consumes her, so that not only is she destroyed as a mother, but not even the condition of a servant is possible for her." All were pleased at Lauretta's explanation, and Alteria, who sat next to her, having been selected as the next speaker, began at once her story without awaiting the Signora's command.

THE SECOND FABLE.

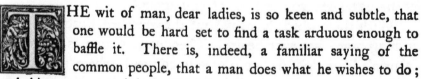

Cassandrino, a noted robber, and a friend of the prætor of Perugia, steals the prætor's bed and his horse Liardo, but afterwards becomes a man of probity and good repute.

THE wit of man, dear ladies, is so keen and subtle, that one would be hard set to find a task arduous enough to baffle it. There is, indeed, a familiar saying of the common people, that a man does what he wishes to do; and this same proverb it is which has suggested to me the tale I am about to tell you. Although it is somewhat ridiculous, it may yield you some pleasure, or even instruction, by demonstrating to you the cunning of those who are thieves by profession.

In Perugia, an ancient and noble city of Romagna, renowned for its learning and for sumptuous living, there abode, not very long ago, a handsome young scapegrace named Cassandrino. So ill was his reputation with the citizens, on account of his many robberies, that frequent and lengthy complaints thereanent were made to the prætor by men of all stations in the city; but this latter, though he rated Cassandrino soundly for his misdeeds, seemed loath to punish him. Now, though Cassandrino was, past gainsaying, a thievish knave, he had one virtue which at least got him credit with the prætor, that is, he did not rob for the mere love of pelf so much as to be able, now and then, to spend magnificently and to offer handsome gifts to those who favoured him. Wherefore, and because he was affable, courteous, and witty, the prætor looked upon him so kindly that he would rarely let pass a day without seeing him.

But since Cassandrino persisted in these more or less reprehensible courses, the prætor was forced to give ear to the complaints which, with full justice, were laid against him. Being still reluctant to bring the culprit to justice, on account of the kindly feeling in his heart, he summoned Cassandrino one day into an inner chamber, and began to admonish him with friendly words, and to exhort him to have done with his evil ways, warning him of the perils he was risking thereby. Cassandrino listened attentively to the prætor's words, and spake thus in reply: 'Sir, I hear and clearly understand the good counsel which you, of your great courtesy, have given to me, and I know full well that it springs from the generous affection in which you hold me, and for which I am most grateful. I am indeed grieved that we should be plagued with certain foolish people jealous of others' well-being, and ever ready to blast their honour with spiteful words. These busybodies, who bear such tales about me, would do better to keep their venomous tongues between their teeth than to let them run on to my hurt.' The prætor, swayed by his affection for the speaker, needed very little persuasion to believe Cassandrino's story and to turn a deaf ear to the plaints of his ravages made by the citizens. It chanced soon after that Cassandrino, being a guest at the prætor's table, told him of a youth who was so marvellously light-fingered that he could steal anything he had a mind to, however carefully guarded and protected it might be. The prætor, when he heard this, laughed and said : 'Cassandrino, this youth can be no other than you yourself, for there cannot be another such a crafty trickster; but, to put you to the test, I will promise you a hundred golden florins if you succeed to-night in stealing the bed out of the chamber in which I sleep.'   Cassandrino seemed somewhat disturbed at these words, and then answered : 'Sir, you evidently take me for a thief; but let me tell you I am not one, nor the son of one. I live by the sweat of my brow, and by my own industry, such as it is, and do for myself the best I can. But if it be your will to bring me to the gallows on this score, I will go there gladly for the sake of the regard I have ever had, and still have, for you.'   After this speech Cassandrino withdrew, for he was very anxious to humour the prætor's whim, and he went about all day cudgelling his brains to devise how he might steal the prætor's bed from under him without betraying himself. At last he hit on the following scheme. A certain doctor of the city had lately died, and on that very day had been buried in his family vault. After mid-night Cassandrino stole to the burying-place, and, having opened the vault, drew therefrom the dead body of the doctor by the feet, and, after he had stripped it, dressed it again in his own clothes, which fitted so well that anyone would have taken it for Cassandrino and not for the doctor. He hoisted the corpse upon his shoulders as well as he could, and, having made his way safely to the palace, he scaled the roof, with the doctor's body on his back, by a ladder which he had provided, and began noiselessly to remove the tiles with an iron crowbar, finally making a large hole in the ceiling of the room in which the prætor was sleeping.

The prætor, who was wide awake, heard distinctly all that was going on, and laughed to himself, though his roof was being pulled to pieces, for he expected every moment to see Cassandrino enter the room and attempt to carry off the bed. 'Ah! Messer Cassandrino,' he said to himself, 'you will not steal my bed to-night.' But while he was thus chuckling and expecting the attempt, Cassandrino let fall the dead body of the doctor through the breach in the ceiling into the prætor's room. The noise it made caused him to jump out of bed and light a candle, and then he saw what he took to be the body of Cassandrino (because it was dressed in that worthy's clothes) lying mangled and huddled together on the floor. When he recognized the garments, he was profoundly grieved, and cried out, 'Ah, what a wretched sight is here! To gratify my silly caprice I have killed this man. What will men say if it be noised abroad that he met his end in my house? Of a truth one needs to be careful.' The prætor, lamenting thus, went to rouse a faithful servant of his, and having awakened him, told him of the unhappy mischance, and begged him go dig a hole in the garden and bury therein the dead body, so as to prevent scandal. Whilst the prætor and his servant were burying the dead body in the garden, Cassandrino, who had silently watched the prætor's movements, as soon as the coast was clear let himself down by a rope, and having made a parcel of the bed, carried it away with all possible haste. After he had buried the body, the prætor returned to his room; but when he prepared to get into bed, no bed was there. He slept little that night, wherefore he had plenty of time to ponder over the cunning and dexterity of his friend Cassandrino.

The next day Cassandrino, according to his wont, went to the palace and presented himself to the prætor, who, as soon as he had set eyes on him, said: 'In truth, Cassandrino, you are the very prince of thieves! who else would have contrived so cunningly to steal my bed?' Cassandrino was silent, feigning the utmost astonishment, as if he had had no part in the affair. 'You have played an excellent trick upon me,' the prætor went on to say, 'but I must get you to play me yet another, in order that I may judge how far your ingenuity can carry you. If you can manage to-night to steal my horse Liardo—the best I ever had—I will give you another hundred florins, in addition to the hundred I have already promised you.' Cassandrino, when he heard of this fresh task which was put upon him, feigned to be much troubled, and loudly lamented that the prætor should hold him in such ill repute, begging him at the same time not to be his ruin. The prætor, deeming that Cassandrino refused assent to his request, grew angry, and said, 'Well, if you will not do as I bid you, look for no other fate than to hang by a halter from the city wall.' Cassandrino, who now saw that his case was dangerous, and in no small measure,[1] replied: 'I will do all I can to gratify you in what you ask, but believe me the task you propose is one beyond my power;' and with these words he departed.

As soon as he was gone, the prætor, who was resolved this time to put Cassandrino's ingenuity to no light trial, called one of his

---

[1] Orig., *ed importar altro, che finocchi.*

servants and thus addressed him: 'Go to the stable, and saddle and
bridle my horse Liardo; then mount him, and keep all night on his
back, taking good heed the while that he be not stolen.' And he
gave orders to another to see that all the doors of the palace were
well secured with bolts. That night Cassandrino took all his im-
plements, and repaired to the principal gate of the palace, where he
found the porter quietly dozing; but, because he knew well all the
secret issues of the place, he let the porter sleep on, and, making
use of another passage, he gained the courtyard, and thence passed
on to the stables, which he found fast locked. With very little
trouble he unfastened the door, and having opened this, he perceived,
to his amazement, that a man was sitting on the prætor's favourite
horse, with the reins in his hand, but when he approached he saw
the fellow was sound asleep. The crafty rascal, noting that the sleeping varlet was senseless as a statue, at once hit upon a plan, clever
beyond belief. He carefully measured the height of the horse, and
then stole away into the garden, from whence he brought back four
stout poles, such as are used in supporting vines on a trellis; and
having sharpened them at the ends, he cunningly cut the reins, which
the sleeping servant held in his hand, and the breast-strap, and the
girths, and the crupper, and every other bond which stood in his way.
Then, having fixed one of the poles in the ground, with the upper
end dexterously inserted under one corner of the saddle, he did exactly
the same on the other side, and repeated the operation at the other two
remaining corners. Next he raised the saddle off the horse's back
(the servant being sound asleep all the while), and let it rest entirely
on the four poles which were firmly fixed in the ground. Then,
there being no obstacle in his way, he haltered the horse and led it off.

The prætor was astir early the next morning, and repaired forthwith to the stable, where he expected to find his horse all safe; but
the sight which met his eyes was his servant, still sitting fast asleep on
the saddle propped up by four poles. The prætor, having awakened
him, loaded him with abuse, and, half dazed with what he had seen,
quitted the stable and returned to the palace. At the usual hour in
the morning Cassandrino betook himself to the palace, and gave the
prætor a merry salute when he appeared. 'Cassandrino,' said the
latter, 'assuredly you carry off the palm amongst thieves. I may
indeed dub you with the title of "King of the thieves," but still
should like to ascertain whether you are a man of wit and cleverness.

You know, I think, Messer Severino, the priest of Sangallo, a village hard by. Well, if you bring him here to me tied up in a sack, I promise to give you as much money again as you have already earned; but if you fail in this, be sure that I will hang you up by the neck.' This Messer Severino was a man of holy life, and of the best repute, but in no wise experienced in worldly affairs, seeing that he cared for nought else but the service of his church. Cassandrino, perceiving that the prætor had set his mind on working him an injury, said to himself: ' This man, I plainly see, is bent on doing me to death; but in this he will find himself mistaken, for I will execute this task if it is to be done.' Cassandrino, being thus anxious to do the prætor's bidding, cast about how he might play a trick upon the priest which would serve the purpose he had in view, and ultimately fixed on the following stratagem. He borrowed from a friend of his a priest's alb, long enough to come down to his heels, and a well-broidered stole, and these he took home to his lodging. Then he got ready a pair of beautiful wings, painted in divers colours, which he had fashioned out of pasteboards, and also a diadem of tinsel, which shone radiantly. At nightfall he stole out of the town with his gewgaws, and went towards the village where Messer Severino abode, and there he hid himself in a thicket of sharp thorns, and lay close till the day began to dawn. Then Cassandrino put on the alb, and the stole round about his neck, and set the diadem on his head, and fixed the wings on his shoulders. Having done this, he hid himself again, and stirred not till the time had come when the priest should go forth to ring the bell for the Ave Maria. Scarcely had Cassandrino vested himself, when Messer Severino, with his acolyte, arrived at the church door, which he left open, and went in to do his morning office. Cassandrino, who was on the watch, saw that the door of the church was standing open while the good priest was ringing the bell, crept out of his hiding-place, stole softly into the church, and, when he had entered, went up to the altar and stood upright, holding open a large sack in his hands. Next he cried out in a low chanting voice: ' Whoever wishes to enter into the joys of paradise, let him get into this sack;' and these words he repeated over and over again. While he was performing this mummery, the acolyte came out of the sacristy, and, when he saw the snow-white alb, and the diadem shining brilliant as the sun, and the wings as gorgeous as a peacock's—to say nothing of the words he heard—he was altogether

E

amazed; but when he had somewhat recovered, he went off to find the priest, and said to him: 'Sir, sir, I have just seen in the church an angel of heaven, holding a sack in his hands, who said: "Whoever wishes to enter into the joys of paradise, let him get into this sack;" and I, for my part, have made up my mind to do as he bids me.'

The priest, who was not over well-furnished in the upper storey, gave full credence to the acolyte's tale, and, as soon as he had issued from the sacristy, saw the angel standing there, clad in celestial garb, as the acolyte had said. Now Messer Severino was powerfully moved by the angel's words, and being mightily anxious to get safe to paradise, and at the same time somewhat in fear lest the clerk should forestall him by getting first into the sack, made believe to have left his breviary behind him at his lodging, and said to the acolyte: 'Go quickly home and search my chamber diligently, and bring back my breviary which I have left somewhere.'

And while the acolyte was gone to search for the breviary the priest approached the angel, making the while a deep reverence, and crept into the sack. Cassandrino, who was full of sharp cunning and mischief, seeing that the game was going as he wished, closed the sack's mouth at once and tied it firmly. Then he took off the alb, the diadem, and the wings, and having made a bundle of these and hoisted it, together with the sack, on his shoulders, he set out for Perugia, where he arrived as soon as it was clear daylight, and at the accustomed hour presented himself before the prætor with the sack on his back. Having untied the mouth, he lugged out Messer Severino, who, finding himself in the presence of the prætor, and more dead than alive—conscious likewise that a fool's trick had been played with him—made a weighty charge against Cassandrino, crying out at the top of his voice that he had been robbed and inveigled by craft into the sack, to his great loss and humiliation, and begging the prætor to make an example of him, nor to let so great a crime go without severe punishment, so as to give a clear warning to all other malefactors. The prætor, who had already fathomed the business from beginning to end, could not contain his laughter, and turning to Messer Severino thus addressed him: 'My good father and my friend, say not another word and do not distress yourself, for you shall never want any favour, nor fail to have justice done to you; although, as I see quite clearly, you have just been made the victim of a joke.' The prætor had to say and do his best to pacify the good priest, and, having taken a little packet wherein were several pieces of gold, he gave it to him and directed that he should be escorted out of the town. Then, turning to Cassandrino, he said to him : 'Cassandrino, Cassandrino, of a truth your knavish deeds outdo your knavish reputation which is spread abroad. Wherefore, take these four hundred golden florins which I promised you, because you have fairly gained them, but take care that you bear yourself more decently in the future than you have borne yourself in the past, for if I hear any more complaints of your knavish pranks, you shall certainly be hanged.'

Cassandrino hereupon took the four hundred golden florins, and having duly thanked the prætor for them, went his way, and with this money he traded skilfully and successfully, and in time became a man of business highly respected by all.

The ladies and gentlemen were much pleased with Alteria's story, and she being called upon by the Signora gave her enigma in the following terms :

> While I my nightly vigil kept,
> A man I spied, who softly crept
> Adown the hall, whereon I said,
> " To bed, Sir Bernard, get to bed.
> Two shall undress you, four with care
> Shut fast the doors, and eight up there
> Shall watch, and bid the rest beware."
> While these deceiving words I said,
> The thievish wight in terror fled.

Alteria, seeing that the hour was late and that no one was likely to solve her riddle, gave this explanation: " A gentleman had gone into the country with all his household, and had left in his palace an old woman, who prudently made a practice of going about the house at nightfall to see if she might espy any thieves, and one evening it chanced that she saw a robber on a balcony, who watched her through a hole. The good old woman refrained from crying out, and wisely made believe that her master was in the house, and a throng of servants as well. So she said : ' Go to bed, Messer Bernardo, and let two servants undress you, and four shut the doors, while eight go upstairs and guard the house.' And while the old woman was giving these orders, the thief, fearing to be discovered, stole away." When Alteria's clever riddle had been solved, Cateruzza, who was seated next to her, remembered that the third story of this first night was to be told by her, so with a smiling face she began.

THE THIRD FABLE.

Pre Scarpafico, having been once duped by three robbers, dupes them thrice in return, and lives happily the rest of his days.

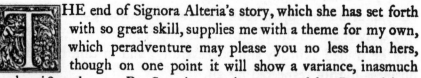

THE end of Signora Alteria's story, which she has set forth with so great skill, supplies me with a theme for my own, which peradventure may please you no less than hers, though on one point it will show a variance, inasmuch as she pictured to us Pre Severino neatly entrapped by Cassandrino; while in the story I am about to tell you, Pre Scarpafico threw the net no less adroitly over divers knaves who were trying to get the better of him.

Near to Imola, a city always plagued by factious quarrels and ultimately destroyed thereby, there lived once upon a time a priest named Scarpafico, who served the village church of Postema. He was well to do, but miserly and avaricious beyond measure, and he had for housekeeper a shrewd and clever woman named Nina, who was so alert and pushing that she would never scruple to tell any man whatever might come into her mind. And because she was faithful and prudent in administering his affairs he held her in high esteem.

Now when good Pre Scarpafico was young he was as jolly a priest as there was to be met in all the country round; but at this time age had made walking on foot irksome to him, so the good Nina was always persuading him to buy a horse, in order that his days might not be shortened through too great fatigue. At last Scarpafico, overborne by the persuasions of his servant, went one day to the market, and having seen there a mule which appeared exactly to suit his need, bought it for seven golden florins.

It happened that there were three merry fellows at the market that day, of the sort which liefer lives on the goods of others than on its own earnings—as sometimes happens even in our own time—and, as soon as they saw the bargain struck, one said to the others, 'Comrades, I have a mind that the mule yonder should belong to us.' 'But how can that be managed?' said the others. Then the first speaker replied, 'We must post ourselves along the road he will take on his journey home, about a quarter of a mile apart one from another, and as he passes each one must affirm positively that the mule he has bought is not a mule at all, but an ass, and if we are brazen enough in our declaration the mule will be ours.'

Accordingly they started from the market and stationed themselves separately on the road, as they had appointed, and when Pre Scarpafico approached the first of the thieves, the fellow, feigning to be on the road to the market, said, 'God be with you, sir!' to which Scarpafico replied, 'And welcome to you, my brother.' 'Whence come you, sir?' said the thief. 'From the market,' Scarpafico answered. 'And what good bargains have you picked up there?' asked the thief. 'This mule,' said Scarpafico. 'Which mule?' exclaimed the robber. 'Why, the mule I am riding,' returned Scarpafico. 'Are you speaking in sober truth, or do you mock me?' asked the thief; 'because it seems to me to be an ass, and not a mule.' 'Indeed,' Scarpafico answered, and without another word he went his way. Before he had ridden far he met the next robber, who greeted him, 'Good morrow, sir, and where may you come from?' 'From the market,' answered Scarpafico. 'And was there aught worth buying?' said the robber. 'Yes,' answered Scarpafico, 'I bought this mule which you see.' 'How, sir,' said the robber, 'do you mean to say you bought that for a mule, and not for an ass? What rascals must be about, seeing you have been thus cheated!' 'An ass, indeed,' replied Scarpafico; 'if anyone else should tell me this same tale, I will make him a present of the beast straightway.' Then going his way, he soon met the third thief, who said to him, 'Good morrow, sir. You come mayhap from the market?' 'I do,' replied Scarpafico. 'And what may you have bought there?' asked the robber. 'I bought this mule which I am riding,' said Scarpafico. 'Mule,' said the fellow; 'do you really mean what you say? Surely you must be joking when you call that beast a mule, while it is really an ass.' Scarpafico, when he heard this tale, said to the fellow, 'Two other men I have met told me the same story, and I did not believe them, but now it appears certain that the beast is an ass,' and having dismounted from the mule, he handed it over to the thief, who, having thanked the priest for it, went off to join his companions, leaving good Pre Scarpafico to make his way home on foot.

As soon as he came to his house he told Nina how he had bought

a nag at the market, thinking it to be a mule, but that it had proved
to be an ass; and how, having been told that he had mistaken one
beast for the other by several people he had met on the road home,
he had given the beast to the last of them. 'Ah, you poor simpleton!' cried Nina. 'Cannot you see they have played you a trick?
I thought you were cleverer than this. In truth, they would not
have fooled me thus.' 'Well, it is no use to grieve over it,' said
Scarpafico. 'They may have played me a trick, but see if I do not
play them two in return. Be sure that these fellows, after having
once fooled me, will not rest content with that, but will soon be
weaving some new plot whereby they may plunder me afresh.'

Not far from Pre Scarpafico's house there lived a peasant, who
had amongst his goats two which were so much alike that it was impossible to tell one from the other. These two goats the priest
bought, and the next day ordered Nina to prepare a good dinner for
himself and some friends he proposed to invite—some boiled veal,
and roast fowls and meat, and to make savoury sauces thereto, and
a tart of the sort she was accustomed to serve him with. Then he
took one of the goats and tied it to a hedge in the garden, and having
given it some fodder, he put a halter round the neck of the other and
led it off to the market, where he was at once accosted by the three
worthies of the late escapade. 'Welcome, good sir, and what may
be your business here to-day? You are come, no doubt, to make
another good purchase?' To which Scarpafico replied, 'I have come
to buy divers provisions, for some friends are coming to dine with
me; and if you will consent to join our feast it will please me greatly.'
The cunning rascals willingly accepted Scarpafico's invitation, and he,
when he had bought everything he required, bestowed all his purchases on the back of the goat, and said to the beast, 'Now go home
and tell Nina to boil this veal, and to roast the fowls and the meat,
and tell her, moreover, to make savoury sauce with these spices, and
a fair tart. Do you understand? Now go in peace.' And with
these words he drove off the laden goat, which, being left to go where
it would, wandered away, and what befell it no one knows. Scarpafico and his companions and some other friends of his strolled
about the market-place till the hour of dinner, and then they all
repaired to the priest's house, where the first thing they saw on entering the garden was the goat which Scarpafico had tied to the hedge,
calmly ruminating after its meal of herbage. The three adventurers

at once set it down as the goat which Pre Scarpafico had despatched home with his purchases, being beyond measure amazed thereat; and when they were all come in, the priest said to Nina, 'Have you prepared everything as the goat told you?' and she, understanding his meaning, replied, 'Yes, sir, in a few minutes the roast loin and the fowls and the boiled veal will be ready, and the sauce made with spices, and the tart likewise; all as the goat told me.'

The three robbers, when they saw set forth the roast and boiled and the tart, and heard what Nina said, were more astonished than ever, and at once began to cast about how they might get possession of the goat by theft; but when the dinner had come to an end, and they found themselves as far as ever from compassing their felonious purpose, they said to Scarpafico, 'Sir, will you do us the favour to sell us that goat of yours?' But Scarpafico replied that he had no wish to part with it, for it was worth more money than the world held; but, after a little, he consented to oblige them, and to take in exchange for it fifty golden florins. 'But,' he added, 'take warning, and blame me not afterwards if the goat does not obey you as it obeys me, for it knows you not or your ways.'

But the three adventurers heeded not this speech of Scarpafico, and, without further parley, carried off the goat, rejoicing in their bargain. When they came to their homes, they said to their wives, 'See that you prepare no food to-morrow save that which we shall send home by the goat.' On the morrow they went to the piazza, where they purchased fowls and divers other viands, and these they packed on the goat's back, and directed it to go home, and to tell to their wives all they ordered. The goat, thus laden, when it was set at liberty, ran away into the country and was never seen again.

When dinner-hour was come the three confederates straightway went home and demanded of their wives whether the goat had come back safely with the provisions, and whether they had duly cooked these according to the directions given. The women, amazed at what they heard, cried out, 'What fools and numskulls you must be to suppose that a beast like that would do your bidding! You surely have been prettily duped. With your cheating other people every day, it was quite certain you would be caught yourselves at last."

As soon as the three robbers saw that Scarpafico had verily made fools of them, besides having eased their pockets of fifty golden florins, they were hotly incensed against him, and, having caught up their arms, they set forth to find him, swearing they would have his life. But the cunning priest, who fully expected that the robbers would seek vengeance upon him when they should discover how he had tricked them, had taken counsel with Nina thereanent. 'Nina,' he said, 'take this bladder, which you see is full, and wear it under your dress; then, when these robbers come, I will put all the blame on you, and in my rage will make believe to stab you; but I will thrust the knife in this bladder, and you must fall down as if you were dead. The rest you will leave to me.'

Scarcely had Scarpafico finished speaking when the confederates arrived, and at once made for Scarpafico as if to kill him. 'Hold, brothers,' he cried, 'what you would bring against me is none of my doing, but the work of this servant of mine, most likely on account of some affront of which I know nothing.' And, turning towards Nina, he struck his knife into the bladder, which he had previously filled with blood, and she forthwith feigned to be dead and fell down, while the blood gushed in streams about where she lay. Then the priest, looking upon his work, made great show of repentance, and bawled out lustily, 'Oh, wretched man that I am! what have I done in thus foolishly slaying this woman who was the prop of my old age? How shall I manage to live without her?' But after a little he fetched a bagpipe, made according to a fancy of his own, and blew a tune upon it, until at last Nina jumped up safe and sound, as if recalled to life.

When the robbers saw what happened they forgot their anger in their astonishment, and, after a little chaffering, they purchased the bagpipe for two hundred florins, and went highly delighted to their homes. A day or two after it chanced that one of them fell out with his wife, and, becoming enraged, stabbed her in the breast with his knife and killed her. The husband at once took the bagpipe which had been bought of Scarpafico, and blew into them as Scarpafico had done in hopes of reviving her; but he spent his wind to no purpose, for the poor woman had verily passed from this life to the next. When the second thief saw what his comrade had done, he cried out, 'What a fool you are! you have bungled the affair. Wait and see how I do it.' And with these words he seized his own wife by the hair, and cut her throat with a razor. Then, taking the bagpipe, he blew with all his might, but with no better result than the first. The third fellow, who was standing by, nothing daunted by the failure of the others, served his own wife in the same way to no better purpose ; so the three were all alike wifeless. With hotter anger against Scarpafico than ever, they hurried to his house, resolved that this time they would pay no heed to his plausible tales, and seized him and thrust him into a sack, purposing to drōwn him in a neighbouring river. But as they bore him along something gave them an alarm, and they ran to hide themselves for a while, leaving Pre Scarpafico in his sack by the wayside.

They had not been gone many minutes before a shepherd, driving his flock to pasture, went by ; and, as he drew nigh, he heard a plaintive voice saying, ' They want me to take her, but I will have none of her ; for I am a priest, and have no concern with such matters.' The shepherd stopped short, somewhat frightened, because he could not discover whence came the voice, which kept repeating the same words over and over again ; but, having looked now here, now there, his eye at last fell on the sack in which Scarpafico was tied up. The shepherd opened the sack and let the priest come forth, demanding why he had been thus tied up, and what he meant by the words he kept uttering. Whereupon Scarpafico declared that the seigneur of the town insisted on marrying him to one of his daughters, but that he himself had no stomach for the match, because, besides being a priest, he was too old to wive. The shepherd, who, like a simpleton, believed every word the cunning priest told him, at once cried out, ' Good father, do you think the seigneur would bestow her upon me ?' ' I believe he would,' said Scarpafico, ' provided you get into this sack and let me tie you up.' The silly shepherd at once crept in, and Scarpafico, having fastened the sack, got away from the place as quickly as he could, driving the poor shepherd's flock before him.

When an hour or so had passed the three thieves returned, and, without examining the sack, they bore it to the river and threw it in, thus sending the wretched shepherd to the fate they had destined for Pre Scarpafico.

They then took their way homewards, and, as they were conversing, they perceived a flock of sheep grazing hard by, and at once began to scheme how they might easiest carry off a couple of lambs. But when they drew anigh, judge their amazement at seeing Pre Scarpafico, whom they believed to be lying at the bottom of the river, tending the flock as a shepherd. As soon as they had recovered from their amazement, they demanded of him how he had managed to get out of the river, and he straightway answered : 'Away with you! you have no more sense than so many jackasses. If you had thrown me a little farther into the stream, I should have come back with ten times as many sheep as you see here.' When the robbers heard this they cried out, 'Ah! Pre Scarpafico, will you at last do us a good turn? Will you put us into sacks and throw us into the river? Then, you see, we shall no longer have need to be footpads and rascals, and will live as honest shepherds.' 'Well,' answered Scarpafico, 'I will do so much for you; indeed, there is no favour in the world I would not grant you, on account of the love I bear you;' and, having got three good sacks of strong canvas, he tied the three thieves therein so firmly that there was no chance of their getting out, and threw them into the river. Thus they went to the place which was their due, and Scarpafico went back to Nina with good store of gold and cattle, and lived many years in happiness and prosperity.

Cateruzza's tale gave great pleasure to all the company, and won high praise, especially the part of it which dealt with Pre Scarpafico's cunning scheme whereby, in exchange for the mule he gave away, he gained much money and a fine flock of sheep. Cateruzza then set forth her enigma :

> A sturdy blacksmith and his wife,
> Who lived a simple honest life,
> Sat down to dine; and for their fare
> A loaf and a half of bread was there.
> But ere they finished came the priest,
> And with his sister joined the feast.
> The loaf in twain the blacksmith cleft,
> So three half loaves for the four were left.
> Each ate a half, each was content.
> Now say what paradox is meant.

The solution of Cateruzza's enigma was, that the blacksmith's wife was the priest's sister. When the husband and wife had sat down to their meal, the priest came in and joined them, and then, apparently, there were four of them, to wit, the blacksmith and his wife, and the priest and his sister; but in reality there were but three. As each one had a third of the bread they were all contented. After Cateruzza had explained her very ingenious enigma, the Signora gave the signal to Eritrea to give them her story, and she forthwith began.

THE FOURTH FABLE.

Tebaldo, Prince of Salerno, wishes to have his only daughter Doralice to wife, but she, through her father's persecution, flees to England, where she marries Genese the king, and has by him two children. These, having been slain by Tebaldo, are avenged by their father King Genese.

I CANNOT think there is one amongst us who has not realized by his own experience how great is the power of love, and how sharp are the arrows he is wont to shoot into our corruptible flesh. He, like a mighty king, directs and governs his empire without a sword, simply by his individual will, as you will be able to understand from the tenour of the story which I am about to tell to you.

You must know, dear ladies, that Tebaldo, Prince of Salerno, according to the story I have heard repeated many times by my elders, had to wife a modest and prudent lady of good lineage, and by her he had a daughter who in beauty and grace outshone all the other ladies of Salerno; but it would have been well for Tebaldo if she had never seen the light, for in that case the grave misadventure which befell him would never have happened. His wife, young in years but of mature wisdom, when she lay a-dying besought her husband, whom she loved very dearly, never to take for his wife any woman whose finger would not exactly fit the ring which she herself wore; and the prince, who loved his wife no less than she loved him, swore by his head that he would observe her wish.

After the good princess had breathed her last and had been honourably buried, Tebaldo indulged in the thought of wedding again, but he bore well in mind the promise he had made to his wife, and was firmly resolved to keep her saying. However, the report that Tebaldo, Prince of Salerno, was seeking another mate soon got noised abroad, and came to the ears of many maidens who, in worth and in estate, were no whit his inferiors; but Tebaldo, whose first care was to fulfil the wishes of his wife who was dead, made it a condition that any damsel who might be offered to him in marriage should first try on her finger his wife's ring, to see whether it fitted, and not having found one who fulfilled this condition—the ring being always found too big for this and too small for that—he was forced to dismiss them all without further parley.

Now it happened one day that the daughter of Tebaldo, whose name was Doralice, sat at table with her father; and she, having espied her mother's ring lying on the board, slipped it on her finger and cried out, 'See, my father, how well my mother's ring fits me!' and the prince, when he saw what she had done, assented.

But not long after this the soul of Tebaldo was assailed by a strange and diabolical temptation to take to wife his daughter Doralice, and for many days he lived tossed about between yea and nay. At last, overcome by the strength of this devilish intent, and fired by the beauty of the maiden, he one day called her to him and said, 'Doralice, my daughter, while your mother was yet alive, but fast nearing the end of her days, she besought me never to take to wife any woman whose finger would not fit the ring she herself always wore in her lifetime, and I swore by my head that I would observe this last request of hers. Wherefore, when I felt the time was come for me to wed anew, I made trial of many maidens, but not one could I find who could wear your mother's ring, except yourself. Therefore I have decided to take you for my wife, for thus I shall satisfy my own desire without violating the promise I made to your mother.' Doralice, who was as pure as she was beautiful, when she listened to the evil designs of her wicked father, was deeply troubled in her heart; but, taking heed of his vile and abominable lust, and fearing the effects of his rage, she made no answer and went out of his presence with an untroubled face. As there was no one whom she could trust so well as her old nurse, she repaired to her at once as the surest bulwark of her safety, to take counsel as to what she should do. The nurse, when she had heard the story of the execrable lust of this wicked father, spake words of comfort to Doralice, for she knew well the constancy and steadfast nature of the girl, and that she would be ready to endure any torment rather than accede to her father's desire, and promised to aid her in keeping her virginity unsullied by such terrible disgrace.

After this the nurse thought of nothing else than how she might best find a way for Doralice out of this strait, planning now this and now that, but finding no method which gained her entire approval. She would fain have had Doralice take to flight and put long distance betwixt her and her father, but she feared the craft of Tebaldo, and lest the girl should fall into his hands after her flight, feeling certain that in such event he would put her to death.

So while the faithful nurse was thus taking counsel with herself, she suddenly hit upon a fresh scheme, which was what I will now tell you. In the chamber of the dead lady there was a fair cassone, or clothes-chest, magnificently carved, in which Doralice kept her richest dresses and her most precious jewels, and this wardrobe the nurse alone could open. So she removed from it by stealth all the robes and the ornaments that were therein, and bestowed them elsewhere, placing in it a good store of a certain liquor which had such great virtue, that whosoever took a spoonful of it, or even less, could live for a long time without further nourishment. Then, having called Doralice, she shut her therein, and bade her remain in hiding until such time as God should send her better fortune, and her father be delivered from the bestial mood which had come upon him. The maiden, obedient to the good old woman's command, did all that was told her; and the father, still set upon his accursed design, and making no effort to restrain his unnatural lust, demanded every day what had become of his daughter; and, neither finding any trace of her, or knowing aught where she could be, his rage became so terrible that he threatened to have her killed as soon as he should find her.

Early one morning it chanced that Tebaldo went into the room where the chest was, and as soon as his eye fell upon it, he felt, from the associations connected with it, that he could not any longer endure the sight of it, so he gave orders that it should straightway be taken out and placed elsewhere and sold, so that its presence might not be an offence to him. The servants were prompt to obey their master's command, and, having taken the thing on their shoulders, they bore it away to the market-place. It chanced that there was at that time in the city a rich dealer from Genoa, who, as soon as he caught sight of the sumptuously carved cassone, admired it greatly, and settled with himself that he would not let it go from him, however much he might have to pay for it. So, having accosted the servant who was charged with the sale of it, and learnt the price demanded, he bought it forthwith, and gave orders to a porter to carry it away and place it on board his ship. The nurse, who was watching the trafficking from a distance, was well pleased with the issue thereof, though she grieved sore at losing the maiden. Wherefore she consoled herself

by reflecting that when it comes to the choice of evils it is ever wiser
to avoid the greater.

The merchant, having set sail from Salerno with his carven chest
and other valuable wares, voyaged to the island of Britain, known to
us to-day as England, and landed at a port near which the country
was spread out in a vast plain. Before he had been there long,
Genese, who had lately been crowned king of the island, happened to
be riding along the seashore, chasing a fine stag, which, in the end,
ran down to the beach and took to the water. The king, feeling
weary and worn with the long pursuit, was fain to rest awhile, and,
having caught sight of the ship, he sent to ask the master of it to
give him something to drink; and the latter, feigning to be ignorant
he was talking to the king, greeted Genese familiarly, and gave him a
hearty welcome, finally prevailing upon him to go on board his vessel.
The king, when he saw the beautiful clothes-chest so finely carved,
was taken with a great longing to possess it, and grew so impatient
to call it his own that every hour seemed like a thousand till he
should be able to claim it. He then asked the merchant the price
he asked for it, and was answered that the price was a very heavy
one. The king, being now more taken than ever with the beautiful
handicraft, would not leave the ship till he had arranged a price with
the merchant, and, having sent for money enough to pay the price
demanded, he took his leave, and straightway ordered the cassone to
be borne to the palace and placed in his chamber.

Genese, being yet over-young to wive, found his chief pleasure in
going every day to the chase. Now that the cassone was transported
into his bedroom, with the maiden Doralice hidden inside, she heard,
as was only natural, all that went on in the king's chamber, and, in
pondering over her past misfortunes, hoped that a happier future was
in store for her. And as soon as the king had departed for the chase
in the morning, and had left the room clear, Doralice would issue
from the clothes-chest, and would deftly put the chamber in order, and
sweep it, and make the bed. Then she would adjust the bed-curtains,
and put on the coverlet cunningly embroidered with fine pearls, and
two beautifully ornamented pillows thereto. After this, the fair
maiden strewed the bed with roses, violets, and other sweet-smelling
flowers, mingled with Cyprian spices which exhaled a subtle odour
and soothed the brain to slumber. Day after day Doralice continued
to compose the king's chamber in this pleasant fashion, without being

seen of anyone, and thereby gave Genese much gratification; for every day when he came back from the chase it seemed to him as if he was greeted by all the perfumes of the East. One day he questioned the queen his mother, and the ladies who were about her, as to which of them had so kindly and graciously adorned his room, and decked the bed with roses and violets and sweet scents. They answered, one and all, that they had no part in all this, for every morning, when they went to put the chamber in order, they found the bed strewn with flowers and perfumes.

Genese, when he heard this, determined to clear up the mystery, and the next morning gave out that he was going to hunt at a village ten leagues distant; but, in lieu of going forth, he quietly hid himself in the room, keeping his eyes steadily fixed on the door, and waiting to see what might occur. He had not been long on the watch before Doralice, looking more beautiful than the sun, came out of the cassone and began to sweep the room, and to straighten the carpets, and to deck the bed, and diligently to set everything in order, as was her wont. The beautiful maiden had no sooner done her kindly and considerate office, than she made as if she would go back to her hiding-place; but the king, who had keenly taken note of everything, suddenly caught her by the hand, and, seeing that she was very fair, and fresh as a lily, asked her who she was; whereupon the trembling girl confessed that she was the daughter of a prince. She declared, however, that she had forgotten what was his name, on account of her long imprisonment in the cassone, and she would say nothing as to the reason why she had been shut therein. The king, after he had heard her story, fell violently in love with her, and, with the full consent of his mother, made her his queen, and had by her two fair children.

In the meantime Tebaldo was still mastered by his wicked and treacherous passion, and, as he could find no trace of Doralice, search as he would, he began to believe that she must have been hidden in the coffer which he had caused to be sold, and that, having escaped his power, she might be wandering about from place to place. Therefore, with his rage still burning against her, he set himself to try whether perchance he might not discover her whereabouts. He attired himself as a merchant, and, having gathered together a great store of precious stones and jewels, marvellously wrought in gold, quitted Salerno unknown to anyone, and scoured all the nations and countries round about, finally meeting by hazard the trader who had originally purchased the clothes-chest. Of him he demanded whether he had been satisfied with his bargain, and into whose hands the chest had fallen, and the trader replied that he had sold the cassone to the King of England for double the price he had given for it. Tebaldo, rejoicing at this news, made his way to England, and when he had landed there and journeyed to the capital, he made a show of his jewels and golden ornaments, amongst which were some spindles and distaffs cunningly wrought, crying out the while, 'Spindles and distaffs for sale, ladies.' It chanced that one of the dames of the court, who was looking out of a window, heard this, and saw the merchant and his goods; whereupon she ran to the queen and told her there was below a merchant who had for sale the most beautiful golden spindles and distaffs that ever were seen. The queen commanded him to be brought into the palace, and he came up the stairs into her presence, but she did not recognize him in his merchant's guise; moreover, she was not thinking ever to behold her father again; but Tebaldo recognized his daughter at once.

The queen, when she saw how fair was the work of the spindles and distaffs, asked of the merchant what price he put upon them. 'The price is great,' he answered, 'but to you I will give one of them for nothing, provided you suffer me to gratify a caprice of mine. This is that I may be permitted to sleep one night in the same room as your children.' The good Doralice, in her pure and simple nature, never suspected the accursed design of the feigned merchant, and, yielding to the persuasion of her attendants, granted his request.

But before the merchant was led to the sleeping chamber, certain ladies of the court deemed it wise to offer him a cup of wine well drugged to make him sleep sound, and when night had come and the merchant seemed overcome with fatigue, one of the ladies conducted him into the chamber of the king's children, where there was prepared for him a sumptuous couch. Before she left him the lady said, 'Good man, are you not thirsty?' 'Indeed I am,' he replied; whereupon she handed him the drugged wine in a silver cup; but the crafty Tebaldo, while feigning to drink the wine, spilled it over his garments, and then lay down to rest.

Now there was in the children's room a side door through which it was possible to pass into the queen's apartment. At midnight, when all was still, Tebaldo stole through this, and, going up to the bed

beside which the queen had left her clothes, he took away a small
dagger, which he had marked the day before hanging from her girdle.
Then he returned to the children's room and killed them both with
the dagger, which he immediately put back into its scabbard, all
bloody as it was, and having opened a window he let himself down
by a cord. As soon as the shopmen of the city were astir, he went
to a barber's and had his long beard taken off, for fear he might be
recognized, and having put on different clothes he walked about the
city without apprehension.

In the palace the nurses went, as soon as they awakened, to
suckle the children; but when they came to the cradles they found
them both lying dead. Whereupon they began to scream and to
weep bitterly, and to rend their hair and their garments, thus laying
bare their breasts. The dreadful tidings came quickly to the ears of
the king and queen, and they ran barefooted and in their night-clothes
to the spot, and when they saw the dead bodies of the babes they wept
bitterly. Soon the report of the murder of the two children was spread
throughout the city, and, almost at the same time, it was rumoured
that there had just arrived a famous astrologer, who, by studying the
courses of the various stars, could lay bare the hidden mysteries of
the past. When this came to the ears of the king, he caused the
astrologer to be summoned forthwith, and, when he was come into
the royal presence, demanded whether or not he could tell the name
of the murderer of the children. The astrologer replied that he could,
and whispering secretly in the king's ear he said, 'Sire, let all the men
and women of your court who are wont to wear a dagger at their side
be summoned before you, and if amongst these you shall find one
whose dagger is befouled with blood in its scabbard, that same will
be the murderer of your children.'

Wherefore the king at once gave command that all his courtiers
should present themselves, and, when they were assembled, he diligently searched with his own hands to see if any one of them might
have a bloody dagger at his side, but he could find none. Then he
returned to the astrologer—who was no other than Tebaldo himself—
and told him how his quest had been vain, and that all in the palace,
save his mother and the queen, had been searched. To which the
astrologer replied, 'Sire, search everywhere and respect no one, and
then you will surely find the murderer.' So the king searched first
his mother, and then the queen, and when he took the dagger which

Doralice wore and drew it from the scabbard, he found it covered with blood. Then the king, convinced by this proof, turned to the queen and said to her, 'O, wicked and inhuman woman, enemy of your own flesh and blood, traitress to your own children! what desperate madness has led you to dye your hands in the blood of these babes? I swear that you shall suffer the full penalty fixed for such a crime.' But though the king in his rage would fain have sent her straightway to a shameful death, his desire for vengeance prompted him to dispose of her so that she might suffer longer and more cruel torment. Wherefore he commanded that she should be stripped and thus naked buried up to her chin in the earth, and that she should be well fed in order that she might linger long and the worms devour her flesh while she still lived. The queen, seasoned to misfortune in the past, and conscious of her innocence, contemplated her terrible doom with calmness and dignity.

Tebaldo, when he learned that the queen had been adjudged guilty and condemned to a cruel death, rejoiced greatly, and, as soon as he had taken leave of the king, left England, quite satisfied with his work, and returned secretly to Salerno. Arrived there he told to the old nurse the whole story of his adventures, and how Doralice had been sentenced to death by her husband. As she listened the nurse feigned to be as pleased as Tebaldo himself, but in her heart she grieved sorely, overcome by the love which she had always borne towards the princess, and the next morning she took horse early and rode on day and night until she came to England. Immediately she repaired to the palace and went before the king, who was giving public audience in the great hall, and, having thrown herself at his feet, she demanded an interview on a matter which concerned the honour of his crown. The king granted her request, and took her by the hand and bade her rise; then, when the rest of the company had gone and left them alone, the nurse thus addressed the king: 'Sire, know that Doralice, your wife, is my child. She is not, indeed, the fruit of my womb, but I nourished her at these breasts. She is innocent of the deed which is laid to her charge, and for which she is sentenced to a lingering and cruel death. And you, when you shall have learnt everything, and laid your hands upon the impious murderer, and understood the reason which moved him to slay your children, you will assuredly show her mercy and deliver her from these bitter and cruel torments. And if you find that I speak falsely in this, I offer myself to suffer the same punishment which the wretched Doralice is now enduring.'

Then the nurse set forth fully from beginning to end the whole history of Doralice's past life ; and the king when he heard it doubted not the truth of it, but forthwith gave orders that the queen, who was now more dead than alive, should be taken out of the earth ; which was done at once, and Doralice, after careful nursing and ministration by physicians, was restored to health.

Next King Genese stirred up through all his kingdom mighty preparations for war, and gathered together a great army, which he despatched to Salerno.   After a short campaign the city was captured, and Tebaldo, bound hand and foot, taken back to England, where King Genese, wishing to know the whole sum of his guilt, had him put upon the rack, whereupon the wretched man made full confession. The next day he was conducted through the city in a cart drawn by four horses, and then tortured with red-hot pincers like Gano di Magazza, and after his body had been quartered his flesh was thrown to be eaten of ravenous dogs.

And this was the end of the impious wretch Tebaldo ; and King Genese and Doralice his queen lived many years happily together, leaving at their death divers children in their place.

All the listeners were both amazed and moved to pity by this pathetic story, and when it was finished Eritrea, without waiting for the Signora's word, gave her enigma :

> I tell you of a heart so vile,
> So cruel, and so full of guile,
> That with its helpless progeny
> It deals as with an enemy.
> And when it sees them plump and sleek,
> It stabs them with its cruel beak.
> For, lean itself, with malice fell,
> It fain would make them lean as well.
> So they grow thin with wasting pain,
> Till nought but plumes and bones remain.

The ladies and gentlemen gave various solutions to this enigma, one guessing this and another that, but they found it hard to believe there could be an animal so vile and cruel as thus barbarously to maltreat its own progeny, but at last the fair Eritrea said with a smile, " What cause is there for your wonder ? Assuredly there are

parents who hate their children as virulently as the rapacious kite
hates its young. This bird, being by nature thin and meagre, when
it sees its progeny fat and seemly—as young birds mostly are—stabs
their tender flesh with its hard beak, until they too become lean
like itself."

This solution of Eritrea's pointed enigma pleased everybody, and
it won the applause of all. Eritrea, having made due salutation to
the Signora, resumed her seat. Then the latter made a sign to
Arianna to follow in her turn, and she rising from her chair began her
fable as follows.

THE FIFTH FABLE.

*Dimitrio the chapman, having disguised himself as a certain Gramottiveggio,
surprises his wife Polissena with a priest, and sends her back to her
brothers, who put her to death, and Dimitrio afterwards marries his
serving-woman.*

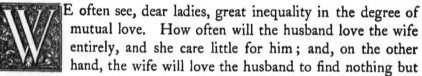

WE often see, dear ladies, great inequality in the degree of
mutual love. How often will the husband love the wife
entirely, and she care little for him; and, on the other
hand, the wife will love the husband to find nothing but
hatred in return. In conditions like these is born the passion of
sudden jealousy, the destroyer of all happiness, rendering a decent
life impossible; likewise dishonourings and unseemly deaths, which
often shed deep disgrace over all our sex. I will say nothing of the
headlong perils, of the numberless ills, into which both men and
women rush on account of this accursed jealousy. It would weary
rather than divert you were I to recount them all to you one by one;
but, as it is my task to bring to an end this evening of pleasant discourse, I will tell you a story of Gramottiveggio, now told for the
first time, and I believe you will gather therefrom no less pleasure
than edification.

The noble city of Venice, famed for the integrity of its magis-
trates, for the justice of its laws, and as being the resort of men from
every nation of the world, is seated on the bosom of the Adriatic sea,
and is named the queen of cities, the refuge of the unhappy, the

asylum of the oppressed. Her walls are the sea and her roof the sky; and, though the earth produces nought, there is no scarcity of anything that life in a great city demands.

In this rich and magnificent city there lived in former days a merchant whose name was Dimitrio, a good and trustworthy man of upright life, though of low degree. He was possessed with a great desire of offspring, wherefore he took to wife a fair and graceful girl named Polissena, whom he loved as dearly as ever man loved woman, letting her clothe herself so sumptuously that there was no dame in all the city—save amongst the nobles—who could outvie her in raiment, or in rings, or in pearls of price. And besides he took care to let her have abundance of delicate victuals, which, not being suitable to one of her humble degree, gave her the look of being more pampered and dainty than she should have been.

It chanced one day that Dimitrio, who on account of his business was often constrained to travel by sea, determined to take ship with a cargo of goods for Cyprus, and, when he had got ready his apparel and stocked the house with provisions and everything that was needful, he left his dear wife Polissena with a fair and buxom serving-maid to bear her company, and set sail on his voyage.

After his departure Polissena went on living luxuriously and indulged herself with every delicacy, and before very long found she was unable to endure further the pricks of amorous appetite, so she cast her eyes upon the parish priest and became hotly enamoured of him. The priest on his part, being young, lively, and well-favoured, came at last to divine the meaning of the glances Polissena cast towards him out of the corner of her eye, and, seeing that she was gifted with a lovely face and a graceful shape, and further endowed with all the charms men desire in a woman, he soon began to return her amorous looks. Thus love grew up between them, and many days had not passed before Polissena brought the young man privily into the house to take her pleasure with him. And thus, for the course of many months, they secretly enjoyed the delights of love in close embraces and sweet kisses, letting the poor husband fare the best he might in the perils of sea and land.

Now when Dimitrio had been some time in Cyprus, and had made there a reasonable profit on his goods, he sailed back to Venice, and, having disembarked, he went to his home and to his dear Polissena, who, as soon as she saw him, burst into tears, and when

Dimitrio asked her the reason of her weeping, she replied, 'I weep because of some bad news which came to me of late, and also for the great joy I feel in seeing you again; for I heard tell by many that all the ships which had sailed for Cyprus were wrecked, and I feared sorely lest some terrible misadventure should have overtaken you. But now, seeing you have by God's mercy returned safe and sound, I cannot keep back my tears for the joy I feel.' The simple Dimitrio, who had returned to Venice to make up—as he thought—to his wife for the solitary time she had passed during his long absence, deemed that the tears and sighs of Polissena sprang from her warm and constant love for him; but the poor dupe never suspected that all the while she was saying in her heart, 'Would to Heaven that he had been drowned at sea! for then I might the more safely and readily take my pleasure with my lover who loves me so well.'

Before a month had passed Dimitrio was forced to set out on his travels once more, whereat Polissena was filled with joy greater than can be imagined, and forthwith sent word to her lover, who showed himself to be no less on the alert; and, when the settled hour for their foregathering had come, he went secretly to her. But the comings and goings of the priest could not be kept secret enough to escape for long the eye of a certain Manusso, a friend of Dimitrio, who lived just opposite. Wherefore Manusso, who held Dimitrio in high esteem for that he was a pleasant companion and one ever ready to do a friendly service, grew mightily suspicious of his young neighbour, and kept a sharp watch over her. When he had satisfied himself that, with a given sign at a certain hour, the door would always be opened to the priest, and that after this the lovers would disport themselves with less circumspection than prudence demanded, he determined that the business, which was as yet a secret, should not be brought to light so as to stir up a scandal, but to let his project have time to ripen by awaiting the return of Dimitrio.

When Dimitrio found himself at liberty to return home, he took ship, and with a favourable breeze sailed back to Venice; and, having disembarked, went straight to his own house and knocked at the door, thus arousing the servant, who, when she had looked out of the window and recognized her master, ran quickly to let him in, weeping with joy the while. Polissena, when she heard her husband had returned, came downstairs forthwith, taking him in her arms and embracing and kissing him as if she had been the most loving

wife in the world.   And because he was weary and altogether worn
out by the sea voyage, he went to bed without taking any food, and
slept so soundly that the morning came before he had taken any
amorous pleasure with his wife.   When the night had passed and
full daylight had come, Dimitrio awoke, and, having left the bed
without bestowing so much as a single kiss upon his wife, took a
little box, out of which he drew a few ornamental trinkets of no
small value, which, on returning to bed, he gave to his wife, who set
little store by them, seeing that her thoughts were running upon
another matter.   Shortly after this it happened that Dimitrio had
occasion to go into Apulia to purchase oil and other merchandise,
and, having announced this to his wife, he began to make ready for
his journey.   She, cunning and full of mischief, and feigning to be
heartbroken at his departure, kissed him lovingly and besought him
to tarry yet a few days longer with her; but in her heart of hearts
she reckoned one day of his presence like a thousand, since it pre-
vented her from taking her pleasure in the arms of her lover.

Now Manusso, who had often espied the priest courting Polissena
and doing divers other things which it is not seemly to mention, felt
that he would be working his friend a wrong if he should not now let
him know all that he had seen.   Therefore he determined, come
what might, to tell him all.   So, having invited him one day to
dinner, he said to him as they sat at table, 'Dimitrio, my friend, you
know, if I am not mistaken, that I have always held, and shall ever
hold you in great affection, so long as there is breath in my body;
nor could you name any task, however difficult, which I would not
undertake for the love I bear you; and, if you would not take it ill,
I could tell you of certain matters which might annoy you rather
than please you, but I fear to speak lest thereby I should disturb
your peace of mind.   Nevertheless, if you will take it—as I hope you
will—circumspectly and prudently, you will not let your anger get
the mastery over you, and thus blind your eyes to the truth.'
'Know you not,' answered Dimitrio, 'that you may say to me anything you please?   If you have, by any mischance, killed a man, tell
me, and do not doubt my fidelity.'   Manusso answered, 'I have
killed nobody, but I have seen another man slay your honour and
your good name.'   'Speak your meaning clearly,' said Dimitrio, 'and
do not beat about the bush with ambiguous words.'   'Do you wish
me to tell it you briefly?' asked Manusso; 'then listen and hear

patiently what I have to say. Polissena your wife, whom you hold so dear, all the time you are away sleeps every night with a priest and takes her pleasure with him.' 'How can this be possible,' said Dimitrio, 'seeing that she loves me so tenderly, never failing when I leave her to shed floods of tears on my bosom and to fill the air with her sighs? If I were to behold this thing with my own eyes I would not believe it.' 'If you are wise, as I believe you to be,' said Manusso, 'if there is any reason in you, you will not shut your eyes, as is the way with so many simpletons and fools. I will let you see with your eyes and touch with your hands all that I have told you; then you may be convinced.' 'Then,' said Dimitrio, 'I shall be content to do whatever you may direct me in order to let you show me all you have promised.' Then Manusso replied, 'But you must take care to keep your secret and put a good face on the matter, otherwise you will wreck the whole plot.[1] When next you have to go abroad, make believe to set sail, but in lieu of quitting Venice come to my lodgings as secretly as you can, and I will clear up the mystery for you.'

When the day came for Dimitrio to start on his journey he embraced his wife tenderly, while he bade her take good care of the house, and having taken leave of her feigned to go on board his ship, but turned and withdrew secretly to the lodging of Manusso. By chance it happened that, before two o'clock had struck, a terrible storm came on, with rain so heavy that it seemed as if the heavens themselves were broken up, and the rain ceased not all through the night. The priest, who had already been advertised of the departure of Dimitrio, and cared neither for wind nor rain, was waiting for the hour of assignation. When he gave the sign the door was opened to him, and, as soon as he was inside, Polissena greeted him with sweet and passionate kisses; while the husband, who was concealed in a passage over the way, saw all that went on, and, being no longer able to contradict his friend's assertion, was altogether overwhelmed, and burst into tears on account of the righteous grief which possessed him. Then said his friend to him, 'Now what do you think? Have you not seen something you would never have believed? But say not a word and keep yourself cool, for if you listen to what I have to say, and do exactly what I shall direct you, you shall see

---

[1] Orig., *altrimenti si guasterebbe la coda al fasiano.*

something more. Take off the clothes you are now wearing, and put on some beggar's rags, and smear your face and your hands with dirt; then go over to your own house as a beggar, and in a counterfeited voice ask for a night's lodging. Most likely the servant, seeing how bad a night it is, will take pity on you and take you in; and if you do this, you will probably see something else you would rather not see.'

Dimitrio, having listened to his friend's counsel, took off his clothes and put on instead the rags of a poor man who had come to the house and asked for lodging in God's name, and, although it still rained smartly, he went over to the door of his own house, at which he knocked thrice, weeping and groaning bitterly the while. The serving-maid having opened the window, cried out who was there, and Dimitrio, in a broken and feigned voice, replied that it was a poor old man, almost drowned by the rain, who begged a night's lodging. Whereupon the kindly girl, who was just as tender-hearted towards the poor and wretched as was her mistress towards the priest, ran to Polissena and begged her to grant the petition of this poor man who was soaked with rain, and to give him shelter till he should be warm and dry. 'He can draw us some water,' she went on, 'and make up the fire, so that the fowls may be the sooner roasted. Then I can prepare the soup, and get ready the spoons, and do other chores about the kitchen.' To this the mistress agreed, and the girl, having opened the door, let him in and bade him sit by the fire and turn the spit. It happened that the priest and Polissena, who had in the meantime been in the chamber, came down into the kitchen holding one another by the hand, and at once began to make mock of the poor wight with his dirty face. Going up to him Polissena asked what was his name. 'I am called Gramottiveggio, signora,' he replied; and Polissena when she heard this began to laugh heartily, showing all her teeth so plainly that a leech might have drawn any one of them. Then she threw her arms round the priest, crying out, 'Come, dear heart, and let me kiss you.' And poor Dimitrio had to look on while they thus kissed and embraced each other. I leave you to fancy what he felt at seeing his wife kissed and fondled by a priest in his very presence.

When the time had come for supper, the servant, when the lovers had sat down, returned to the kitchen and said to the poor man: 'Well now, father, I must just tell you that my mistress has for a husband as good a man as you would find in all Venice, one who lets her want for nothing, and God only knows where the poor man is in this dreadful weather, while she, an ungrateful hussy, caring nothing for his person and less for his honour, has let herself be blinded by this lecherous passion—always fondling this lover, and shutting the door to everybody but him alone. But, I pray you, let us go softly to the door of the chamber; then you will see what they are doing, and how they bear themselves at table.' And when they came to the door they espied the two lovers within, making good play with the viands, and carrying on all sort of amorous dalliance the while.

When the hour of bedtime came, the two lovers retired to rest, and, after a little playful pastime, began to sport in good earnest,[1] and made so much ado that the poor Dimitrio, who was abed in a chamber adjoining, did not close his eyes all night, and understood completely what was going on. As soon as morning came he repaired to the lodgings of Manusso, who, as soon as he saw him, said, laughing, ' Well, friend, how is the business going on ? Is all you have seen to your taste?' 'No, indeed,' answered Dimitrio; 'I would never have believed it had I not seen it with my own eyes; but, patience! since my ill luck will have it so.' Then Manusso, who was a crafty fellow, said, ' My friend, I would have you do what I shall tell you. Wash yourself well and put on your own clothes, and go straightway to your house, and make believe that by great good luck you had not embarked before the storm broke. Take good care that the priest steal not away; for, as soon as you enter, he will assuredly hide himself somewhere, and will lie there till he can make his retreat safely. Meantime, summon all your wife's relations to a banquet at your house, and then, when you have dragged the priest from his hiding-place in their presence, you can do anything else which may seem good to you.'

Dimitrio was highly pleased at his friend's advice, and as soon as he had stripped himself of his ragged clothes went over to his house and knocked at the door. The servant, when she saw it was her master, ran forthwith to Polissena, who was yet in bed with the priest, and said to her, ' Signora, my master is come back.' Her mistress, when she heard these words, was beside herself with fright, and, getting up with what despatch she could, she hid the priest, who was in his shirt, in the coffer where she kept all her choicest raiment, and then ran in her fur-lined cloak, all shoeless as she was, to open the

---

[1] Orig., *cominciorono macinare à raccolta.*

door to Dimitrio. 'My dear husband,' she cried, 'you are indeed welcome. I have not closed my eyes for love of you, wondering always how fortune might be using you, but God be praised for that you have come back safe and sound.' Dimitrio, as soon as he entered the chamber, said, 'Polissena, my love, I scarcely slept a wink last night on account of the bad weather, so that now I would fain rest a little; and in the meanwhile let the servant go to your brothers' house and bid them dine with us to-day.' To this Polissena replied, 'Would it not be better to wait till another day, seeing that it rains so heavily, and the girl is busy calendering our body linen and sheets and other napery?' 'To-morrow the weather will mend, and I shall have to set forth,' said Dimitrio. Polissena then said, 'But you might go yourself; or, if you are too weary, go ask your friend Manusso to do you this service.' 'That is a good suggestion,' said Dimitrio, and, having sent for his friend, he carried the affair out exactly as it had been settled.

The brothers of Polissena came, and they dined jovially together. When the table was cleared, Dimitrio cried: 'Good brothers-in-law of mine, I have never properly let you see my house, nor the fine apparel which I have given to Polissena, my wife and your sister, so that you might judge therefrom how I treat her. Now go, Polissena, my good wife, get up and show your brothers over the house.' Dimitrio then rose and showed them his storehouses full of wheat and timber and oil and other merchandise, then casks of malvoisie and Greek wine and other delicacies. Next he said to his wife: 'Bring out the rings and the pearls which I have bought for you. Just look at these fine emeralds in this little casket; the diamonds, the rubies, and other rings of price. Does it seem to you, my brothers, that your sister is well treated by me?' 'We knew all this well, brother,' they replied, 'and if we had not been satisfied with your worth, we would not have given you our sister to wife.'

But Dimitrio had not yet finished, for he next directed his wife to open all her coffers, and to bring out her fair raiment; but Polissena, her heart sinking with dread, replied, 'What need can there be to open the coffers and show my clothes? Do not my brothers know well enough that you always let me be attired full honourably—more sumptuously indeed than our station calls for?' But Dimitrio cried out, 'Open this coffer, and that, at once,' and when they were opened he went on showing all her wardrobe to her brothers.

Now when they came to the last coffer the key of this was nowhere to be found, for the good reason that the priest was hidden therein. Dimitrio, when he saw the key was not forthcoming, took up a hammer and beat the lock so lustily that it gave way, and then he opened the coffer.

The priest, shaking with fear, could in no way hide himself, or escape being recognized by all the bystanders. The brothers of Polissena, when they saw how the matter stood, were so strongly moved by anger that they were within a little of slaying her and her lover as well on the spot with the daggers they wore, but the husband was averse to this course, deeming it shameful to kill a man in his shirt, however stout a fellow he might be. He spake to the brothers thus : ' What think ye now of this trull of a wife of mine ? ' Then, turning to Polissena, he said : ' Have I deserved such a return as this from you ? Wretched woman ! who has any right to keep me back from cutting your throat ? ' The poor wretch, who could in no wise excuse herself, was silent, because her husband told her to her face all he had seen of her doings the night before so clearly that she could not find a word to say in her defence. Then, turning to the priest, who stood with his head bent down, he said : ' Take your clothes and go quickly from this place, and bad luck go with you. Let me never see your face again, for I have no wish to soil my hands in your accursed blood for the sake of a guilty woman. Now begone; why do you tarry ? ' The priest, without opening his mouth, stole away, fancying as he went that Dimitrio and his brothers-in-law were close behind him with their knives. Then Dimitrio, turning to his brothers-in-law, said : ' Take your sister where you will, for I will not have her before my eyes any longer.' And the brothers, inflamed with rage, took her out of the house and slew her forthwith. When news of this was brought to Dimitrio, he cast his eyes on the serving-maid, who was indeed a very comely lass, and he bore in mind, moreover, the kind turn she had done him. So he made her his wife. He gave her, likewise, all the jewels and raiment of his first wife, and lived many years with her in joy and peace.

As soon as Arianna had brought her story to an end, the company with one voice cried out that the worth and the constancy of the unlucky Dimitrio was most noteworthy, even when he saw before his very eyes the priest who had wrought him this dishonour, and quite as noteworthy was the terror of the culprit, who, clad only in his shirt, and seeing the husband and brothers of his mistress close upon him, trembled like a leaf shaken by the wind. And then the Signora, perceiving that discussion on the matter promised to be overmuch, called for silence, and directed Arianna to give her enigma, whereupon she, with her gracious manner and pleasant smile, set it forth in these words:

> Three jolly friends sat down to eat,
> A merrier crew you could not meet.
> They tried and emptied every dish,
> For better fare they could not wish.
> The varlet next before them placed
> A dish with three fat pigeons graced.
> Each ate his pigeon, bones and all,
> But pigeons twain were left withal.

This enigma seemed to the company to be one very difficult to solve, and finally it was judged to be impossible, for no one saw how, after each had eaten his pigeon, two out of the three could remain on the board, but they did not look for the snake which was hidden in the grass. When, therefore, Arianna saw that the secret of her enigma had not been grasped, and that the solution was impossible, she turned her fair and delicate face towards the Signora and said: "It seems, dear lady, that my enigma is not to be solved, and yet it is not so difficult but that it may be easily disentangled. The answer is this: Out of the three jolly friends one bore the name of Each. As they sat together at the same table they ate as if they had been famished wolves, and when, at the end of the feast, the varlet brought them three roast pigeons, two out of the three revellers were so full that they could eat no more, but the one whose name was Each finished his neatly, so there were two pigeons left when they rose from the table."

The solution of this obscure riddle was greeted with great laughter and applause, for not one of the company could have solved it. Thus, the last story of this present night having been told, the Signora directed everyone to go home to rest. And by the flare of torches, which shed over all the place a white light, the ladies and gentlemen were escorted to the landing-place.

The End of the First Night.

Night the Second.

The Fables and Enigmas of Messer
Giovanni Francesco Straparola da Caravaggio.

Night the Second.

HŒBUS had already plunged his golden wheels into the salt waves of the Indian ocean, his rays no longer gave light to the world, his horned sister now ruled the universe with her mild beams, and the sparkling stars had spread their fires thickly over the sky, when the courtly and honourable company met once more at the accustomed spot. And when they had seated themselves according to their rank, the Signora Lucretia gave the word that they should observe, this night, the same order in their entertainment as hitherto. And, seeing that five of the damsels had not told their stories, the Signora bade the Trevisan to write the names of these on paper, then to place the billets in a golden vase, and to draw them out one after another, as they had done last night. The Trevisan hastened to obey her command, and the first paper which was taken out of the vase bore the name of Isabella, the second that of Fiordiana, the third that of Lionora, the fourth that of Lodovica, and the fifth that of Vicenza. Then the flutes struck up a tune, and they all began to sing and dance in a circle, Antonio Molino and Lionora leading the revel; and they all laughed so loud and heartily, that meseems the sound of their merriment is still to be heard. And when the measure had come to an end they all sat down, and the damsels sang a fair carol in praise of the Signora.

SONG.

What once we sang we sing to-day,
And ever will we tune our lay,
To praise thee, lady, as the queen
Of beauty, and of all our bene ;
The loftiest theme the poet sings,
The sweetest chord that shakes the strings,
The fairest shape the painter gives,
The peer of all in thee survives.

He who never owns the spell
Which moves us now thy praise to tell,
Wins no kindly word from me.
He the bliss shall never see
That flows on earth from faithful love,
And waits on spirits blest above.

At the close of this pleasant song Isabella, who had been chosen
to begin the entertainment of the second night, began to tell the
story which follows.

THE FIRST FABLE.

𝕲aleotto, 𝕶ing of 𝕬nglia, has a son who is born in the shape of a pig.
This son marries three wives, and in the end, having thrown off his
semblance, becomes a handsome youth.

FAIR ladies, if man were to spend a thousand years in
rendering thanks to his Creator for having made him in
the form of a human and not of a brute beast, he could
not speak gratitude enough. This reflection calls to
mind the story of one who was born as a pig, but afterwards became
a comely youth. Nevertheless, to his dying day he was known to the
people over whom he ruled as King Pig.

You must know, dear ladies, that Galeotto, King of Anglia, was
a man highly blest in worldly riches, and in his wife Ersilia, the
daughter of Matthias, King of Hungary, a princess who, in virtue
and beauty, outshone all the other ladies of the time. And Galeotto
was a wise king, ruling his land so that no man could hear complaint
against him. Though they had been several years married they had

no child, wherefore they both of them were much aggrieved. While Ersilia was walking one day in her garden she felt suddenly weary, and remarking hard by a spot covered with fresh green turf, she went up to it and sat down thereon, and, overcome with weariness and soothed by the sweet singing of the birds in the green foliage, she fell asleep.

And it chanced that while she slept there passed by three fairies who held mankind somewhat in scorn, and these, when they beheld the sleeping queen, halted, and gazing upon her beauty, took counsel together how they might protect her and throw a spell upon her. When they were agreed the first cried out, 'I will that no man shall be able to harm her, and that, the next time she lie with her husband, she may be with child and bear a son who shall not have his equal in all the world for beauty.' Then said the second, 'I will that no one shall ever have power to offend her, and that the prince who shall be born of her shall be gifted with every virtue under the sun.' And the third said, 'And I will that she shall be the wisest among women, but that the son whom she shall conceive shall be born in the skin of a pig, with a pig's ways and manners, and in this state he shall be constrained to abide till he shall have three times taken a woman to wife.'

As soon as the three fairies had flown away Ersilia awoke, and straightway arose and went back to the palace, taking with her the flowers she had plucked. Not many days had passed before she knew herself to be with child, and when the time of her delivery was come, she gave birth to a son with members like those of a pig and not of a human being. When tidings of this prodigy came to the ears of the king and queen they lamented sore thereanent, and the king, bearing in mind how good and wise his queen was, often felt moved to put this offspring of hers to death and cast it into the sea, in order that she might be spared the shame of having given birth to him. But when he debated in his mind and considered that this son, let him be what he might, was of his own begetting, he put aside the cruel purpose which he had been harbouring, and, seized with pity and grief, he made up his mind that the son should be brought up and nurtured like a rational being and not as a brute beast. The child, therefore, being nursed with the greatest care, would often be brought to the queen and put his little snout and his little paws in his mother's lap, and she, moved by natural affection, would caress him by stroking his bristly back with her hand, and embracing and kissing him as if he had been of human form.   Then he would wag his tail and give other signs to show that he was conscious of his mother's affection.

The pigling, when he grew older, began to talk like a human being, and to wander abroad in the city, but whenever he came near to any mud or dirt he would always wallow therein, after the manner of pigs, and return all covered with filth.   Then, when he approached the king and queen, he would rub his sides against their fair garments, defiling them with all manner of dirt, but because he was indeed their own son they bore it all.

One day he came home covered with mud and filth, as was his wont, and lay down on his mother's rich robe, and said in a grunting tone, 'Mother, I wish to get married.'   When the queen heard this, she replied, 'Do not talk so foolishly.   What maid would ever take you for a husband, and think you that any noble or knight would give his daughter to one so dirty and ill-savoured as you?'   But he kept on grunting that he must have a wife of one sort or another. The queen, not knowing how to manage him in this matter, asked the king what they should do in their trouble: 'Our son wishes to marry, but where shall we find anyone who will take him as a husband?'   Every day the pig would come back to his mother with the same demand: 'I must have a wife, and I will never leave you in peace until you procure for me a certain maiden I have seen to-day, who pleases me greatly.'

It happened that this maiden was a daughter of a poor woman who had three daughters, each one of them being very lovely.   When the queen heard this, she had brought before her the poor woman and her eldest daughter, and said, 'Good mother, you are poor and burdened with children.   If you will agree to what I shall say to you, you will be rich.   I have this son who is, as you see, in form a pig, and I would fain marry him to your eldest daughter.   Do not consider him, but think of the king and of me, and remember that your daughter will inherit this whole kingdom when the king and I shall be dead.'

When the young girl listened to the words of the queen she was greatly disturbed in her mind and blushed red for shame, and then said that on no account would she listen to the queen's proposition; but the poor mother besought her so pressingly that at last she yielded.

When the pig came home one day, all covered with dirt as usual, his
mother said to him, ' My son, we have found for you the wife you
desire.'   And then she caused to be brought in the bride, who by this
time had been robed in sumptuous regal attire, and presented her to
the pig prince.   When he saw how lovely and desirable she was he
was filled with joy, and, all foul and dirty as he was, jumped round
about her, endeavouring by his pawing and nuzzling to show some
sign of his affection.   But she, when she found he was soiling her
beautiful dress, thrust him aside; whereupon the pig said to her,
' Why do you push me thus?   Have I not had these garments made
for you myself?'   Then she answered disdainfully, ' No, neither you
nor any other of the whole kingdom of hogs has done this thing.'
And when the time for going to bed was come the young girl said to
herself, ' What am I to do with this foul beast?   This very night,
while he lies in his first sleep, I will kill him.'   The pig prince, who
was not far off, heard these words, but said nothing, and when the
two retired to their chamber he got into the bed, stinking and dirty
as he was, and defiled the sumptuous bed with his filthy paws and
snout.   He lay down by his spouse, who was not long in falling to
sleep, and then he struck her with his sharp hoofs and drove them
into her breast so that he killed her.

The next morning the queen went to visit her daughter-in-law,
and to her great grief found that the pig had killed her; and when
he came back from wandering about the city he said, in reply to the
queen's bitter reproaches, that he had only wrought with his wife as
she was minded to deal with him, and then withdrew in an ill humour.
Not many days had passed before the pig prince again began to
beseech the queen to allow him to marry one of the other sisters, and
because the queen at first would not listen to his petition he persisted
in his purpose, and threatened to ruin everything in the place if he
could not have her to wife.   The queen, when she heard this, went
to the king and told him everything, and he made answer that perhaps
it would be wiser to kill their ill-fated offspring before he might work
some fatal mischief in the city.   But the queen felt all the tenderness
of a mother towards him, and loved him very dearly in spite of his
brutal person, and could not endure the thought of being parted from
him; so she summoned once more to the palace the poor woman, together with her second daughter, and held a long discourse with her,
begging her the while to give her daughter in marriage.   At last the

girl assented to take the pig prince for a husband; but her fate
was no happier than her sister's, for the bridegroom killed her,
as he had killed his other bride, and then fled headlong from the
palace.

When he came back, dirty as usual and smelling so foully that no
one could approach him, the king and queen censured him gravely for
the outrage he had wrought; but again he cried out boldly that if he
had not killed her she would have killed him. As it had happened
before, the pig in a very short time began to importune his mother
again to let him have to wife the youngest sister, who was much more
beautiful than either of the others; and when this request of his was
refused steadily, he became more insistent than ever, and in the end
began to threaten the queen's life in violent and bloodthirsty words,
unless he should have given to him the young girl for his wife. The
queen, when she heard this shameful and unnatural speech, was wellnigh broken-hearted and like to go out of her mind; but, putting all
other considerations aside, she called for the poor woman and her
third daughter, who was named Meldina, and thus addressed her:
'Meldina, my child, I should be greatly pleased if you would take
the pig prince for a husband; pay no regard to him, but to his father
and to me; then, if you will be prudent and bear patiently with him,
you may be the happiest woman in the world.' To this speech
Meldina answered, with a grateful smile upon her face, that she was
quite content to do as the queen bade her, and thanked her humbly
for deigning to choose her as a daughter-in-law; for, seeing that she
herself had nothing in the world, it was indeed great good fortune
that she, a poor girl, should become the daughter-in-law of a potent
sovereign. The queen, when she heard this modest and amiable
reply, could not keep back her tears for the happiness she felt; but
she feared all the time that the same fate might be in store for
Meldina as her sisters.

When the new bride had been clothed in rich attire and decked
with jewels, and was awaiting the bridegroom, the pig prince came in,
filthier and more muddy than ever; but she spread out her rich gown
and besought him to lie down by her side. Whereupon the queen
bade her to thrust him away, but to this she would not consent, and
spoke thus to the queen: 'There are three wise sayings, gracious
lady, which I remember to have heard. The first is that it is folly
to waste time in searching for that which cannot be found. The

second is that we should believe nothing we may hear, except those things which bear the marks of sense and reason. The third is that, when once you have got possession of some rare and precious treasure, prize it well and keep a firm hold upon it.'

When the maiden had finished speaking, the pig prince, who had been wide awake and had heard all that she had said, got up, kissed her on the face and neck and bosom and shoulders with his tongue, and she was not backward in returning his caresses; so that he was fired with a warm love for her. As soon as the time for retiring for the night had come, the bride went to bed and awaited her unseemly spouse, and, as soon as he came, she raised the coverlet and bade him lie near to her and put his head upon the pillow, covering him carefully with the bed-clothes and drawing the curtains so that he might feel no cold. When morning had come the pig got up and ranged abroad to pasture, as was his wont, and very soon after the queen went to the bride's chamber, expecting to find that she had met with the same fate as her sisters; but when she saw her lying in the bed, all defiled with mud as it was, and looking pleased and contented, she thanked God for this favour, that her son had at last found a spouse according to his liking.

One day, soon after this, when the pig prince was conversing pleasantly with his wife, he said to her : 'Meldina, my beloved wife, if I could be fully sure that you could keep a secret, I would now tell you one of mine; something I have kept hidden for many years. I know you to be very prudent and wise, and that you love me truly ; so I wish to make you the sharer of my secret.' 'You may safely tell it to me, if you will,' said Meldina, 'for I promise never to reveal it to anyone without your consent.' Whereupon, being now sure of his wife's discretion and fidelity, he straightway shook off from his body the foul and dirty skin of the pig, and stood revealed as a handsome and well-shaped young man, and all that night rested closely folded in the arms of his beloved wife. But he charged her solemnly to keep silence about this wonder she had seen, for the time had not yet come for his complete delivery from this misery. So when he left the bed he donned the dirty pig's hide once more. I leave you to imagine for yourselves how great was the joy of Meldina when she discovered that, instead of a pig, she had gained a handsome and gallant young prince for a husband. Not long after this she proved to be with child, and when the time of her delivery came she gave birth to a fair and shapely boy. The joy of the king and queen was unbounded, especially when they found that the new-born child had the form of a human being and not that of a beast.

But the burden of the strange and weighty secret which her husband had confided to her pressed heavily upon Meldina, and one day she went to her mother-in-law and said : ' Gracious queen, when first I married your son I believed I was married to a beast, but now I find that you have given me the comeliest, the worthiest, and the most gallant young man ever born into the world to be my husband. For know that when he comes into my chamber to lie by my side, he casts off his dirty hide and leaves it on the ground, and is changed into a graceful handsome youth. No one could believe this marvel save they saw it with their own eyes.' When the queen heard these words she deemed that her daughter-in-law must be jesting with her, but Meldina still persisted that what she said was true. And when the queen demanded to know how she might witness with her own eyes the truth of this thing, Meldina replied : ' Come to my chamber to-night, when we shall be in our first sleep ; the door will be open, and you will find that what I tell you is the truth.'

That same night, when the looked-for time had come, and all were gone to rest, the queen let some torches be kindled and went, accompanied by the king, to the chamber of her son, and when she had entered she saw the pig's skin lying on the floor in the corner of the room, and having gone to the bedside, found therein a handsome young man in whose arms Meldina was lying. And when they saw this, the delight of the king and queen was very great, and the king gave order that before anyone should leave the chamber the pig's hide should be torn to shreds. So great was their joy over the recovery of their son that they wellnigh died thereof.

And King Galeotto, when he saw that he had so fine a son, and a grandchild likewise, laid aside his diadem and his royal robes, and advanced to his place his son, whom he let be crowned with the greatest pomp, and who was ever afterwards known as King Pig. Thus, to the great contentment of all the people, the young king began his reign, and he lived long and happily with Meldina his beloved wife.

When Isabella's story was finished, the whole company broke into laughter at the notion of the pig prince, all dirty and muddy as he was, kissing his beloved spouse and lying by her side. " But let us give over laughter," cried Signora Lucretia, " in order that Isabella's enigma may be given in due course." And forthwith Isabella, with a smile, propounded her riddle.

> I prithee, sir, to give to me,
> What never did belong to thee,
> Or ever will, what though thy span
> Of life exceed the wont of man.
> Dream not this treasure to attain;
> Thy longing will be all in vain;
> But if you deem me such a prize,
> And pine for me with loving eyes,
> Give me this boon, my wish fulfil,
> For you can grant it if you will.

When Isabella had set forth her cunningly devised enigma, the listeners were all in a state of bewilderment, for no one could understand how a man could give what he did not possess or ever could possess. But Isabella, when she saw that they were troubled overmuch, said, with much good taste and judgment: "There is no reason for wonder, my good friends, for a man certainly can give to a woman that which he has not or ever will have; that is to say, a man has no husband nor ever will have one, but it is an easy matter for him to give one to a lady." The whole company received this solution with much applause, and when silence had once more been imposed on the assembly, Fiordiana, who sat next to Isabella, arose from her seat and, smiling merrily, said: "Signora, and you gentle folks all, does it not seem meet to you that Signor Molino, our good friend, should enliven this honourable company with one of his merry conceits; and I say this, not because I want to escape the task of telling my own story (for I have ready more than one), but because I feel that a tale, told with all his accustomed pleasant grace and style, would, just now, give the company the greater delight. He, as you well know, is ingenious and full of wit, and gifted with all those good parts which pertain to a man of breeding. And as for ourselves, dear ladies, it is better that we should ply our needles than be always telling stories."

All agreed with these prudent and well-timed words of Fiordiana, and warmly applauded them, and the Signora, casting her eyes towards Molino, said: "Come, Signor Antonio, it is now your turn to enliven us with an example of your graceful wit." And she signed to him to begin. Molino, who had not reckoned on being named as a storyteller for this evening, first gave his thanks to Fiordiana for the flatter-

ing words she had spoken of him, and then in obedience to the Signora's
direction began his fable.

THE SECOND FABLE.

*Filenio Sisterno, a student of Bologna, having been tricked by certain
ladies, takes his revenge upon them at a feast to which he has bidden
them.*

SHOULD never have believed or imagined that the
Signora would have laid upon me the task of telling a
story, seeing that in the due order of things we should
call upon Signora Fiordiana to give us one.   But since
it is the pleasure of the company, I will take upon myself to tell you
something which may peradventure fit in with your humour.   But
if by chance my narrative (which God forbid) should prove tiresome
to you, or should overstep the bounds of civility, I must crave your
indulgence therefor, and that the blame may be laid on Signora
Fiordiana, to whom it is in fact due.

In Bologna, the chief city of Lombardy, the parent of learning,
and a place furnished with everything needful for its high and
flourishing estate, there lived a young scholar of graceful and amiable
parts named Filenio Sisterno, born in the island of Crete.   It chanced
one day that a magnificent feast was given, to which were invited the
most beautiful and distinguished ladies of Bologna, and many gentlemen, and certain of the scholars, amongst whom was Filenio.   After
the manner of gallants, he went dallying now with this and now with
that fair dame, and finding no difficulty in suiting his taste, resolved
to lead out one of them for a dance.   His choice fell upon the Signora Emerentiana, the wife of a certain Messer Lamberto Bentivogli,
and she, who was very gracious, and no less sprightly than beautiful,
did not say him nay.   During the dance, which Filenio took care
should be very gentle and slow, he wrung her hand softly, and thus
addressed her in a whisper: 'Ah! Signora, how great is your beauty;
surely it transcends any that has yet met my eye; surely the lady
does not live who could ensnare my heart as you have ensnared it.
If only I might hope you would give me back the like, I should be

the happiest man in the world; but if you should prove cruel, you
will soon see me lying dead at your feet, and know yourself as the
cause of my bane. Seeing that I love you so entirely—and indeed I
could do no other thing—you ought to take me for your servant,
disposing both of my person and of the little I can call mine as if
they were your own. Higher favour from heaven I could not
obtain than to find myself subject to such a mistress, who has taken
me in the snare of love as if I had been a bird.' Emerentiana, while
she listened earnestly to these sweet and gracious speeches, like a
modest gentlewoman made as though she had no ears, and held her
peace. When the measure had come to an end, Emerentiana sat
down, and straightway Filenio led out another lady as his partner,
but the dance had scarcely begun before he began to address her in
like fashion: 'Of a truth, most gracious Signora, there is no need
for me to waste words in setting forth how deep and ardent is the
love I have for you, and ever shall have, so long as this soul of mine
inhabits and rules my unworthy frame. And I would hold myself
blest indeed if I could possess you as the lady of my heart and my
peculiar mistress. Therefore, loving you as I do, and being wholly
yours, as you may easily understand, I beg you will deign to take
me for your most humble servant, seeing that my life and everything
I have to live for depends on you and on no other.' The young lady,
whose name was Panthemia, although she understood all this, made
no reply, but modestly went on with the dance, and, when it had come
to an end, she sat down with the other ladies, smiling a little the
while.

But short time had passed before the gallant scholar took a third
partner by the hand; this time the most seemly, the most gracious,
and the fairest lady in Bologna, and began to tread a measure with
her, making all those who pressed round to admire her, give way;
and before the dance was ended he thus addressed her: 'Most
estimable lady, perhaps I shall seem to you out of measure presumptuous to reveal the secret love which I have borne, and still bear
towards you, but for this offence blame not me, but your own
beauty, which raises you high above all others, and makes me your
slave. I speak not now of your delightful manners, nor of your
surpassing virtues, which are great enough and many enough to
bring all the world to your feet. If then your loveliness, the work
of nature, and owing nought to art, fascinates everyone, there is no

wonder that it should constrain me to love you and to guard your image in my inmost heart. I beseech you then, sweet lady, the one comfort of my life, to spare some tenderness for one who dies for you a thousand times a day. If you grant me this grace I shall know I owe my life to you; so to your kindness I now recommend myself.'

The fair lady, who was called Sinforosia, when she heard the sweet and loving words which came from Filenio's ardent bosom, could not forbear sighing, but taking heed of her honour as a married woman she answered him nought, and when the dance was come to an end returned to her seat.

It happened that all these three ladies found themselves sitting in a ring close to one another, and disposed for sprightly talk, when Emerentiana, the spouse of Messer Lamberto, moved by jocund humour and not by spite, said to her two companions, 'Dear friends, I have to tell you of a diverting adventure which has this evening befallen me.' 'And what is it?' they inquired. Said Emerentiana, 'This evening, in the course of the dancing, I have gotten for myself a cavalier, the handsomest, the trimmest, the most gracious you could find anywhere, who protests himself to be so hotly inflamed with my beauty that he can find no rest day or night.' And word by word she related all that the scholar had said to her. As soon as Panthemia and Sinforosia heard her story, they told her that the same had happened to them, and before they left the feast they had satisfied themselves that it was the same gallant who had made love to all three of them. Wherefore they clearly comprehended that the words of this gallant sprang not from loyal feeling, but from deceit and feigning of love, and they gave to them no more credence than one is wont to give to the babblings of a sick man or to the romancer's fables, and they did not go from thence before they had agreed, each one of them, to put a trick upon him such as he would not readily forget; for ladies, too, may play jokes. Filenio meantime was bent on amorous design, and went on making love now to one lady now to another. Judging from their carriage that they looked not unkindly upon him, he set himself the task, if it were possible, of moving each one of them to grant him the supremest favour of love, but the issue of the affair was not according to his desire, for all his schemes went astray.

Emerentiana, who could no longer bear with the mock love-making of the silly scholar, called to a pretty buxom handmaid of hers, and charged her to find some excuse for speaking with Filenio, in order to disclose to him the love which her mistress had conceived for him, and to let him know that he might whenever he would spend a night with her in her own house. When Filenio heard this he was much elated, and said to the maid, 'Hasten home forthwith and commend me to your mistress, and tell her in my behalf that she may expect me this evening at her house, provided that her husband be not at home.' When this word had been brought to Emerentiana, she straightway caused to be collected a great store of prickly thorns, and having strewn these under the bed where she lay at night, she awaited the coming of her gallant. When it had become dusk the scholar took his sword and stole towards the house of his fancied mistress, and the door, when he had given the password, was immediately opened. Then, when the two had held some little converse and supped daintily, they withdrew into the bedchamber for the night.

Scarcely had Filenio taken off his clothes to go to bed when Messer Lamberto was heard without, and hereupon the lady, feigning to be at her wits' end where she should hide her lover, bade him get under the bed. Filenio, seeing how great the danger was, both to the lady and to himself, made haste to betake himself thither, without putting on any more clothes than the shirt he wore, and was in consequence so grievously pricked by the thorns prepared for him that there was no part of his body, from the crown of his head to the sole of his foot, which was not running with blood. And the more he essayed in this dark hole to defend himself from the pricks, the more grievously was he wounded, and he dared not make a sound lest Messer Lamberto should hear him and slay him. I leave you to figure in what plight the poor wretch found himself that night, seeing that he dared not call out, though he was like to lose a good part of his breech through the torment he was suffering. When the morning was come, and the husband had left the house, the wretched scholar clothed himself as best he could, and made his way back to his lodging, bleeding and in great fear lest he should die. But being well treated by his physician, he got well and recovered his former health.

Many days had not passed before Filenio essayed another bout of love-making, casting amorous eyes on the other two ladies, Panthemia and Sinforosia, and went so far as to find one evening an occasion to

address Panthemia, to whom he rehearsed his continued woes and torments, and besought her that she would have pity upon him.   Panthemia, who was full of tricks and mischief, while feigning to compassionate him, made excuse that it was not in her power to do his will ;
but at last, as if vanquished by his tender prayers and ardent sighs, she
brought him into her house.   And when he was undressed, and ready to
go to bed with her, she bade him go into a cabinet adjacent, where she
kept her orange water and perfumes, to the intent that he might well
perfume his person, and then get to bed.   The scholar, never suspecting the cunning of this mischief-working dame, entered the cabinet,
and, having set his foot upon a board unnailed from the joist which
held it up, he and the board as well fell down into a warehouse below,
in which certain merchants kept their store of cotton and wool, and
although he fell so far he suffered no ill.   The scholar, finding himself in this dark place, began to search for some ladder or door to serve
his exit, but coming upon none he cursed the hour and the place where
he had first set eyes on Panthemia.   The morning dawned at last, and
then the unhappy wight began to realize by degrees the full treachery
of Panthemia.   He espied on one side of the storehouse certain out-
lets in the wall, through which streamed in a dim light, and, finding
the masonry to be old and moss-grown, he set to work with all his
strength to pull out the stones in the spot which had fallen most to
decay, and soon made a gap big enough to let him out.   And, finding himself in an alley, clad only in his shirt, and stockingless, he stole
back to his lodging without being seen of any.

And next it happened that Sinforosia, having heard of the tricks
which the two others had played the scholar, resolved to treat him
with a third, no less noteworthy ; so, the next time she saw him, she
began to ogle him with the tail of her eye, by way of telling him that
a passion for him was burning her up.   Filenio, forgetting straightway his former mishaps, began to walk up and down past her house, and
play the lover.   Sinforosia, when she saw from this that he was deeply
smitten with love for her, sent him a letter by an old woman to let
him know that he had so completely captured her fancy by his fine
person and gracious manners that she could find rest neither night nor
day, and to beg him that, whenever it might please him, he would come
and hold converse with her, and give her a pleasure greater than any
other.   Filenio took the letter, and having mastered the contents, was
at once filled with more glee and happiness than he had ever known

before, clean forgetting all the tricks and injuries he had suffered hitherto. He took pen and ink, and wrote a reply, that, though she might be enamoured of him, he, on his part, was just as much in love with her, or even more, and that at any time she might appoint he would hold himself at her service and commands. When she had read this reply, Sinforosia made it her business to find full soon an opportunity for the scholar to be brought to her house, and then, after many feigned sighs, she said : ' O my Filenio, of a truth I know of no other gallant who could have brought me into such plight, but you alone ; since your comeliness, your grace, and your discourse have kindled such fire in my heart that I burn like dry wood.' The scholar, while he listened, took it for certain that she was melting with love for him, and, poor simpleton as he was, kept on some time bandying sweet and loving words with her, till it seemed to him that the time had come to go to bed and to lie down beside her. Then Sinforosia said : ' Before we go to bed it seems meet that we should regale ourselves somewhat.' And having taken him by the hand, she led him into an adjoining cabinet, where there was a table spread with sumptuous cakes and wines of the finest, in which the mischievous dame had caused to be mingled a certain drug, potent to send her gallant to sleep for a certain time. Filenio took a cup and filled it with wine, and suspecting no fraud he emptied it straightway. Enlivened by the banquet, and having washed himself in orange water and dainty perfumes, he got into bed, and then immediately the drug began to work, and he slept so sound that even the uproar of great artillery would scarce have awakened him. Then, when Sinforosia perceived that he was in a heavy slumber and that the drug was doing its work well, she called one of her maids, a strong wench whom she had made privy to the jest, and the two of them took Filenio by the legs and arms, and, having opened the door softly, they placed him in the street, about a stone's cast from the house, and there left him.

It was about an hour before dawn when, the drug having spent its force, the poor wretch came to himself, and, believing that he had been in bed with the lady, found himself instead stockingless, and clad only in his shirt, and half dead with cold through lying on the bare ground. Almost helpless in his arms and legs, he found it a hard matter to get on his feet, and, when he had done so much, it was with difficulty that he kept from falling again ; but he managed, as best he could, to regain his lodging and to care for his health.

Had it not been for his lusty youth, he would surely have been
maimed for life ; but he regained his former health, and when he
went abroad again he showed no signs of remembering the injuries
and vexations which had been put upon him ; but, on the other hand,
he bore himself towards the three ladies as if he loved them as well
as ever, and feigned, now to be enamoured of one, and now of
another. The ladies, never suspecting malice on his part, put a good
face on the matter, and treated him graciously as if they were dealing with a real lover. Filenio was many times tempted to give his
hand free play, and to mark their faces for them, but he prudently
took thought of the condition of the ladies, and of the shame that
would be cast on him should he offer violence to them, and restrained
his wrath. Day and night he considered how he might best wreak
his vengeance on them, and when he could hit on no plan he was in
great perplexity. But in the course of time he devised a scheme by
which he might readily work his purpose, and fortune aided him to
prosecute it as he had designed. He hired for himself in the city a
very fine house, containing a magnificent hall and many dainty
chambers, and in this he purposed to give a great and sumptuous
feast, and to invite thereto a company of gentlefolk, Emerentiana,
and Panthemia, and Sinforosia amongst the rest. They accepted the
scholar's invitation without demur, suspecting nothing sinister in the
same, and when they were come to the feast the wily scholar led them
with many courteous speeches into a room and begged them to take
some refreshment. As soon as the three ladies—foolish and impru-
dent indeed—had entered the room, Filenio locked the door, and,
advancing towards them, said : ' Now, my pretty ladies, the time is
come for me to take my revenge upon you, and to give you some
repayment for all the ills you put upon me, just because I loved you
so well.' When they heard these words, they seemed more dead
than alive, and began to repent heartily that they had ever abused
him, and at the same time to curse their own folly in having trusted
the word of one they ought to have treated as a foe. Then the
scholar with fierce and threatening looks commanded them that they
should, if they set any store on their lives, strip themselves naked,
and the ladies, when they heard this speech, exchanged glances one
with the other and began to weep, begging him the while, not only
for the sake of love, but also for the sake of his natural gentleness,
that their honour might be left to them. Filenio, exulting in his

deed, was exceedingly polite to them, but at the same time informed them that he could not suffer them to remain clothed in his presence. Hereupon the ladies cast themselves down at Filenio's feet, and with piteous weeping humbly besought him not to be the cause of so great shame to them. But he, whose heart was now grown as hard as a stone, cried out that what he would do to them was in no sense blameworthy: it was nothing but just revenge; so the ladies were forced to take off their clothes and to stand as naked as when they were born, in which condition they appeared fully as fair as when apparelled. When this had come to pass even Filenio began to feel some pity for them; but, remembering his recent wrongs, and the mortal perils he had undergone, he chased away his pitying humour and once more hardened his heart. He then craftily conveyed all the clothes and linen they had lately worn into a neighbouring cabinet, and bade them with threatenings all to get into one bed. The ladies, altogether astounded and shaking with terror, cried out, 'Wretched fools that we are! What will our husbands and our friends say when it shall be told to them that we have been found here slain in this shameful case?' The scholar, seeing them lying one by the other like married folk, took a large sheet of linen, very white, but not fine enough to suffer their bodies to be seen and recognized, and covered them therewith from head to foot; then he left the chamber, locking the door behind him, to go and find the three husbands, who were dancing in the hall. Their dance being finished, Filenio led them with him into the chamber where the ladies were lying in the bed, and said to them: 'Gentlemen, I have brought you hither for your diversion, and to show you the prettiest sight you have ever seen;' and, having led them up to the bed with a torch in his hand, he began softly to lift up the covering at their feet, and to turn it back so as to disclose the fair limbs beneath it as far as the knees, thus giving the three husbands something wondrous fair to look upon. Next he uncovered them as far as their stomachs, which he then disclosed entirely by lifting the sheet in the same way. I leave you to imagine how great was the diversion the three gentlemen got from this jest of Filenio's, also in what distressful plight these poor wretched ladies found themselves when they heard their husbands join in mocking them. They lay quite still, not daring even to cough, lest they should be discovered, while their husbands kept urging the scholar to uncover their faces; but he, wiser in other men's wrongs

than in his own, would not oblige them so far. Not content with
this, he brought forth their garments, which he showed to their
husbands, who, when they looked thereon, were astonished and somewhat perturbed at heart, and, after examining them closely, said one
to another : 'Is not this the gown which I once had made for my
wife?' 'Is not this the coif which I bought for her?' 'Is not this
the pendant that she hangs round her neck? Are not these the rings
she wears on her fingers?'

At last Filenio brought the three gentlemen out of the chamber,
and bade them, so as not to break up the company, to remain to
supper. The scholar, learning that the supper was ready and everything
set in order by the majordomo, gave the word for everyone to take
his place. And while the guests were setting their teeth to work,
Filenio returned to the chamber where the three ladies were, and as he
uncovered them said : 'Good evening, fair ladies; did you hear what
your husbands were saying? They are now without, waiting impatiently to see you. Get up; surely you have slept enough; give
over yawning and rubbing your eyes. Take your clothes and don
them without delay, and go into the hall where the other guests await
you.' With such words as these he mocked them; while they, dis-
consolate and despairing, feared lest this adventure might come to
some fatal issue, and wept bitterly. At last, full of anguish and terror
and looking for nothing less than death at his hands, they arose and
turning to the scholar said to him : 'Filenio, you have taken more
than vengeance upon us. Now nothing remains but for you to draw
your sword and make an end of our lives, for we desire death beyond
any other thing. And if you will not grant us this boon, at least
suffer us to return unobserved to our homes, so that our honour may
be saved.'

Filenio, seeing that he had carried the affair far enough, gave them
back their garments, and directed them to clothe themselves quickly,
and when this was done he sent them out of the house by a secret
door, and they went back to their homes. At once they laid aside
their fine clothes, which they had lately worn, and put them away in
their presses, and with great prudence sat down to work instead of
going to bed. When the feast had come to an end, the three husbands thanked the scholar for the fine entertainment he had given
them, and in particular for the sight of the beauties laid out for their
benefit in the chamber, beauties surpassing the sun himself, and,

having taken leave of him, they returned to their homes, where they found their wives sewing beside the hearth. Now the sight of the clothes, and the rings, and the jewels, which the scholar had exhibited to them, had made them somewhat suspicious; so each one now demanded of his wife where she had spent that evening, and where her best garments were. To this questioning each lady replied boldly that she had not left the house that evening, and, taking the keys of the coffers wherein was disposed her apparel, she showed this to her husband, with the rings and other jewels which he had given her. When the husbands saw these they were silent, and knew not what to say, but after a little they told their wives word by word what they had seen that evening. The ladies made as if they knew nothing of it, and, after jesting a little over the matter, they undressed and went to bed. And in after times Filenio often met the three ladies in the streets, and would always inquire of them: 'Which of you was in the greatest fear? and did I suffer most from your jests, or you from mine?' But they always held their eyes down on the ground, and said nothing. And in this fashion the scholar avenged himself as well as he could of the tricks he had suffered, without violence or outrage.

When they had listened to the story of Molino, the Signora and all the other ladies declared that the revenge, worked upon the three gentlewomen by the scholar for the tricks they had played him, was no less revolting than cowardly; but when they came to consider the severe punishment which the poor fellow had suffered in couching upon the thorns, and the danger of breaking his bones he had incurred in falling down into the warehouse, and the biting cold he had been exposed to when laid out in the open street to sleep upon the bare earth clad only in his shirt, they admitted that his vengeance was no heavier than was due. The Signora, though she had excused Fiordiana from telling her story in due order, now demanded of her that she should at least give her enigma, which ought to have some reference to the story of the scholar; and she, in obedience to this word, said: "Signora, it happens that the enigma which I have to submit to the company has nothing in keeping with deeds of grave and terrible vengeance such as the ingenious Signor Antonio has set forth in his fable, but at the same time it will be one which may be of interest to every studious youth." And without further delay she propounded her enigma:

From two dead blocks a living man
Gave life to one whose spirit ran
To vivify another wight,
Who thus from darkness rose to light.
Two living ones together bide,
The creature by the maker's side,
And by the creature's radiance led,
The master communes with the dead.

This subtle riddle of the Signora Fiordiana was interpreted in various wise, but not one of the company hit upon its exact meaning. And seeing that Fiordiana kept on shaking her head at the essays made by the company, Bembo remarked with a quiet smile, " Signora Fiordiana, it seems to me to be foolishness to waste our time in this fashion. Tell us what you will, and we shall be contented." " Since this noble company decrees," replied Fiordiana, " that I should be my own interpreter, I will gladly do this; not because I deem myself in any way competent for this task, but because I wish to oblige all you here, to whom I am bound by so many kindnesses. My enigma shows simply a student who rises from bed early in the morning, and he, a living thing, by the working of two dead things, the flint and the steel, gives life to the dead tinder, and this in its turn enlivens the dead candle. Thus the first living one, the student, by the help of these other two living ones who lately were dead, sits down to converse with the dead, that is, with the books writ by learned men of times long past." The explication of this most ingenious riddle by Fiordiana pleased the company greatly, and the Signora directed Lionora to begin her story at once.

THE THIRD FABLE.

Carlo da Rimini vainly pursues Theodosia with his love, she having resolved to live a virgin. In striving to embrace her he meets with divers misadventures, and is well beaten by his own servants to boot.

DEAR ladies, the clever story just told to us by Molino has made me give up all thought of relating to you the one I had in my mind, and to offer in its place another which, if I am not mistaken, will be equally pleasing to you ladies as Molino's was to the gentlemen. Mine will certainly be shorter than his, and, I think I may say, more decent in the subject it treats.

I must tell you then that Carlo da Rimini—as I think many of you know—was a man whose trade was fighting, a despiser of God, a blasphemer of the saints, brutal and a cutthroat, and at the same time given over to all kinds of effeminate luxury. So great indeed was his malignity and the corruption of his nature, that his equal could not be found. Now in the days when he was a handsome, seemly young man, it chanced that he became hotly enamoured of a certain maiden, the daughter of a poor widow, who, though she was very poor and only contrived to find a living for herself and her child with much difficulty, would rather have died with hunger than have consented to live on the wages of her daughter's sin.

The maiden, whose name was Theodosia, was very fair and graceful in her person, and no less honest and discreet in her conduct; moreover, she was of a prudent, sober temper, and had already determined to devote herself to the religious life and to prayer, holding all worldly things to be of small account. Carlo, therefore, burning with lascivious passion, was in the habit of molesting her with his attentions every day, and on any day when he might not chance to see her he was like to die of vexation.

With flatteries and gifts and solicitations he made frequent trial to win the maiden's consent to his wishes, but all his importunities were in vain; for, like a wise and good girl, she would have none of his presents, and every day she prayed to God to turn away from his heart these dishonest wishes. At last there came a time when he

could no longer hold within bounds his ardent lust and bestial desire,
and, feeling gravely affronted at these continual rebuffs by one
whom he loved more dearly than his own life, he made up his mind
to ravish her and satisfy his lecherous appetite, let the consequence
be what it might. But he feared to stir up a commotion through
any public scandal, lest the people, who held him in great hatred,
should rise and slay him.

But at last, being overcome by his unbridled desire, with his
mind distempered with rage as if he had been a mad dog, he made a
plan with two of his underlings—desperate ruffians both of them—
to carry her off and then to ravish her. Therefore one day, when
the evening dusk had fallen, he armed himself and went with the
two desperadoes to the young girl's dwelling-place, the door of which
he found open; but before entering he charged his men to keep on
the alert, and to take care, as they valued their own lives, that no
other person should enter the house or come out therefrom until he
himself should rejoin them. The two ruffians, who were full willing
to obey their leader's behests, gave answer that whatever he might
command should be carried out.

But Theodosia (by some means unknown to me) had got tidings
of Carlo's intent, and had shut herself up in a small kitchen, and Carlo,
when he had mounted the staircase of the poor little house, found
there the old mother, who, suspecting nothing of any such surprise,
had taken to her spinning. He demanded forthwith where was her
daughter, for whom he had such great love and desire, and the poor
old woman, as soon as she perceived that the young lecher was fully
armed and manifestly more inclined to evil than to good, was greatly
confounded in her mind, and her face became as white as the face of
a corpse, and she was on the point of screaming aloud; but, perceiving that her outcries would be of no use, she determined to hold her
peace, and put her honour in the keeping of God, whom she altogether
trusted. So, plucking up her courage, she turned to Carlo and said:
'Carlo, I know not what humour or what insolent spirit may have
brought you here to defile the soul of this girl, who desires to live
honestly. If by chance you should be come with righteous intent,
then may God grant you fulfilment of every just and honourable wish;
but if it should be otherwise, which God forbid, you are guilty of a
great wickedness in trying to attain by outrage that which can never
be yours. Therefore, cast away and have done with this unbridled

lust, and no longer strive to ravish from my daughter that which you can never give back to her, to wit, the chastity of her body. And the more you lust after her, the more she will hate you, seeing that her mind is firm set to dedicate herself to virginity.'

Carlo, when he heard these moving words spoken by the poor old mother, instead of being awakened to pity or turned away from his evil intent, raged like a madman, and began to search for Theodosia in every corner of the house, without finding any trace of her, until he came to the little kitchen, where, seeing that the door was fast close, he thought (and thought rightly) that she must be concealed. Then, spying through a crack in the door, he perceived Theodosia, who was at her prayers, and with honeyed words he began to beseech her that she would open to him the door, addressing her in these terms: 'Theodosia, life of my life, be sure that I am not come here to sully your honour, which is more dear to me than my own self and my own good name, but to take you as my wife, provided that my offer be acceptable to you and to your good mother. And, beyond this, I swear I will have the life of anyone who may in any way affront your honour.'

Theodosia, who listened attentively to Carlo's speech, answered him straightway in these terms: 'Carlo, I beseech you to give over this obstinate prosecution of your desire. I can never marry you, seeing that I have offered my virginal service to Him who sees and governs us all. And if cruel fortune should suffer you to defile violently this body of mine, at least you will have no power to blacken the purity of my soul, which from the hour of my birth I have dedicated to my Creator. God has given you freedom of will so that you may know the evil from the good, and may do that which seems best to you. Follow, therefore, after the good, and you will be of good report, and turn aside from evil.' Carlo, when he found that his flattery availed him nothing, and that the maiden refused to have aught to say to him, could no longer keep under the fire which was burning in his heart, and, more maddened than ever, trusted no longer to words, but resorted to violence, bursting open by force the door, which, being none of the strongest, soon gave way as he willed.

When Carlo entered the little kitchen and cast his eyes upon the maiden, so full of grace and fair beyond belief, his passion grew hotter than ever, and, thinking only of satisfying to the full his inordinate lust, he threw himself upon her from behind, just as if he had been an

eager famishing greyhound, and she a timid hare.   And the ill-fated
Theodosia, with her golden hair loose over her shoulders, and grasped
tightly round the neck by Carlo, grew pale, and felt so deadly a languor
coming over her that she could scarcely move.   Then she commended
her soul to heaven and demanded help of God above, and scarcely
had she finished her mental prayer, when, in miraculous wise, her body
seemed to melt away out of Carlo's grip; and at the same time God
dazzled so completely his eyesight and understanding that he no longer
knew rightly what were the things around him, and while he deemed
he was holding the maid in his embrace and covering her with kisses
and endearments, he was, in sooth, embracing nothing better than the
pots and pans, spits and cauldrons, and other kitchen gear lying about
the place.   Though his lust was in some measure satisfied, he soon
felt his wounded heart stirring again, and again he flew to embrace a
huge kettle, fancying all the while that he held in his arms the fair
form of Theodosia.   In thus handling the kettles and cauldrons his
hands and face were so besmirched with soot that he looked less like
Carlo da Rimini than the devil.   In the end, feeling that his desire
was for the nonce satisfied, and conscious that it was time to retreat,
he made his way out by the staircase all blackened as he was, but the
two ruffians, who were keeping guard near the door lest anyone should
enter or leave the house, when they saw him thus transformed, with
his face all disfigured, and looking more like a beast than a human
being, imagined that he must be some ghost or evil spirit, and were
fain to take to their heels and save themselves from this monster.
But having taken heart to stand up to him, and to look closely into
his face, which seemed to them mightily disfigured and ugly, they
began to drub him with cudgels and with their fists, which were as
hard as iron, so that they mangled cruelly his face and his shoulders
with hearty goodwill, and left not a hair on his head.   Not content
with this, they threw him down on the ground, stripping off the
clothes from his back, and dealing him as many kicks and cuffs as he
could endure, and the blows fell so thick and fast that Carlo had no
time allowed him to open his mouth and ask the reason of his cruel
chastisement.   Nevertheless, he made shift at last to break away from
their hold, when he ran as for his life, always suspecting, however,
that the ruffians were close behind him.

Thus Carlo, having been soundly beaten [1] by his servants, his eyes

---

[1] Orig., *essendo da suoi servi senza pettine oltra modo carminato.*

being so discoloured and swollen from their lusty pummelling that he could scarcely see, ran towards the piazza, clamouring and complaining loudly of the ill-handling he had got from his own men. The town-guard, when he heard these shouts and lamentations, went towards him, and, marking his disfigured state and his face all bedaubed with dirt, took him for a madman. And since no one recognized him, the whole crowd began to mock at him, and to cry : ' Give it to him, give it to him, for he is a lunatic.' Then some hustled him, others spat in his face, and others took dust and cast it in his eyes ; and they kept on maltreating him thus for a good space of time, until the uproar came to the ears of the prætor, who, having risen from his bed and gone to the window which overlooked the piazza, demanded what had happened to cause so great a tumult. One of the guards thereupon answered that there was a madman who was turning the piazza topsy-turvy, and the prætor gave order that he should be securely bound and brought before him, which command was forthwith carried out.

Now Carlo, who up to this time had been the terror of all, find-ing himself thus bound and ill-treated and insulted, without a notion as to the cause of it, was utterly confounded in his mind, and broke out into so violent a rage that he wellnigh burst the bonds that held him. But as soon as he was brought before the prætor, the latter recognized him straightway as Carlo da Rimini, and at once set down the filthy condition of his prisoner as the work of Theodosia, for he was privy to the fact that Carlo was inflamed with passion for the girl. Therefore he at once began to use soft speech and to soothe Carlo, promising to make smart sharply those who had brought upon him such a shameful mischance. Carlo, who suspected not that his face was like that of a blackamoor, could not at first gather the purport of these words, but in the end, when it had been made known to him how filthy his condition was, how that he resembled a brute beast rather than a man, he, like the prætor, attributed his discomfiture to Theodosia, and, letting his rage have free course, he swore an oath that unless the prætor would punish her he would take revenge by his own hand. When the morning was come, the prætor sent for Theodosia, deeming that she had wrought this deed by magic arts. But she gave good heed to the plight in which she stood, and com-pletely realized the great danger thereof; so she betook herself to a convent of nuns of holy life, where she abode secretly, serving God for the rest of her days with a cheerful heart.

M

It happened after this that Carlo was sent to lay siege to a strong place, and, when in the assault he pressed on to a more desperate essay than he had power to accomplish, he found himself caught like a rat in a trap; for, as he mounted the walls of the citadel to plant thereon the banner of the Pope, he was smitten by a great stone, which crushed him and dashed him to pieces in such manner that no time was allowed to him to make his peace with heaven. Thus the wicked Carlo made a wretched end of his days, according to his deserts, without having plucked that fruit of love he desired so ardently.

Before Lionora had come to the end of her concisely-told fable, all her good companions began to laugh over the stupidity of Carlo in kissing and embracing the pots and kettles, thinking all the while that he was enjoying his beloved Theodosia; nor did they make less merry in the case of the cuffs and blows he got from the hands of his own men in the rough handling they gave him. And after a good spell of laughter Lionora, without waiting for further word from the Signora, set forth her enigma:

> I am fine and pure and bright,
> At my best am snowy white.
> Maid and matron scourge and flout me,
> Yet they cannot do without me,
> For I serve both young and old,
> Shield their bodies from the cold.
> A parent mighty mothered me,
> Mother of all mothers she.
> And, my time of service past,
> I'm torn and beaten at the last.

This cleverly-worded enigma won the praise of all the company, but since it seemed to be beyond the power of anyone to solve it, Lionora was requested to divulge its meaning; whereupon she said with a smile: "It is scarcely becoming that one of parts so slender as mine should presume to teach you, ladies and gentlemen, who are so much better versed in knowledge. But since this is your will, and since your will to me is law, I will tell you forthwith what I mean by my enigma. It means nothing else than linen cloth, fine and white, which is by ladies pierced by scissors and needles, and beaten. And it serves as a covering to us all, and comes from the mother of us all, the earth; moreover, when it grows old we no longer send it to the fuller, but let it be torn up small and made into paper."

Everyone was pleased with the interpretation of this clever enigma and commended it highly. The Signora having already remarked that Lodovica, who was chosen to tell the next story, was troubled with a bad headache, turned to the Trevisan and said, "Signor Benedetto, it is indeed the duty of us ladies to provide the stories to-night; but seeing that Lodovica is gravely troubled in her head, we beg you to take her place this evening, and grant you free field to tell whatever may please you best." To which speech the Trevisan thus replied: "It happens, Signora, that I am little skilled in these matters; nevertheless (since your will commands my entire obedience) I will use my best effort to satisfy you all, begging you at the same time to hold me excused if I fail therein." And having made due salutation, he rose from his seat and began his story in the following words:

THE FOURTH FABLE.

The devil, having heard divers husbands railing over the humours of their wives, makes trial of matrimony by espousing Silvia Balastro, and, not being able to endure his wife for long, enters into the body of the Duke of Malphi.

HE frivolity and want of judgment which nowadays is to be found amongst most women (I speak of those who, without heed, give full licence to their eyes and fancy in straining to compass their unbridled lust), offers me occasion to tell to this noble concourse a story which may not be familiar. And, although you may find it somewhat short, and ill put together, it may, nevertheless, serve as a wholesome lesson to you wives to be less irksome and exacting to your husbands than you have been heretofore. And if I seem to lay on the lash too heavily, blame not me, who am but the humble servant of all you others, but make your complaint to the Signora, who, as you have heard, has given me leave to set before you whatever story might commend itself to my taste.

I will first tell you, gracious ladies, that many years ago the devil, becoming weary of the unceasing and clamorous accusations made by husbands against their wives, determined to test the truth of

these by making trial of marriage himself, and, that he might the
better compass this design, he took the shape of a goodly young man
of courtly manners, and well furnished with lands and gold, Pancrazio
Stornello by name.   As soon as the bruit of his intention got abroad
in the city, divers matchmakers waited upon him with plentiful choice
of comely women, well dowered, for his wife, and from amongst
these he settled upon Silvia Balastro, a noble maiden.   Never before
had the city witnessed such magnificent nuptials and rejoicings.   The
kinsfolk of the bride came from far and near, and for the best man
the bridegroom chose one Gasparino Boncio, a townsman of repute.
A few days after the marriage the devil addressed Sylvia, saying,
' My dear wife, I need scarcely tell you that I love you better than I
love myself, seeing that I have already given you many tokens of my
affection; therefore, for the sake of this love of mine, I am about to
beg of you a favour which will be easy for you to grant, and most
acceptable to me.   This favour is nought else than that you should
demand of me all that you want now, and all that you will ever be
likely to want, of raiment, jewellery, pearls, and other things of the
same sort which ladies love ; for I have determined, on account of the
great love I have for you, to give you all you may demand, though
it may cost a kingdom.   I make but one condition, which is, that you
shall never trouble me about such matters again ; so be careful that
you get all you can possibly require for the rest of our married life,
and be careful likewise never to demand aught of me more, for you
will ask in vain.'   Silvia begged for time to consider this proposition,
and, having betaken herself to Signora Anastasia, her mother, a
worldly-wise old lady, she laid bare the offer of her husband, and
asked for advice thereanent.   Anastasia, who knew well enough how
to play a game of this sort, took pen and paper and wrote out a list
of articles, such as would need two days to describe by word of mouth,
and said to Silvia, ' Take this paper, and ask your husband to give
you everything that is here written down.   If he agrees, you may be
well content with him.'   Hereupon Silvia departed, and, having found
her husband, she asked him to give her all that was written on the
list, and he, when he had carefully read it over, said, ' Are you quite
sure, dearest Sylvia, that you have put down here all you want—that
there is nothing missing for which at some future time you may have
to ask me ? for I warn you that, if this should be so, neither your
prayers nor your sighs nor your tears will avail to get it for you.'

Silvia could think of nothing else to ask for, and agreed to the conditions of her husband, who at once commanded to be made vast store of rich vestments studded with big pearls, and rings and all sorts of jewels the most sumptuous that were ever seen. And over and above these he gave her coifs and girdles embroidered with pearls, and all manner of other dainty baubles which can be better imagined than described. When Silvia was arrayed in these, and conscious of being the best dressed woman in the city, she became somewhat saucy. There was nothing else she could ask her husband for, so well had he cared for her needs.

It chanced, soon after this, that the city was all agog concerning a great feast to which were bidden all the nobles of the place, and amongst these was naturally included Silvia, who was amongst the most beautiful and distinguished ladies in the city. And the more to honour this festival, the other ladies met and devised all sorts of new fashions of dress, altering them so much that anyone accoutred in those in vogue heretofore would hardly have been recognized. There was no mother's daughter in the town—just as if it had happened to-day—who was not bent on mounting the newest fashion to do honour to the festival, and each one vied to outdo the other in pomp and magnificence.

When there came to Silvia's ears the news that the fashion of dress was to be changed, she was at once beset with fear that the store of raiment she had lately received from her husband would be found of unfashionable shape and unfit to be worn at the feast, and, in consequence, fell into a melancholy humour, neither eating nor sleeping, and making the house resound with her sighs and groans. The devil, who fathomed the trouble in his wife's heart, feigned to know nothing of it, and one day addressed her : 'What is troubling you, Silvia, that you look so unhappy? Have you no heart for the coming festival?' Silvia, seeing her opportunity, plucked up courage and said: 'What is the festival to me? How can I go there in these old-fashioned clothes of mine? I am sure you will not force me thither to be mocked at by the others.' Then said Pancrazio to her: 'Did I not give you everything you would want for the rest of your days? How comes it that you now ask me for more after agreeing to the conditions I then made?' These words only made Silvia weep the more, and, bewailing her unhappy fate, cry out that she could not go to the feast because she had no clothes fit to wear.

Then said the devil, 'I gave you at first all that was necessary for the rest of your days, but I will once more gratify your wishes. You may ask of me for anything you want, and your request shall be granted; but never again. If, after this, you make a like petition, the issue will be something you will never forget.'

Silvia straightway put off her peevish humour, and wrote out another list of braveries as long as the last, which Signor Pancrazio procured for her without delay. In the course of time the ladies of the city once more set to work to make another change in the fashion of dress, and once more Silvia found herself clad in dresses of outworn cut. No other lady could boast of jewels so costly, or of robes of such rich and sumptuous web; but this was no solace to her, and she went mourning all day long, without daring to make another appeal to her husband, who, marking her tristful face, and knowing well enough what was vexing her, said, 'Silvia, my love, why are you so sad?' Then she took courage and said, 'Is there not cause enough for me to be sad, seeing that I have no raiment in the new fashion, and that I cannot show my face amongst the other ladies of the city without their making a mock of me, and bringing reproach upon you as well as upon myself? and the respect and fidelity I have towards you do not merit such a return of shame and humiliation.' At these words the devil was terribly wroth and said: 'What cause have you for complaint? Have I not twice over given you all you have asked for? Your desires are insatiable, and beyond my power to satisfy. I will once more give you everything you may demand, but I will straightway go away and you will never see my face again.' The devil was as good as his word, and, after he had given Silvia a goodly store of new garments, all after the latest fashion, he left her without taking leave of her, and went to Malphi, where, for a diversion, he entered into the body of the duke and tormented him grievously.

Now it chanced that, soon after this, Gasparino Boncio, the gallant who had acted at Pancrazio's nuptials as best man, was forced to fly from his city on account of some offence against good manners. Wherefore he betook himself to Malphi, where he managed to live by gambling and by a lot of cunning tricks of which he was master, and rumour would have it that he was a man of parts, though he was indeed nought but a sorry knave. One day, when at the cards with some gentlemen of the place, he went a step too far, and roused their wrath so hotly that, but for fear of the law, they would certainly have made an end of him. One of these, smarting under some special wrong, vowed that he would bring Master Gasparino into such a plight as he would never forget. And forthwith he betook himself to the duke, and, having made a profound obeisance, he said: 'Your excellency, there is in this town a man named Gasparino, who makes boast that he can cast out evil spirits—whether of this world or of the nether one—which may have entered the bodies of men; therefore, methinks, you would do wisely to bid him try his skill to deliver you from your torment.' On hearing these words the duke sent forthwith for Gasparino, who, being summoned, went into the duke's presence at once.

'Signor Gasparino,' said the duke, 'they tell me you profess to be an exorcist of evil spirits. I, as no doubt you have heard, am sorely tormented by one of these, and I pledge my faith to you that, if you will work your spells upon him and drive him out, I will deal with you so that you may live for the rest of your days free from care.' Gasparino was utterly confounded by this speech, and, as soon as the duke was silent, he began to stammer and to protest loudly that he knew nought of such matters, and had never boasted of any such power; but the gentleman, who was standing by, came forward and said: 'Do you not remember, Signor Gasparino, that, on a certain day, you told me this and that?' Gasparino persisted in denying any such speech, and, while they were wrangling together, the duke broke in and said: 'Come, come, hold your peace, both of you! As for you, Master Gasparino, I give you three days to work up your charms, and, if you can deliver me from this misery, I promise you the most beautiful castle in my dominions, and you may ask of me whatever you will. But, if you fail in this, before eight days have passed I will have you strangled between two of these columns.'

Gasparino, when he listened to the duke's command, was utterly confounded and filled with grief, and, having withdrawn from the duke's presence, began to ruminate day and night as to how he might accomplish the task laid upon him. On the day fixed for the incantation he went to the palace, and, having ordered to be spread on the floor a large carpet, began to conjure the evil spirit to come out, and to cease his torment. The devil, who was quite at his ease in the duke's body, did not reply, but breathed so strong a

blast of wind through the duke's throat that he was like to choke
him. When Gasparino renewed his conjurations the devil cried out:
'My friend, you can enjoy your life; why can't you leave me at peace
here, where I am very comfortable? Your mummery is all in vain.'
And here the devil began to deride him. But Gasparino was not to
be daunted by this, and for the third time he called upon the devil to
come out, asking him so many questions that at last he got to know
the evil spirit to be no other than his whilom friend, Pancrazio
Stornello. 'And I know you, too,' the devil went on; 'you are
Gasparino Boncio, my very dear friend. Don't you remember those
merry nights we spent together?' 'Alas! my friend,' said Gasparino,
'why have you come here to torment this poor man?' 'That is my
secret,' answered the devil; 'why do you refuse to go away and
leave me here, where I am more at my ease than ever I was before?'
But Gasparino went on with his questioning so long and so adroitly
that he induced the devil at last to tell him the story of his wife's insatiable greed, of the violent aversion he had conceived for her thereanent, and how he had fled from her and taken up his abode in the
body of the duke, and that no consideration would induce him to
return to her. Having learnt so much, Gasparino said: 'And now,
my dear friend, I want you to do me a favour.' 'What may it be?'
the devil inquired. 'Nothing more than to get you gone from the
body of this poor man.' 'Friend Gasparino,' quoth the devil, 'I
never set you down as a wise man, but this request of yours tells me
you are a downright fool.' 'But I beg you, I implore you for the
sake of the merry bouts we have enjoyed together, to do as I ask,'
said Gasparino. 'The duke has heard that I have power to cast out
spirits, and has imposed this task upon me. Unless I fulfil it I shall
be hanged, and you will be chargeable with my death.' 'Pooh!'
said the devil, 'our camaraderie lays no such duties upon me. You
may go to the lowest depths of hell for all I care. Why didn't you
keep your tongue between your teeth, instead of going about boasting
of powers you do not possess?' And with this he roared most horribly, and threw the poor duke into a fit which nearly made an end
of him.

But after a little the duke came to himself again, and Gasparino
thus addressed him: 'My lord, take courage; for I see a way of
ridding you of this evil spirit. I must ask you to command all the
players of music in the city to assemble at the palace to-morrow

morning, and at a set moment to strike their instruments, while the
bells all ring loudly, and the gunners let off their cannon as a sign of
rejoicing for victory. The more noise they make the better for my
purpose. The rest you may leave to me.'

The next morning Gasparino went to the palace, and duly began
his incantations, and, as it had been settled, the trumpets and cymbals
and tambours gave out their music, and the bells and artillery clanged
and roared so loud and long that it seemed as if the uproar would
never cease. At last the devil asked Gasparino, 'Isn't there a hideous
medley of sound about the place? What is the meaning of it? Ah,
I begin to hear it plain now!' 'Begin to hear it!' said Gasparino.
'Surely there has been clamour enough for the last half-hour to have
deafened even you.' 'I dare say,' the devil replied; 'but you must
know that the bodies of you mortals are gross and dull enough to
shut out the sound from the hearing of one in my place; but, tell
me, what is the reason of this noise?' 'I'll tell you in a very few
words,' said Gasparino, 'if in the meantime you let the duke have a
little ease.' 'It shall be as you wish,' said the devil. And then
Gasparino brought out his story.

'You must know, my dear friend and former comrade,' he began,
'that it has come to the duke's ears how you were forced to run
away from your wife on account of the woes you suffered through
her greed for attire, and he has in consequence invited her to
Malphi. The noise you hear is part of the rejoicing of the city
over her arrival.' 'I see your hand in this, honest Signor Gasparino,' said the devil. 'Well, you have outdone me in cunning.
Was there ever a loyal friend? Was I not right in belittling the
claims of comradeship? However, you have won the game. The
distaste and horror in which I hold my wife are so great that I will
do your bidding and betake myself elsewhere; indeed, rather than
set eyes on her again, I prefer to depart for the nethermost hell.
Farewell, Gasparino, you will never see me or hear of me again.'

Immediately after these words the poor duke began to throttle
and choke, and his eyes rolled about in ghastly wise; but these
frightful tokens only gave warning that the evil spirit had at last
taken flight. Nothing remained to tell of his presence save an
appalling smell of sulphur. Gradually the duke came to himself,
and, when he had regained his former health, he sent for Gasparino,
and, to prove his gratitude, gave him a stately castle, and a great

sum of money, and a crowd of retainers to do him service. Though assailed by the envy of certain of the courtiers, Gasparino lived happily for many years; but Silvia, when she saw all the treasures her husband had given her turn to smoke and ashes, lost her wits, and died miserably.

The Trevisan told his story with great wit, and the men greeted it with hearty applause and laughter; but the ladies demurred some-what thereat, so that the Signora, hearing them murmuring amongst themselves while the men kept on their merriment, commanded silence and directed the Trevisan to give his enigma, and he, with-out excusing himself to the ladies for the sharp pricks against their sex dealt out in his story, thus began:

> In our midst a being proud
> Lives, with every sense endowed.
> Keen his wit, though brainless he,
> Reasoning with deep subtlety.
> Headless, handless, tongueless too,
> He kens our nature through and through.
> Born but once and born for ever,
> Death shall touch or mar him never.

The abstruse riddle of the Trevisan was no light task for the wit of the company, and it was in vain that each one essayed its unravel-ling. At last the Trevisan, seeing that their guesses were all wide of the mark, said: "It does not seem meet for me to perplex any longer the ingenuity of this honourable company. By your leave I will now unfold its meaning, unless you had rather wait for some cunning wit to fathom it." With one voice they prayed him to unveil its purport, and this he did in these terms: "My enigma signifies nothing else than the immortal soul of man, which, being spiritual, has neither head nor hands nor tongue, yet it makes its working known to all, and, whether it be judged in heaven or in hell, lives eternally." This learned unfolding of the Trevisan's obscure riddle pleased the company vastly.

Inasmuch as the night was now far spent, and the clamour of the cocks foretelling the dawn was heard, the Signora made sign to Vicenza, who was bespoken to tell the finishing story of the second night, to begin her task. But Vicenza, red in the face through choler at the Trevisan's story, and not from bashfulness, cried out: "Signor Benedetto, I looked for a better turn from you than this, that

ou would aim at something higher than the character of a mere railer
against women; but since you take so bitter a tone, meseems you
must have been vexed by some lady who has asked more of you than
you could give. Surely you lack justice if you judge us all alike; your
eyes will tell you that some of us, albeit all of the same flesh and
blood, are gentler and more worshipful than others. If you rate us
in such wise, wonder not if some day you find your beauty marred
by some damsel's finger-nails. Then you will sing your songs in vain."

To her the Trevisan replied: "I did not tell my story to hurt
the feelings of anyone, nor for spite of my own; but to give counsel
and warning to those ladies who may be going to marry, to be modest
and reasonable in the calls they make on their husbands." "I care
nought what may have been your object," said Vicenza, "nor do these
ladies either; but I will not sit silent and let it be thought I allow
these charges of yours against women to have any worth. I will tell
you a story which you may find to be one for your own edification," and
having made obeisance she began.

THE FIFTH FABLE.

*Messer Simplicio di Rossi is enamoured of Giliola, the wife of Ghirotto
Scanferla, a peasant, and having been caught in her company is ill-
handled by her husband therefor.*

NE cannot deny, dear ladies, the gentle nature of love, but
love rarely accords a happy issue to the enterprises it
inflames us to undertake. And thus it fell out in the
case of the lovesick Messer Simplicio di Rossi, who,
when he flattered himself that he was about to enjoy the person of
the woman he desired so ardently, had to fly from her laden with as
many buffets as he well could carry. All this history I will duly set
forth, if, as is your gracious custom, you will lend your ears to the
fable I purpose to relate to you.

In the village of Santa Eufemia, situated just below the plain of
San Pietro, in the territory of the famous and illustrious city of Padua,
there lived, some years ago, one Ghirotto Scanferla, a man rich and
influential enough for a man in his station, but at the same time a

factious, wrangling fellow, and he had for a wife a young woman named Giliola, who, albeit that she was peasant born, was very fair and graceful. With her Simplicio di Rossi, a citizen of Padua, fell violently in love. Now it happened that he had a house which stood not far removed from that of Ghirotto, and he was accustomed frequently to roam about the neighbouring fields with his wife, a very beautiful lady, whom however he held in but little esteem, although she had many good qualities which ought to have bound him to her. So great was his passion for Giliola that he got no rest day or night, but he let this passion lie closely hidden in his heart, partly because he feared lest he might in any way arouse the husband's wrath, partly on account of Giliola's good name, and partly for fear of giving offence to his own wife. Now close to Messer Simplicio's house there was a fountain from which gushed forth a stream of water, much sought by all the people round, and so clear and delicious that even a dead man might have been tempted to drink thereof; and hither every morning and evening Giliola would repair, with a copper pail, to fetch water for her household needs. Love, who of a truth spares nobody, spurred on Messer Simplicio in his passion; but he, knowing what her life was and the good name she bore, did not venture to manifest his love by any sign, and simply sustained himself and comforted his heart by gazing now and then upon her beauty. For her part she knew nothing of all this, nor was she cognizant at all of his admiration; for, as became a woman of honest life, she gave heed to nothing else but to her husband and her household affairs.

Now one day it happened that Giliola, when she went according to her custom to fetch water, met Messer Simplicio, to whom she said, in her simple, courteous way, as any woman might, 'Good morrow, Signor,' and to this he replied by uttering the word 'Ticco.' His thought was to divert her somewhat by a jest of this sort, and to make her familiar with his humour. She, however, took no heed thereof, nor said another word, but went straightway about her business. And as time went on the same thing happened over and over again, Simplicio always giving back the same word to Giliola's greeting. She had no suspicion of Simplicio's craftiness, and always went back to her home with her eyes cast down upon the ground; but after a time she determined that she would tell her husband what had befallen her. So one day, when they were conversing pleasantly together, she said to him, 'Oh! my husband, there is something I should

like to tell you, something that perhaps will make you laugh.'
'And what may this thing be?' inquired Ghirotto. 'Every time I
go to the well to draw water,' said Giliola, 'I meet Messer Simplicio,
and when I give him the good morning he answers to me " Ticco."
Over and over again I have pondered over this word, but I cannot
get at the meaning thereof.' 'And what answer did you give
him?' said Ghirotto, and Giliola replied that she had answered him
nothing. 'Well,' said Ghirotto, 'take care that when he next says
" Ticco" to you you answer him "Tacco." See that you give
good heed to this thing I tell you, and be sure not to say another
word to him, but come home according to your wont.' Giliola
went at the usual time to the well to fetch the water, and met Messer
Simplicio and gave him good day, and he, as hitherto, answered her
'Ticco.' Then Giliola, according to her husband's directions,
replied 'Tacco,' whereupon Messer Simplicio, suddenly inflamed,
and deeming that he had at last made his passion known to her, and
that he might now have his will of her, took further courage and
said, 'And when shall I come?' But Giliola, as her husband had
instructed her, answered nothing, but made her way home forthwith,
and being questioned by him how the affair had gone, she told him
how she had carried out everything he had directed her to do ; how
Messer Simplicio had asked her when he might come, and how she
had given him no reply.

Now Ghirotto, though he was only a peasant, was shrewd enough,
and at once grasped the meaning of Messer Simplicio's watchword,
which perturbed him mightily ; for it struck him that this word
meant more than mere trifling.[1] So he said to his wife, 'If the next
time you go to the well he should ask of you, " When shall I
come?" you must answer him, " This evening." The rest you can
leave to me.'

The next day, when Giliola went according to her wont to draw
water at the well, she found there Messer Simplicio, who was waiting
for her with ardent longing, and greeted him with her accustomed
'Good morning, Signor.' To this the gallant answered 'Ticco,'
and she followed suit with 'Tacco.' Then he added, 'When shall
I come?' to which she replied, 'This evening.' 'Let it be so then,'
he said. And when Giliola returned to her house she said to her

---

[1] Orig., *infilzar perle al scuro.*

husband, ' I have done everything as you directed.' ' What did he answer?' said Ghirotto. ' He said he would come this evening,' his wife replied.

Now Ghirotto, who by this time had got a bellyful of something else besides vermicelli and maccaroni, spake thus to his wife: 'Giliola, let us go now and measure a dozen sacks of oats, for I will make believe that I am going to the mill, and when Messer Simplicio shall come, you must make him welcome and give him honourable reception. But before this, have ready an empty sack beside those which will be full of oats, and as soon as you hear me come into the house make him hide himself in the sack thus prepared, and leave the rest to me.' ' But,' said Giliola, 'we have not in the house enough sacks to carry out the plan you propose.' ' Then send our neighbour Cia,' said the husband, ' to Messer Simplicio to beg him to lend us two, and she can also let it be known that I have business at the mill this evening.' And all these directions were diligently carried out. Messer Simplicio, who had given good heed to Giliola's words, and had marked, moreover, that she had sent to borrow two of his sacks, believed of a truth that the husband would be going to the mill in the evening, and found himself at the highest pitch of felicity and the happiest man in the world, fancying the while that Giliola was as hotly inflamed with love for him as he was for her; but the poor wight had no inkling of the conspiracy which was being hatched for his undoing, otherwise he would assuredly have gone to work with greater caution than he used.

Messer Simplicio had in his poultry yard good store of capons, and he took two of the best of these and sent them by his bodyservant to Giliola, enjoining her to let them be ready cooked by the time when he should be with her according to their agreement. And when night had come he stole secretly out and betook himself to Ghirotto's house, where Giliola gave him a most gracious reception. But when he saw the oat-sacks standing there he was somewhat surprised, for he expected that the husband would have taken them to the mill; so he said to Giliola, ' Where is Ghirotto? I thought he had gone to the mill, but I see the sacks are still here; so I hardly know what to think.' Then Giliola replied, ' Do not murmur, Messer Simplicio, or have any fear. Everything will go well. You must know that, just at vesper-time, my husband's brother-in-law came to the house and brought word that his sister was lying gravely

ill of a persistent fever, and was not like to see another day. Wherefore he mounted his horse and rode away to see her before she dies.'
Messer Simplicio, who was indeed as simple as his name imports, took
all this for the truth and said no more.

Whilst Giliola was busy cooking the capons and getting ready
the table, lo and behold ! Ghirotto her husband appeared in the courtyard, and Giliola, as soon as she saw him, feigned to be grief-stricken
and terrified, and cried out, 'Woe to us, wretches that we are ! We
are as good as dead, both of us ; ' and without a moment's hesitation
she ordered Messer Simplicio to get into the empty sack which was
lying there; and when he had got in—and he was mightily unwilling to enter it—she set the sack with Messer Simplicio inside it
behind the others which were full of oats, and waited till her husband
should come in. And when Ghirotto entered and saw the table duly
set and the capons cooking in the pot, he said to his wife: 'What is
the meaning of this sumptuous supper which you have prepared for
me?' and Giliola made answer : 'I thought that you must needs come
back weary and worn out at midnight, and, in order that you might
fortify and refresh yourself somewhat after the fatigues you so constantly have to undergo, I wished to let you have something succulent
for your meal.' 'By my faith,' said Ghirotto, 'you have done well,
for I am somewhat sick and can hardly wait to take my supper before
I go to bed, and moreover I want to be astir in good time to-morrow
morning to go to the mill. But before we sit down to supper I want
to see whether the sacks we got ready for the mill are all in order
and of just weight.' And with these words he went up to the sacks
and began to count them, and, finding there were thirteen, he feigned
to have made a miscount of them, and began to count them over
again, and still he found there were thirteen of them ; so he said to
his wife : 'Giliola, what is the meaning of this? How is it that I
find here thirteen sacks while we only got ready twelve? Where
does the odd one come from?' And Giliola answered : 'Yes, of a
certainty, when we put the oats into the sacks there were only twelve,
and how this one comes to be here I cannot tell.'

Inside the sack, meantime, Messer Simplicio, who knew well
enough that there were thirteen sacks on account of his being there,
kept silent as a mouse and went on muttering paternosters beneath
his breath, at the same time cursing Giliola, and his passion for her,
and his own folly in having put faith in her. If he could have cleared

himself from his present trouble by flight, he would have readily taken to his heels, for he feared the shame that might arise thereanent, rather than the loss. But Ghirotto, who knew well enough what was inside the sack, took hold of it and dragged it outside the door, which he had by design left open, in order that the poor wretch inside the sack, after he should have been well drubbed, might get out of the sack and have free field to go whithersoever he listed. Then Ghirotto, having caught up a knotty stick which he had duly prepared for the purpose, began to belabour him so soundly that there was not a square inch of his carcass which was not thrashed and beaten; indeed, a little more would have made an end of Messer Simplicio. And if it had not happened that the wife, moved by pity or by fear lest her husband should have the sin of murder on his soul, wrenched the cudgel out of Ghirotto's hand, homicide might well have been the issue.

At last, when Ghirotto had given over his work and had gone away, Messer Simplicio slunk out of his sack, and, aching from head to foot, made his way home, half dreading the while that Ghirotto with his stick was close behind him; and in the meantime Ghirotto and his wife, after eating a good supper at Messer Simplicio's cost, went to bed. And after a few days had passed, Giliola, when she went to the well, saw Simplicio, who was walking up and down the terrace in his garden, and with a merry glance greeted him, saying, 'Ticco, Messer Simplicio;' but he, who still felt the pain of the bruises he had gotten on account of this word, only replied:

> Neither for your good morning, nor for your tic nor your tac,
> Will you catch me again, my lady, inside your sack.

When Giliola heard this she was struck silent, and went back to her house with her face red for shame, and Messer Simplicio, after the sorry usage he had received, changed his humour and gave the fullest and most loving service to his own wife, whom he had hitherto disliked, keeping his eyes and his hands off other men's goods, so that he might not again be treated to a like experience.

When Vicenza had made an end of her story, all the ladies cried out with one voice: "If the Trevisan treated badly the women he dealt with in his fable, Vicenza has in hers given the men yet worse measure in letting Messer Simplicio be thus beaten and mauled in the mishandling he got." And while they were all laughing, one at this thing and another at that, the Signora made a sign for silence in order that Vicenza might duly propound her enigma; and the latter, feeling that she had more than avenged the insult put upon her sex by the Trevisan, gave her enigma in these terms:

> I blush to tell my name aright,
> Rough to touch, and rude to sight.
> Wide and toothless is my mouth,
> Red of hue my lips uncouth;
> Black all round, and from below
> Ardour oft will make me glow;
> Rouse my passion closely pent,
> Make me foam till I am spent.
> A scullion base may e'en abuse me,
> And all men at their pleasure use me.

The men were hard pressed to keep from laughing when they saw the ladies cast down their eyes into their laps, smiling somewhat the while. But the Signora, to whom modest speech was more pleasing than aught that savoured of ribaldry, bent a stern and troubled glance upon Vicenza and thus addressed her: "If I had not too much respect for these gentlemen, I would tell you to your face what really is the meaning of this lewd and immodest riddle of yours; but I will forgive you this once, only take good heed that you offend not again in such fashion; for, if you should, I will let you feel and know what my power over you really is." Then Vicenza, blushing like a morning rosebud at hearing herself thus shamefully reproved, plucked up her courage and gave answer in these terms: "Signora, if I have uttered a single word which has offended your ears, or the ears of any of the modest gentlewomen I see around me, I should assuredly deserve not only your reproof, but severe chastisement to boot. But, seeing that my words were in themselves simple and blameless, they scarcely merited so bitter a censure; for the interpretation of my riddle, which has been apprehended by you in a mistaken sense, will show my words to be true and prove my innocence at the same time. The thing which my enigma describes is a stockpot, which is black all round, and when fiercely heated by the fire boils over and scatters foam on all sides. It has a wide mouth and no teeth, and takes everything that may be thrown into it, and any scullion may take out what he will when the dinner is being prepared for his master."

When they heard from Vicenza this modest solution of her riddle, all the listeners, men as well as women, gave her hearty praise, deeming the while that she had been wrongfully reproved by the Signora. And now, because the hour was late, and the rosy tints of morning already visible in the sky, the Signora, without excusing herself in any way for the scolding she had given Vicenza, dismissed the company, bidding them all under pain of her displeasure to assemble in good time the following evening.

The End of the Second Night.

Night the Third.

The Fables and Enigmas of Messer
Giovanni Francesco Straparola da Caravaggio.

Night the Third.

LREADY the sister of the sun had begun her reign in the sky over the forests and the gloomy gorges of the hills, and showed her golden circle over the half of heaven; already the car of Phœbus had sunk beneath the western wave, the moving stars had lighted their lamps, and the pretty birds, ceasing their pleasant songs and bickerings, sought repose in their nests set amongst the green boughs, when the ladies and the gallant youths as well met on the third evening in the accustomed spot to renew their story-telling. And as soon as they were all seated according to their rank, the Signora Lucretia commanded that the vase should be brought forth as before, and in it she caused to be placed the names of five damsels, who, according to the order determined by lot, should that evening tell in turn their stories. The first name which was drawn from the vase was that of Cateruzza, the second that of Arianna, the third that of Lauretta, the fourth that of Alteria, and the fifth that of Eritrea. Then the Signora gave the word for the Trevisan to take his lute, and Molino his viol, and for all the rest to tread a measure to Bembo's leading. And when the dance had come to an end, and the sweet lyre and the divine strings of the hollow lute were silent, the Signora directed Lauretta to begin her song, and she, anxious to obey the Signora in everything, took hands with her companions, and having made respectful salutation, sang in clear and mellow tone the following song:

SONG.

Lady, while thy face I scan,
Where love smiling holds his court,
Lo ! from out your beauteous eyes
Light so radiant doth arise,
That it shows us Paradise.

All my sighs and all my tears,
Which I foolish shed in vain ;
All the anguish of my heart,
All my hidden woe and smart,
With my faint desire have part.

Then to love's last mood I fly,
Recking nought that earth and sky
Stand beneath me and above ;
So my soul is drawn by love
To the heights of passion free,
And I learn that fate's decree
Binds me, whatsoe'er betide,
Dead or living, to thy side.

After Lauretta and her companions had given sign by their silence
that their song had come to an end, the Signora, bending her gaze
upon the fair and open countenance of Cateruzza, said that the task
of making a beginning of the story-telling of that third evening fell
upon her, and Cateruzza, with a becoming blush upon her cheek and
laughing lightly, began in these terms.

THE FIRST FABLE.

*A simple fellow, named Peter, gets back his wits by the help of a tunny fish
which he spared after having taken it in his net, and likewise wins for
his wife a king's daughter.*

THERE is proof enough, dear ladies, both in the chronicles
of the past and in the doings of our own day, that a fool,
whether by lucky accident or by sheer force of blundering,
may sometimes score a success where a wise man might fail.
Therefore it has come into my mind to tell you the story of one of
these fools, who, through the issue of a very foolish deed, got for his

wife the daughter of a king and became a wise man himself into the bargain.

In the Ligurian Sea there is an island called Capraia, which, at the time I am describing, was ruled by King Luciano. Amongst his subjects was a poor widow named Isotta, who lived with her only son Peter, a fisher-lad, but from Peter's fishing she would scarce have kept body and soul together, for he was a poor silly creature known to all the neighbours as Peter the Fool. Though he went fishing every day he never caught anything, but in spite of his ill-success he would always come up from his boat shouting and bellowing so that all the town might hear him: 'Mother, mother, bring out your tubs and your buckets and your pails; bring them out all, great and small, for Peter has caught a boatful of fish.' The poor woman soon got to know the value of Peter's bragging, but in spite of this she always prepared the vessels, only to find herself jeered at by the silly youth, who, as soon as he came near, would thrust out his long tongue in ridicule, and otherwise mock at her.

Now it chanced that the widow's cottage stood just opposite to the palace of King Luciano, who had only one child, a pretty graceful girl about ten years old, Luciana by name. She, it happened, was looking out of the window of the palace one day when Peter came back from fishing, crying out to his mother to bring out her tubs and her buckets and her pails to hold the fish with which he was laden, and so much was she diverted at the silly antics of the fool, that it seemed likely she would die with laughing. Peter, when he saw that he was made sport of, grew very angry, and threw some ugly words at her, but the more he raged the more she—after the manner of wilful children—laughed and made mock at him. Peter, however, went on with his fishing day after day, and played the same trick on his mother every evening on his return; but at last fortune favoured him, and he caught a fine tunny, very big and fat. Overjoyed at his good luck, he began to shout and cry out over and over again, 'Mother and I will have a good supper to-night,' when, to his amazement, he heard the tunny which he had just caught begin to speak: 'Ah! my dear brother, I pray you of your courtesy to give me my life. When once you have eaten me, what farther benefit do you think you will get from me? but if you will let me live there is no telling what service I may not render you.' But Peter, whose thoughts just then were set only on his supper, hoisted the fish on his shoulders and set off homewards; but the tunny still kept on beseeching his captor to spare his life, promising him first as many fish as he could want, and finally to do him any favour he might demand. Peter was not hard-hearted, and, though a fool, fancied he might profit by sparing the fish, so he listened to the tunny's petition and threw him back into the sea. The fish, sensible of Peter's kindness, and not wishing to seem un-grateful, told Peter to get into his boat again and tilt it over so that the water could run in. This advice Peter at once followed, and, having leant over on one side, he let the boat be half filled with water, which brought in with it such a huge quantity of fish that the boat was in danger of sinking. Peter was wellnigh beside himself with joy when he saw what had happened, and, when he had taken as many fish as he could carry, he betook himself homewards, crying out, as was his wont, when he drew near to the cottage : ' Mother, mother, bring out your tubs and your buckets and your pails; bring out them all, great and small, for Peter has caught a boatful of fish.' At first poor Isotta, think-ing that he was only playing his old fool's game, took no heed; but at last, hearing him cry out louder than ever, and fearing that he might commit some greater folly if he should not find the vessels prepared as usual, got them all ready. What was her surprise to see her simple-ton of a son at last coming back with a brave spoil! The Princess Luciana was at the palace window, and hearing Peter bellowing louder than ever, she laughed louder than ever, so that Peter was almost mad with rage, and having left his fish, he rushed back to the seashore, and called aloud on the tunny to come and help him. The fish, hearing Peter's voice, came to the marge of the shore, and putting his nose up out of the waves, asked what service was required of him. ' What service !' cried Peter. ' Why I would that Luciana, that saucy minx, the daughter of our king, should find herself with child at once.'

What followed was a proof that the tunny had not made an empty promise to Peter, for before many days had passed the figure of the young girl, who was not twelve years old, began to show signs of maternity. Her mother, when she marked this, fell into great trouble, but she could not believe that a child of eleven could be pregnant, and rather set down the swelling to the working of an incurable disease; so she brought Luciana to be examined by some women expert in such cases, and these, as soon as they saw the girl, declared that she was certainly with child. The queen, overwhelmed by this terrible news, told it also to the king, and he, when he heard it, cried aloud for death rather than such ignominy. Strict inquisition was made to discover who could have violated the child, but nothing was found out; so Luciano, to hide her dire disgrace, determined to have his daughter secretly killed.

The queen, on hearing this, begged her husband to spare the unfortunate Luciana till the child should be born, and then do with her what he would. The king, moved with compassion for his only daughter, gave way so far; and in due time Luciana was delivered of a boy so fine and beautiful that the king could no longer harbour the thought of putting them away, but, on the other hand, gave order to the queen that the boy should be well tended till he was a year old. When this time was completed the child had become beautiful beyond compare, and then it came into the king's mind that he would again make a trial to find out who the father might be. He issued a proclamation that every man in the city who had passed fourteen years should, under pain of losing his head, present himself at the palace bearing in his hand some fruit or flower which might attract the child's attention. On the appointed day, in obedience to the proclamation, all those summoned came to the palace, bearing, this man one thing and that man another, and, having passed before the king, sat down according to their rank.

Now it happened that a certain young man as he was betaking himself to the palace met Peter, and said to him, ' Peter, why are you not going to the palace like all the others to obey the order of the king ?' ' What should I do in such a crowd as that ? ' said Peter. ' Cannot you see I am a poor naked fellow, and have hardly a rag to my back, and yet you ask me to push myself in amongst all those gentlemen and courtiers? No.' Then the young man, laughing at him, said, ' Come with me, and I will give you a coat. Who knows whether the child may not turn out to be yours?' In the end Peter let himself be persuaded to go to the young man's house, and having put on a decent coat, they went together to the palace; but when they arrived there Peter's heart again failed him, and he hid himself behind a door. By this time all the men had presented themselves to the king, and were seated in the hall. Then Luciano commanded the nurse to bring in the child, thinking that if the father should be there the sense of paternity would make him give some sign. As the nurse carried the child down the hall everyone, as he passed, began to caress him and to give him, this one a fruit and that one a

flower; but the infant, with a wave of his hand, refused them all.
When the nurse passed by the entrance door the child began to laugh
and crow, and threw himself forward so lustily that he almost jumped
out of the woman's arms, but she, not knowing that anyone was
there, walked on down the hall. When she came back to the same
place, the child was more delighted than ever, laughing and pointing
with his finger to the door; so that the king, who had already
noticed the child's actions, called to the nurse, and asked her who was
behind the door. The nurse, being somewhat confused, said that
surely some beggar must be hidden there. By the king's command
Peter was at once haled forth, and everybody recognized the town
fool; but the child, who was close to him, stretched out his arms and
clasped Peter round the neck, and kissed him lovingly. The king,
recognizing the sign, was stricken to the heart with grief, and having
discharged the assembly, commanded that Peter and Luciana and the
child should be put to death forthwith.

The queen, though assenting to this doom, was fearful lest the
public execution of the victims might draw down upon the king the
anger of the people; so she persuaded him to have made a huge cask
into which the three might be put and cast into the sea to drift
at random; then, at least, no one might witness their dying agony.
This the king agreed to; and when the cask was made, the condemned ones were put therein, with a basket of bread and a flask of
wine, and a drum of figs for the child, and thrust out into the rough
sea, with the expectation that the waves would soon dash it to pieces
against the rocks; but this was not to be their fate.

Peter's poor old mother, when she heard of her son's misfortune,
died of grief in a few days; and the unhappy Luciana, tossed about
by the cruel waves, and seeing neither sun nor moon, would have
welcomed a similar fate. The child, since she had no milk to give
it, had to be soothed to sleep with now and then a fig; but Peter
seemed to care for nothing, and ate the bread and drank the wine
steadily, laughing the while. 'Alas! alas!' cried Luciana in despair,
' you care nothing for this evil which you have brought upon me, a
poor innocent girl. You eat and drink and laugh without a thought
of the danger around us.' 'Why,' replied Peter, 'this misfortune
is more your own fault than mine. If you had not mocked me so,
it would never have happened; but do not lose heart, our troubles
will soon be over.' 'I believe that,' cried Luciana, 'for the cask

will soon be split on a rock, and then we must all be drowned.'
'No, no,' said Peter, 'calm yourself. I have a secret, and were you
to know what it is, you would be vastly surprised and vastly delighted too, I believe.' 'What secret can you know,' said Luciana,
'which will avail us in such danger as this?' 'I will soon tell you,'
Peter replied. 'I have a faithful servant, a great fish, who will do
me any service I ask of him, and there is nothing he cannot do. I
may as well tell you it was through his working that you became
with child.' 'That I cannot believe,' said Luciana; 'and what may
this fish of yours be called?' 'His name is Signor Tunny,' replied
Peter. 'Then,' said Luciana, 'to put your fish to the test, I will ask
you to transfer to me the power you exercise over him, and to command him to do my bidding instead of yours.' 'Be it as you will,'
said Peter; and without more ado he called the tunny, who at once rose
up near the cask, whereupon Peter commanded him to do everything
that Luciana might require of him. She at once exercised her power
over the fish by ordering him to make the waves cast the cask ashore
in a fair safe cleft in the rocks on an island, a short sail from her
father's kingdom. As soon as the fish had worked her will so far,
she laid other and much harder tasks upon him: one was to change
Peter from the ugly fool he was into a clever, handsome gallant;
another was, to have built for her forthwith a rich and sumptuous
palace, with lofty halls and chambers, and girt with carven terraces.
Within the court there was to be laid out a beautiful garden, full of
trees which should bear, instead of fruit, pearls and precious stones,
and in the midst of it two fountains, one of the freshest water and
the other of the finest wine. All these wonders were wrought by
the fish almost as soon as Luciana had spoken.

Now all this time the king and the queen were in deep misery in
thinking of the cruel death they had contrived for Luciana and her
child, how they had given their own flesh and blood to be eaten by
the fishes; therefore, to find some solace in their woe, they determined
to go to Jerusalem and to visit the Holy Land. So they ordered a
ship to be put in order for them, and furnished with all things suited
to their state. They set sail with a favouring wind, and before they
had gone a hundred miles they came in sight of an island upon which
they could see a stately palace, built a little above the level of the
sea. Seeing that this palace was so fair and sumptuous, and standing,
moreover, within Luciano's kingdom, they were seized with a longing

to view it more closely ; so, having put into a haven, they landed on the island.   Before they had come to the palace Luciana and Peter saw and recognized them, and, having gone forth to meet them, greeted them with a cordial welcome, but the king and queen did not know their hosts for the great change which had come over them.   The guests were taken first into the palace, which they examined in every part, praising loudly its great beauty, and then they were led by a secret staircase into the garden, the splendour of which pleased them so amazingly that they swore they had never at any time before looked upon a place so delightful.   In the centre of this garden there stood a noble tree, which bore on one of its branches three golden apples.   These the keeper of the garden was charged to guard jealously against robbers, and now, by some secret working which I cannot unravel, the finest of these apples was transported into the folds of the king's robe about his bosom, and there hidden.   Luciano and the queen were about to take their leave when the keeper approached and said to Luciana, ' Madam, the most beautiful of the three golden apples is missing, and I can find no trace of the thief.'

Luciana forthwith gave orders that the whole household should be searched, one by one, for such a loss as this was no light matter. The keeper, after he had searched thoroughly everyone, came back and told Luciana that the apple was nowhere to be found.   At these words Luciana fell into great confusion, and, turning to the king, said : ' Your majesty must not be wroth with me if I ask that even you allow yourself to be searched, for I prize the golden apple that is lost almost as highly as my life.'   The king, unsuspicious of any trick, and sure of his innocence, straightway loosened his robe, and lo ! the golden apple fell from it to the ground.

The king stood as one dazed, ignorant as to how the golden apple could have come into his robe, and Luciana spoke : ' Sire, we have welcomed you to our house with all the worship fitting to your rank, and now, as a recompense, you would privily rob our garden of its finest fruit.   Meseems you have proved yourself very ungrateful.'   The king, in his innocence, attempted to prove to her that he could not have taken the apple, and Luciana, seeing his confusion, knew that the time had come for her to speak, and reveal herself to her father.   ' My lord,' she said, with the tears in her eyes, ' I am Luciana, your hapless daughter, whom you sentenced to a cruel death along with my child and Peter the fisher-boy.   Though I bore a child,

I was never unchaste. Here is the boy, and here is he whom men were wont to call Peter the Fool. You wonder at this change. It has all been brought about by the power of a marvellous fish whose life Peter spared when he had caught it in his net. By this power Peter has been turned into the wisest of men, and the palace you see has been built. In the same way I became pregnant without knowledge of a man, and the golden apple was conveyed into the folds of your robe. I am as innocent of unchastity as you are of theft.'

When the king heard these words his eyes were opened, and he knew his child. Then, weeping with joy, they embraced each other, and all were glad and happy. After spending a few days on the island, they all embarked and returned together to Capraia, where with sumptuous feastings and rejoicings Peter was duly married to Luciana, and lived with her in great honour and contentment, until Luciano died, and then he became king in his stead.

The story of Cateruzza had at one time moved the ladies to tears; but, when its happy issue was made known to them, they rejoiced and thanked God therefor. Then the Signora, when Cateruzza had ended, commanded her to continue in the order they had followed hitherto, and she, not willing to hold in suspense the attention of her hearers, smilingly proposed to them the following enigma :

> Sir Redman stands behind a tree,
> Now hidden, now in sight is he.
> To him four runners speed along,
> Bearing a warrior huge and strong.
> Two darts into the trunk he wings,
> And Redman from his lair upsprings,
> And smites him from behind with skill ;
> Thus ten little men one giant kill.
> Now he who shall this speech unfold,
> Shall be a witty rogue and bold.

Cateruzza's graceful and ingenious enigma was received by the whole company with applause. Many interpretations were put forth ; but none came so near the mark as Lauretta : " Our sister's enigma can have but one meaning—the wild bull of the forest,' she said. ' He has four runners to carry his huge bulk. The sight of a red rag maddens him, and thinking to rend it, he strikes his horns into the tree. Straightway the huntsman, who was hidden behind the trunk, comes forth and kills him with a dart sped by ten little men, that is, the ten fingers of his two hands."

This speedy solution of her riddle raised an angry humour in Cateruzza's heart, for she had hoped it might prove beyond the wit of any; but she had not reckoned for Lauretta's quickness. The Signora, who perceived that the two were fain to wrangle, called for silence, and gave the word to Arianna to begin a story which should please them all, and the damsel, somewhat bashful, began as follows.

THE SECOND FABLE.

Dalfreno, King of Tunis, had two sons, one called Listico and the other Livoretto. The latter afterwards was known as Porcarollo, and in the end won for his wife Bellisandra, the daughter of Attarante, King of Damascus.

IT is no light matter for the steersman, let him be ever so watchful, to bring his tempest-strained bark safely into a sheltered port when he may be vexed by envious and contrary fortune, and tossed about amongst the hard and ragged rocks. And so it happened to Livoretto, son of the great King of Tunis, who, after many dangers hardly to be believed, heavy afflictions, and lengthened fatigues, succeeded at last, through the valour of his spirit, in trampling under foot his wretched fortune, and in the end reigned peacefully over his kingdom in Cairo. All this I shall make abundantly clear in the fable I am about to relate to you.

In Tunis, a stately city on the coast of Africa, there reigned, not long ago, a famous and powerful king named Dalfreno. He had to wife a beautiful and wise lady, and by her begot two sons, modest, well-doing and obedient in everything to their father, the elder being called Listico, and the younger Livoretto. Now it happened that by royal decree, as well as by the approved usage of the state, these youths were barred in the succession to their father's throne, which ran entirely in the female line. Wherefore the king, when he saw that he was by evil fortune deprived of female issue, and was assured by knowledge of himself that he was come to an age when he could hardly expect any further progeny, was sorely troubled, and felt his heart wrung thereanent with unbounded grief. And his sorrow was

all the heavier because he was haunted by the dread that after his
death his sons might be looked at askance, and evilly treated, and
driven with ignominy from his kingdom.

The unhappy king, infected by these dolorous humours, and
knowing not where might lie any remedy therefor, turned to the
queen, whom he loved very dearly, and thus addressed her : ' Madam,
what shall we do with these sons of ours, seeing that we are bereft
of all power to leave them heirs to our kingdom both by the law and
by the ancient custom of the land ? '   The sagacious queen at once
made answer to him in these words : ' Sire, it seems to me that, as
you have a greater store of riches than any other king in the world,
you should send them away into some foreign country where no man
would know them, giving them first a great quantity of money and
jewels.   In such case they may well find favour in the sight of some
well-disposed sovereign, who will see that no ill befall them.   And if
(which may God forbid) they should happen to come to want, no one
will know whose sons they are.   They are young, fair to look upon,
of good address, high-spirited, and on the alert for every honourable
and knightly enterprise, and let them go where they will they will
scarcely find any king or prince or great lord who will not love them
and set great store upon them for the sake of the rich gifts which
nature has lavished upon them.'   This answer of the prudent queen
accorded fully with the humour of King Dalfreno, and having summoned into his presence his sons Listico and Livoretto, he said to
them : ' My well-beloved sons, you must by this time know that,
after I am dead, you will have no chance of succeeding to the sovereignty of this my kingdom ; not, indeed, on account of your vices or
from your ill manner of living, but because it has been thus determined by law and by the ancient custom of the country.   You being
men, created by mother nature and ourselves, and not women, are
barred from all claim.   Wherefore your mother and I, for the benefit
and advantage of you both, have determined to let you voyage into
some strange land, taking with you jewels and gems and money in
plenty ; so that whenever you may light upon some honourable
position you may gain your living in honourable wise, and do credit
to us at the same time.   And for this reason I look that you shall
show yourselves obedient to our wishes.'

Listico and Livoretto were as much pleased at this proposition as
the king and the queen themselves had been, because both one and

other of the young men desired ardently to see new lands and to
taste the pleasures of the world.   It happened that the queen (as is
not seldom the way with mothers) loved the younger son more tenderly than she loved the elder, and before they took their departure
she called him aside and gave him a prancing high-mettled horse,
flecked with spots, with a small shapely head, and high courage
shining in its eye.   Moreover, in addition to all these good qualities
with which it was endowed, it was gifted with magic powers, but this
last fact the queen told only to Livoretto, her younger son.

As soon, then, as the two sons had received their parents' benediction, and secured the treasure prepared for them, they departed
secretly together; and after they had ridden for many days without
lighting upon any spot which pleased them, they began to be sorely
troubled at their fate.   Then Livoretto spoke and addressed his
brother : ' We have all this time ridden in one another's company,
and narrowly searched the country without having wrought any deed
which could add aught to our repute.   Wherefore it seems to me
wiser (supposing what I propose contents you also) that we should
separate one from the other, and that each one should go in search
of adventures for himself.'

Listico, having taken thought of his brother's proposition, agreed
thereto, and then, after they had warmly embraced and kissed each
other, they bade farewell and went their several ways.   Listico, of
whom nothing more was ever heard, took his way towards the West,
while Livoretto journeyed into the East.   And it happened that,
after he had consumed a great space of time in going from one place
to another, and seen almost every country under the sun, and spent
all the jewels and the money and the other treasures his good father had
given him, save and except the magic horse, Livoretto found himself at
last in Cairo, the royal city of Egypt, which was at that time under
the rule of a sultan whose name was Danebruno, a man wise in all
the secrets of statecraft, and powerful through his riches and his high
estate, but now heavily stricken in years.   But, notwithstanding his
advanced age, he was inflamed with the most ardent love for Bellisandra, the youthful daughter of Attarante, the King of Damascus,
against which city he had at this time sent a powerful army with
orders to camp round about it, and to lay siege to it, and to take it
by storm, in order that, either by love or by force, he might win
for himself the princess to wife.   But Bellisandra, who had already

a certain foreknowledge that the Sultan of Cairo was both old and ugly, had made up her mind once for all that, rather than be forced to become the wife of such a man, she would die by her own hand.

As soon as Livoretto had arrived at Cairo, and had gone into the city, and wandered into every part thereof, and marvelled at all he saw, he felt this was a place to his taste, and seeing that he had by this time lavished all his substance in paying for his maintenance, he determined that he would not depart thence until he should have taken service with some master or other. And one day, when he found himself by the palace of the sultan, he espied in the court thereof a great number of guards and mamelukes and slaves, and he questioned some of these as to whether there was in the court of the sultan lack of servants of any sort, and they answered him there was none. But, after a little, one of these, calling to mind that there was room in the household for a man to tend the pigs, shouted after him, and questioned him whether he would be willing to be a swineherd, and Livoretto answered ' Yes.' Then the man bade him get off his horse, and took him to the pigsties, asking at the same time what was his name. Livoretto told him, but hereafter men always called him Porcarollo, the name they gave him.

And thus it happened that Livoretto, now known by the name of Porcarollo, settled himself in the court of the sultan, and had no other employ than to let fatten the pigs, and in this duty he showed such great care and diligence that he brought to an end easily in two months tasks which would have taken any other man six months to accomplish. When, therefore, the guards and the mamelukes and the slaves perceived what a serviceable fellow he was, they persuaded the sultan that it would be well to provide some other employment for him, because his diligence and cleverness deserved some better office than the low one he now held. Wherefore, by the decree of the sultan, he was put in charge of all the horses in the royal stables, with a large augmentation of his salary, a promotion which pleased him mightily, because he deemed that, when he should be the master of all the other horses, he would be the better able to see well to his own. And when he got to work in his new office he cleaned and trimmed the horses so thoroughly, and made such good use of the currycomb, that their skins shone like satin.

Now, amongst the other horses there was an exceedingly beautiful high-spirited young palfrey, to which, on account of its good looks,

he paid special attention in order to train it perfectly, and he trained
it so well that the palfrey, besides going anywhere he might be told
to go, would curve his neck, and dance, and stand at his whole height
on his hind legs and paw the air so rapidly that every motion seemed
like the flight of a bolt from a crossbow. The mamelukes and slaves,
when they saw what Livoretto had taught the palfrey to do by his
training, were thunderstruck with amazement, for it seemed to them
that such things could hardly ensue in the course of nature. Wherefore
they determined to tell the whole matter to the sultan, in order that he
might take pleasure in witnessing the marvellous skill of Porcarollo.

The sultan, who always wore an appearance of great melancholy,
whether from the torture of his amorous passion or by reason of his
great age, cared little or nothing for recreation of any sort ; but,
weighed down by his troublesome humours, would pass the time in
thinking of nothing else besides his beloved mistress. However, the
mamelukes and the slaves made so much ado about the matter, that
before long the sultan was moved to take his stand at the window one
morning, and there to witness all the various wonderful and dexterous
feats of horsemanship which Porcarollo performed with his trained
palfrey, and, seeing what a good-looking youth he was, and how well
formed in his person, and finding, moreover, that what he had seen was
even more attractive than he had been led to expect, he came to the con-
clusion that it was mighty ill management (which now he began greatly
to regret) to have sent so accomplished a youth to no better office than
the feeding and tending of beasts. Wherefore, having turned the
matter over in his mind, and considered it in every light, he realized
to the full the eminent qualities, hitherto concealed, of the graceful
young man, and found there was nothing lacking in him. So he
resolved at once to remove him from the office he now filled, and to
place him in one of higher consideration ; so, having caused Porcarollo
to be summoned into his presence, he thus addressed him : 'Porcarollo,
it is my will that you do service no longer in the stables, as heretofore,
but that you attend me at my own table and do the office of cupbearer,
and taste everything that may be put before me, as a guarantee that I
may eat thereof without hurt.'

The young man, after he had duly entered upon the office of cupbearer to the sultan, discharged his duties with so great art and skil-
fulness that he won the approbation, not only of the sultan, but of all
those about the court. But amongst the mamelukes and slaves there

arose against him such a bitter hatred and envy on account of the
great favour done to him by the sultan that they could scarce bear the
sight of him, and, had they not been kept back by the fear of their
master, they would assuredly have taken his life.   Therefore, in order
to deprive the unfortunate youth of the favour of the sultan, and to
let him either be slain or driven into perpetual exile, they devised a
most cunning and ingenious plot for the furtherance of their design.
They made beginning in this wise.   One morning a slave named
Chebur, who had been sent in his turn to do service to the sultan,
said, 'My lord, I have some good news to give you.'   'And what
may this be?' inquired the sultan.   'It is,' replied the slave, 'that
Porcarollo, who bears by right the name of Livoretto, has been boasting that he would be able to accomplish for you even so heavy a task
as to give into your keeping the daughter of Attarante, King of
Damascus.'   'And how can such a thing as this be possible?' asked
the sultan.   To whom Chebur replied, 'It is indeed possible, O my
lord! but if you will not put faith in my words, inquire of the mamelukes and of the other slaves, in whose presence he has boasted more
than once of his power to do this thing, and then you will easily know
whether the tale I am telling you be false or true.'   After the sultan
had duly assured himself that what the slave had told to him was just,
he summoned Livoretto into his presence, and demanded of him
whether this saying concerning him which was openly bruited about
the court, was true.   Then the young man, who knew nothing of
what had gone before, gave a stout denial, and spake so bluntly that
the sultan, with his rage and animosity fully aroused, thus addressed
him : 'Get you hence straightway, and if within the space of thirty
days you have not brought into my power the Princess Bellisandra,
the daughter of Attarante, King of Damascus, I will have your head
taken off your shoulders.'   The young man, when he heard this cruel
speech of the sultan, withdrew from the presence overwhelmed with
grief and confusion, and betook himself to the stables.

As soon as he had entered, the fairy horse, who remarked at once
the sad looks of his master and the scalding tears which fell so plentifully from his eyes, turned to him and said : 'Alas! my master, why
do I see you so deeply agitated and so full of grief?'   The young man,
weeping and sighing deeply the while, told him from beginning to
end all that the sultan had required him to perform.   Whereupon the
horse, tossing his head and making signs as if he were laughing,

managed to comfort him somewhat, and went on to bid him be of
good heart and fear not, for all his affairs would come to a prosperous
issue in the end.   Then he said to his master : ' Go back to the sultan
and beg him to give you a letter patent addressed to the captain-
general of his army who is now laying siege to Damascus, in which
letter he shall write to the general an express command that, as
soon as he shall have seen and read the letter patent sealed with the
sultan's great seal, he shall forthwith raise the siege of the city, and
give to you money and fine clothing and arms in order that you may
be able to prosecute with vigour and spirit the great enterprise which
lies before you.   And if peradventure it should happen, during your
voyage thitherward, that any person or any animal of whatever sort
or condition should entreat you to do them service of any kind, take
heed that you perform the favour which may be required of you, nor,
as you hold your life dear to you, refuse to do the service asked for.
And if you should meet with any man who is anxious to purchase me
of you, tell him that you are willing to sell me, but at the same time
demand for me a price so extravagant that he shall give up all thought
of the bargain.   But if at any time a woman should wish to buy me,·
bear yourself gently towards her, and do her every possible courtesy,
giving her full liberty to stroke my head, my forehead, my eyes and
ears, and my loins, and to do anything else she may have a mind to,
for I will let them handle me as they will without doing them the
least mischief or hurt of any kind.'

When he heard these words the young man, full of hope and
spirit, went back to the sultan and made a request to him for
the letter patent and for everything else that the fairy horse had
named to him.   And when he had procured all these from the
sultan, he straightway mounted the horse and took the road which
led to Damascus, giving by his departure great delight to all the
mamelukes and slaves, who, on account of the burning envy and
unspeakable hate they harboured against him, held it for certain
that he would never again come back alive to Cairo.   Now it
happened that, when Livoretto had been a long time on his journey,
he came one day to a pool, and he marked, as he passed by the end
thereof, that the shore gave forth a very offensive smell, the cause of
which I cannot tell, so that one could hardly go near to the place,
and there upon the shore he saw lying a fish half dead.   The fish,
when it saw Livoretto approaching, cried out : ' Alas ! kind gentle-

man, I beseech you of your courtesy to set me free from this foul-smelling mud, for I am, as you may see, wellnigh dead on account of it. The young man, taking good heed of all that the fairy horse had told him, forthwith got down from his saddle and drew the fish out of the ill-smelling water, and washed it clean with his own hands. Then the fish, after it had returned due thanks to Livoretto for the kindness he had done for it, said to him: 'Take from my back the three biggest scales you can find, and keep them carefully by you; and if at any time it shall happen that you are in need of succour, put down the scales by the bank of the river, and I will come to you straightway and will give you instant help.'

Livoretto accordingly took the three scales, and, having thrown the fish, which was now quite clean and shining, into the clear water, remounted his horse and rode on until he came to a certain place where he found a peregrine falcon which had been frozen into a sheet of ice as far as the middle of its body, and could not get free. The falcon, when it saw the young man, cried out: 'Alas! fair youth, take pity on me, and release me from this ice in which, as you see, I am imprisoned, and I promise, if you will deliver me from this great misfortune, I will lend you my aid if at any time you should chance to stand in need thereof.' The young man, overcome by compassion and pity, went kindly to the succour of the bird, and having drawn a knife which he carried attached to the scabbard of his sword, he beat and pierced with the point thereof the hard ice round about the bird so that he brake it, and then he took out the falcon and cherished it in his bosom in order to bring back somewhat of warmth to its body. The falcon, when it had recovered its strength and was itself again, thanked the young man profusely for his kindness, and as a recompense for the great service he had wrought, it gave him two feathers which he would find growing under its left wing, begging him at the same time to guard and preserve them most carefully for the sake of the love it bore him; for if in the future he should chance to stand in need of any succour, he might take the two feathers to the river and stick them in the bank there, and then immediately it would come to his assistance. And having thus spoken the bird flew away.

After Livoretto had continued his journey for some days he came to the sultan's army encamped before the city, and there he found the captain-general, who was vexing the place with fierce

assaults. Having been brought into the general's presence, he
drew forth the sultan's letter patent, and the general, as soon as
he had mastered the contents thereof, immediately gave orders that
the siege should be raised, and this having been done he marched
back to Cairo with his whole army. Livoretto, after watching the
departure of the captain-general, made his way the next morning into
the city of Damascus by himself, and having taken up his quarters
at an inn, he attired himself in a very fair and rich garment, all
covered with most rare and precious gems, which shone bright
enough to make the sun envious, and mounted his fairy horse, and
rode into the piazza in front of the royal palace, where he made the
horse go through all the exercises he had taught it with so great
readiness and dexterity, that everyone who beheld him stood still in
amazement and could look at nought beside.

Now it happened that the noise made by the tumultuous crowd
in the piazza below roused from sleep the Princess Bellisandra, and
she forthwith arose from her bed. Having gone out upon a balcony,
which commanded a view of all the square beneath, she saw there a
very handsome youth; but what she marked especially was the beauty
and vivacity of the gallant and high-mettled horse on which he sat.
In short, she was seized with a desire to get this horse for her own,
just as keen as the passion of an amorous youth for the fair maiden
on whom he has set his heart. So she went at once to her father
and besought him most urgently to buy the horse for her, because
ever since she had looked upon his beauty and grace she had come
to feel that she could not live without him. Then the king, for the
gratification of the fancy of his daughter, whom he loved very tenderly, sent out one of his chief nobles to ask Livoretto whether he
would be willing to sell his horse for any reasonable price, because
the only daughter of the king was taken with the keenest desire to
possess it. On hearing this Livoretto answered that there was
nothing on earth precious and excellent enough to be accounted as a
price for the horse, and demanded therefor a greater sum of money
than there was in all the dominions which the king had inherited
from his fathers. When the king heard the enormous price asked
by Livoretto, he called his daughter and said to her: ' My daughter,
I cannot bring myself to lavish the value of my whole kingdom in
purchasing for you this horse and in satisfying your desire. Wherefore have a little patience, and live happy and contented, for I will

make search and buy you another horse even better and more beautiful than this.'

But the effect of these words of the king was to inflame Bellisandra with yet more ardent longing to possess the horse, and she besought her father more insistently than ever to buy it for her, no matter how great might be the price he had to pay for it. Then the maiden, after much praying and intercession, found that her entreaties had no avail with her father, so she left him, and betook herself to her mother, and feigning to be half dead and prostrate with despair, fell into her arms. The mother, filled with pity, and seeing her child so deeply grief-stricken and pale, gave her what gentle consolation she could, and begged her to moderate her grief, and suggested that, as soon as the king should be out of the way, they two should seek out the young man and should bargain with him for the purchase of the horse, and then perhaps (because they were women) he would let them have it at a more reasonable price. The maiden, when she heard these kindly words of her beloved mother, was somewhat comforted, and as soon as the king was gone elsewhere the queen straightway despatched a messenger to Livoretto, bidding him to come at once to the palace and to bring his horse with him; and he, when he heard the message thus delivered to him, rejoiced greatly, and at once betook himself to the court. When he was come into the queen's presence, she forthwith asked him what price he demanded for the horse which her daughter so much desired to possess, and he answered her in these words: 'Madam, if you were to offer to give me all you possess in the world for my horse it could never become your daughter's as a purchase, but if it should please her to accept it as a gift, she can have it for nothing. Before she takes it as a present, however, I had rather that she should make trial of it, for it is so gentle and well-trained that it will allow anybody to mount it without difficulty.' With these words he got down from the saddle and helped the princess to mount therein; whereupon she, holding the reins in her hand, made it go here and there and managed it perfectly. But after a little, when the princess had gone on the horse about a stone's throw distant from her mother, Livoretto sprang suddenly upon the crupper of the horse, and struck his spurs deep into the flanks of the beast, and pricked it so sharply that it went as quickly as if it had been a bird flying through the air. The maiden, bewildered at this strange conduct, began to cry out: ' You wicked and

disloyal traitor! Whither are you carrying me, you dog, and son of a
dog?' However, all her cries and reproaches were to no purpose,
for there was no one near to give her aid or even to comfort her
with a word.

It happened as they rode along that they came to the bank of a
river, and in passing this the maiden drew off from her finger a very
beautiful ring which she wore thereon, and cast it secretly into the water.
And after they had been for many days on their journey, they arrived
at last at Cairo, and as soon as Livoretto had come to the palace he
immediately took the princess and presented her to the sultan, who,
when he saw how lovely and graceful and pure she was, rejoiced
greatly, and bade her welcome with all sorts of kindly speeches.
And after a while, when the hour for retiring to rest had come, and
the sultan had retired with the princess to a chamber as richly adorned
as it was beautiful in itself, the princess spake thus to the sultan:
'Sire, do not dream that I will ever yield to your amorous wishes
unless you first command that wicked and rascally servant of yours
to find my ring which fell into the river as we journeyed hither.
When he shall have recovered it and brought it back to me you
will see that I shall be ready to comply with your desire.' The
sultan, who was by this time all on fire with love for the deeply
injured princess, could deny her nothing which might please her; so
he turned to Livoretto and bade him straightway set forth in quest
of the ring, threatening him that if he should fail in his task he
should be immediately put to death.

Livoretto, as soon as he heard the words of the sultan, perceived
that these were orders which must be carried out at once, and that he
would put himself in great danger by running counter to his master's
wishes; so he went out of his presence deeply troubled, and betook
himself to the stables, where he wept long and bitterly, for he was
altogether without hope that he would ever be able to recover the
princess's ring. The fairy horse, when he saw his master thus heavily
stricken with grief and weeping so piteously, asked him what evil could
have come to him to make him shed such bitter tears; and after Livoretto had told him the cause thereof, the horse thus addressed his master:
'Ah, my poor master! cease, I pray you, to talk in this strain.
Remember the words that the fish spake to you, and open your ears
to hear what I shall say, and take good heed to carry out everything
as I shall direct you. Go back to the sultan and ask him for all you

may need for your enterprise, and then set about it with a confident spirit, and have no doubts.' Livoretto therefore did exactly what the horse commanded him to do, no more and no less; and, after having travelled for some time, came at last to that particular spot where he had crossed the river with the princess, and there he laid the three scales of the fish on the green turf of the bank. Whereupon the fish, gliding through the bright and limpid stream, leaping now to this side and now to that, swam up to where Livoretto stood with every manifestation of joy and gladness, and, having brought out of his mouth the rare and precious ring, he delivered it into Livoretto's hand, and when he had taken back his three scales he plunged beneath the water and disappeared.

As soon as Livoretto had got the ring safely back, all his sorrow at once gave place to gladness, and without any delay he took his way home to Cairo, and when he had come into the sultan's presence and had made formal obeisance to him, he presented the ring to the princess. The sultan, as soon as he saw that her wishes had been fulfilled by the restoration of the precious ring she had desired so ardently, began to court her with the most tender and amorous caresses and flattering speeches, hoping thereby to induce her to lie with him that night; but all his supplications and wooings were in vain, for the princess said to him: 'Sir, do not think to deceive me with your fine words and false speeches. I swear to you that you shall never take your pleasure of me until that ruffian, that false rascal who entrapped me with his horse and conveyed me hither, shall have brought me some of the water of life.' The sultan, who was anxious not to cross or contradict in any way this lady of whom he was so much enamoured, but did all in his power to please her, straightway summoned Livoretto, and bade him in a severe tone to go forth and to bring back with him some of the water of life, or to lose his head.

Livoretto, when he heard the impossible demand that was made upon him, was terribly overcome with grief; moreover, the wrath which was kindled in his heart burst out into a flame, and he complained bitterly that the sultan should offer him so wretched a return as this for all the faithful service he had given, and for all the heavy and prolonged fatigue he had undergone, putting his own life the while in the most imminent danger. But the sultan, burning with love, was in no mind to set aside the purpose he had formed for

R

satisfying the wishes of the lady he loved so much, and let it be known that he would have the water of life found for her at any cost. So when Livoretto went out of his master's presence he betook himself, as was his wont, to the stables, cursing his evil fortune and weeping bitterly all the while. The horse, when he saw the heavy grief in which his master was, and listened to his bitter lamentations, spake to him thus : 'O my master! why do you torment yourself in this fashion? Tell me if any fresh ill has happened to you. Calm yourself as well as you can, and remember that a remedy is to be found for every evil under the sun, except for death.' And when the horse had heard the reason of Livoretto's bitter weeping, it comforted him with gentle words, bidding him recall to memory what had been spoken to him by the falcon which he had delivered from its frozen bonds of ice, and the valuable gift of the two feathers. Whereupon the unhappy Livoretto, having taken heed of all the horse said to him, mounted it and rode away. He carried with him a small phial of glass, well sealed at the mouth, and this he made fast to his girdle. Then he rode onward and onward till he came to the spot where he had set the falcon at liberty, and there he planted the two feathers in the bank of the river according to the direction he had received, and suddenly the falcon appeared in the air and asked him what his need might be. To this Livoretto answered that he wanted some of the water of life ; and the falcon, when he heard these words, cried out, ' Alas, alas, gentle knight! the thing you seek is impossible. You will never get it by your own power, because the fountain from which it springs is always guarded and narrowly watched by two savage lions and by two dragons, who roar horribly day and night without ceasing, and mangle miserably and devour all those who would approach the fountain to take of the water. But now, as a recompense for the great service you once rendered me, take the phial which hangs at your side, and fasten it under my right wing, and see that you depart not from this place until I shall have returned.'

When Livoretto had done all this as the falcon had ordered, the bird rose up from the earth with the phial attached to its wing, and flew away to the region where was the fountain of the water of life, and, having secretly filled the phial with the water, returned to the place where Livoretto was, and gave to him the phial. Then he took up his two feathers and flew away out of sight.

Livoretto, in great joy that he had indeed procured some of the
precious water, without making any more delay returned to Cairo in
haste, and, having arrived there, he presented himself to the sultan,
who was passing the time in pleasant converse with Bellisandra, his
beloved lady.   The sultan took the water of life, and in high glee
gave it to the princess, and, as soon as she could call this precious
fluid her own, he recommenced his entreaties that she would, according to her promise, yield herself to his pleasure.   But she, firm as
a strong tower beaten about by the raging winds, declared that she
would never consent to gratify his desire unless he should first cut
off with his own hands the head of that Livoretto who had been to
her the cause of so great shame and disaster.   When the sultan heard
this savage demand of the cruel princess, he was in no degree moved
to comply with it, because it seemed to him a most shameful thing
that, as a recompense for all the great labours he had accomplished,
Livoretto should be thus cruelly bereft of life.   But the treacherous
and wicked princess, resolutely determined to work her nefarious
purpose, snatched up a naked dagger, and with all the daring and
violence of a man struck the youth in the throat while the sultan
was standing by, and, because there was no one present with courage
enough to give succour to the unhappy Livoretto, he fell dead.

And not content with this cruel outrage, the bloody-minded girl
hewed off his head from his shoulders, and, having chopped his flesh
into small pieces, and torn up his nerves, and broken his hard bones
and ground them to a fine powder, she took a large bowl of copper,
and little by little she threw therein the pounded and cut-up flesh,
compounding it with the bones and the nerves as women of a household are wont to do when they make a great pasty with a leavened
crust thereto.   And after all was well kneaded, and the cut-up flesh
thoroughly blended with the powdered bones and the nerves, the
princess fashioned out of the mixed-up mass the fine and shapely
image of a man, and this she sprinkled with the water of life out of
the phial, and straightway the young man was restored to life from
death more handsome and more graceful than he had ever been
before.

The sultan, who felt the weight of his years heavy upon him,
no sooner saw this amazing feat and the great miracle which was
wrought, than he was struck with astonishment and stood as one
confounded.   Then he felt a great longing to be made again a youth,

so he begged Bellisandra to treat him in the same way as she had treated Livoretto. Then the princess, who tarried not a moment to obey this command of the sultan, took up the sharp knife which was still wet with Livoretto's blood, and, having seized him by the throat with her left hand, held him fast while she dealt him a mortal blow in the breast. Then she commanded the slaves to throw the body of the sultan out of the window into the deep ditch which ran round the walls of the palace, and thus, instead of being restored to youth as was Livoretto, he became food for dogs after the miserable end he made.

After she had wrought this terrible deed the Princess Bellisandra was greatly feared and reverenced by all in the city on account of the strange and marvellous power that was in her, and when the news was brought to her that the young man was a son of Dalfreno, King of Tunis, and that his rightful name was Livoretto, she wrote a letter to the old father, giving him therein a full account of all the amazing accidents which had befallen his son, and begging him most urgently to come at once to Cairo in order that he might be present at the nuptials of herself and Livoretto. And King Dalfreno, when he heard this good news about his son—of whom no word had been brought since he left Tunis with his brother—rejoiced greatly, and, having put all his affairs in good order, betook himself to Cairo and was welcomed by the whole city with the most distinguished marks of honour. After the space of a few days Bellisandra and Livoretto were married amidst the rejoicings of the whole people, and thus with the princess as his lawful spouse, with sumptuous triumphs and feastings, and with the happiest omens, Livoretto was made the Sultan of Cairo, where for many years he governed his realm in peace and lived a life of pleasure and tranquillity. Dalfreno tarried in Cairo a few days after the nuptials, and then took leave of his son and daughter-in-law and returned to Tunis safe and sound.

As soon as Arianna had come to the end of her interesting story, she propounded her enigma forthwith, in order that the rule which governed the entertainment might be strictly kept :

> Small what though my compass be,
> A mighty furnace gendered me.
> The covering which round me clings,
> Is what from marshy plain upsprings.
> My soul, which should be free as air,

Is doomed a prisoner close to fare.
It is a liquor bland and sweet.
No jest is this which I repeat :
All silken are my festal clothes,
And man will put me to his nose,
To make me all my charms disclose.

All those assembled listened with the keenest attention to the ingenious enigma set forth by Arianna, and they made her repeat it over and over again, but not one of the whole company proved to have wit sharp enough for the disentangling thereof. At last the fair Arianna gave the solution in these words : " Ladies and gentlemen, my enigma is supposed to describe a little flask of rose water, which has a body of glass born in a fiery furnace. Its covering comes from the marshes, for it is made of straw, and the soul which is contained within is the rose water. The gown or robe with which it is surrounded is the vessel, and whosoever sees it puts it under his nose to enjoy the odour thereof."

As soon as Arianna had given the solution of her enigma, Lauretta, who was seated next to her, remembered that it was her turn to speak. Wherefore without waiting for any further command from the Signora she thus began.

THE THIRD FABLE.

Biancabella, the daughter of Lamberico, Marquis of Monferrato, is sent away by the stepmother of Ferrandino, King of Naples, in order that she may be put to death; but the assassins only cut off her hands and put out her eyes. Afterwards she, her hurts having been healed by a snake, returns happily to Ferrandino.

IT is praiseworthy, or even absolutely necessary, that a woman, of whatever state or condition she may be, should bear herself with prudence in each and every undertaking she may essay, for without prudence nothing will bring itself to a commendable issue. And if a certain stepmother, of whom I am about to tell you, had used it with due moderation when she plotted wickedly to take another's life, she would not herself have

*

been cut off by divine judgment in such fashion as I will now relate to you.

Once upon a time, now many years ago, there reigned in Monferrato a marquis called Lamberico, very puissant, both on account of his lordships and his great wealth, but wanting in children to carry on his name. He was, forsooth, mighty anxious for progeny, but this bounty of heaven was denied to him. Now one day it chanced that the marchioness his wife was walking for her pleasure in the palace garden, and, being suddenly overcome by sleep, she sat down at the foot of a tree and slumber fell upon her. While she slept gently there crept up to her side a very small snake, which, having passed stealthily under her clothes without arousing her by its presence, made its way into her body, and by subtle windings penetrated even into her womb, and there lay quiet. Before long time had elapsed the marchioness, with no small pleasure to herself, and with the highest delight of all the state, proved to be with child, and, when the season of her lying-in came, she was delivered of a female child, round the neck of which there was coiled three times something in the similitude of a serpent. When the midwives, who were in attendance upon the marchioness, saw this, they were much affrighted; but the snake, without causing any hurt whatsoever, untwined itself from the infant's neck, and, winding itself along the floor and stretching itself out, made its way into the garden.

Now when the child had been duly cared for and clothed, the nurses having washed it clean in a bath of clear water and swathed it in snow-white linen, they began to see, little by little, that round about its neck was a collar of gold, fashioned with the most subtle handiwork. So fine was it, and so lovely, that it seemed to shed its lustre from between the skin and the flesh, just as the most precious jewels are wont to shine out from a closure of transparent crystal, and, moreover, it encircled the neck of the infant just as many times as the little serpent had cast its folds thereabout. The little girl, to whom, on account of her exceeding loveliness, the name of Biancabella was given, grew up in such goodliness and beauty that it seemed as if she must be sprung from divine and not from human stock. When she had come to the age of ten years it chanced that one day she went with her nurse upon a terrace, from whence she observed a fair garden full of roses and all manner of other lovely flowers. Then, turning towards the nurse who had her in charge, she demanded of her what garden that was which she had never seen before. To this the nurse replied that it was a place which her mother called her own garden, and one, moreover, in which she was wont often to take her recreation. Then said the child to her : ' I have never seen anything so fair before, and I had fain go into it and walk there.' Then the nurse, taking Biancabella by the hand, led her into the garden, and, having suffered the child to go a little distance apart from her, she sat down under the shade of a leafy beech-tree and settled herself to sleep, letting the little girl take her pleasure the while in roaming about the garden. Biancabella, who was altogether charmed with the loveliness of the place, ran about, now here and now there, gathering flowers, and, at last, when she felt somewhat tired, she sat down under the shadow of a tree. Now scarcely had the child seated herself upon the ground when there appeared a little snake, which crept up close to her side. Biancabella, as soon as she saw the beast, was mightily alarmed, and was about to cry out, when the snake thus addressed her : ' Cry not, I beg you, neither disturb yourself, nor have any fear, for know that I am your sister, born on the same day as yourself and at the same birth, and that Samaritana is my name. And I now tell you that, if you will be obedient to what I shall command you, I will make you happy in your life ; but if, on the other hand, you disobey me, you will come to be the most luckless, the most wretched woman the world has ever yet seen. Wherefore, go your way now, without fear of any sort, and to-morrow cause to be brought into this garden two vessels, of which let one be filled with pure milk, and the other with the finest water of roses. Then you must come to me by yourself without companions.'

When the serpent was gone the little girl rose up from her seat and went back to seek her nurse, whom she found still sleeping, and, having aroused her, she returned with her to the palace without saying aught of what had befallen her. And when the morrow had come Biancabella chanced to be with her mother alone in the chamber, and the mother remarked that the child bore upon her face a melancholy look. Whereupon she said : ' Biancabella, what ails you that you put on so discontented a face ? You are wont to be lively and merry enough, but now you seem all sad and woebegone.' To this Biancabella replied : ' There is nothing amiss with me ; it is only that I want to have taken into the garden two vessels, of which one shall be filled with pure milk and the other of the finest water of roses.' The

mother answered: 'And why do you let yourself be troubled by so
small a matter as this, my child? Do you not know that everything
here belongs to you?' Then the marchioness caused to be brought
to her two vessels, large and beautiful, filled, the one with milk and
the other with rose water, and had them carried into the garden.

When the hour appointed by the serpent had come, Biancabella,
without taking any other damsel to bear her company, repaired to
the garden, and, having opened the door thereof, she went in and
made fast the entrance, and then seated herself upon the ground at
the spot where the two vessels had been placed. Almost as soon as
she had sat down the serpent appeared and came near her, and
straightway commanded her to strip off all her clothes, and then,
naked as she was, to step into the vessel which was filled with milk.
When she had done this, the serpent twined itself about her, thus
bathing her body in every part with the white milk and licking her
all over with its tongue, rendering her pure and perfect in every part
where, peradventure, aught that was faulty might have been found.
Next, having bid her come out of the vessel of milk, the serpent
made her enter the one which was filled with rose water, whereupon
all her limbs were scented with odours so sweet and restorative that
she felt as if she were filled with fresh life. Then the serpent bade
her put on her clothes once more, giving her at the same time express
command that she should hold her peace as to what had befallen her,
and to speak no word thereanent even to her father and mother. For
the serpent willed that no other woman in all the world should be
found to equal Biancabella in beauty or in grace. And finally, after
she had bestowed upon her every good quality, the serpent crept away
to its hiding-place.

When this was done Biancabella left the garden and returned to
the palace. Her mother, when she perceived how her daughter had
become more lovely and gracious than ever, and fairer than any other
damsel in the world, was astonished beyond measure and knew not
what to say. Wherefore she questioned the young girl as to what
she had done to indue herself with such surpassing loveliness; but
Biancabella had no answer to give her. Hereupon the marchioness
took a comb and began to comb and dress her daughter's fair locks,
and forthwith from the girl's hair there fell down pearls and all
manner of precious stones, and when Biancabella went to wash her
hands roses and violets and lovely flowers of all sorts sprang up

around them, and the odours which arose from these were so sweet
that it seemed as if the place had indeed become an earthly paradise.
Her mother, when she saw this marvel, ran to find Lamberico her
husband, and, full of maternal pride, thus addressed him : ‘ My lord,
heaven has bestowed upon us a daughter who is the sweetest, the
loveliest, and the most exquisite work nature ever produced.   For
besides the divine beauty and grace in her, which is manifest to all
eyes, pearls and gems and all other kinds of precious stones fall from
her hair, and—to name something yet more marvellous—round about
her white hands spring up roses and violets and all manner of flowers
which give out the sweetest odours to all those who may come near
her to wonder at the sight. All this I tell to you I assuredly would
never have believed had I not looked thereon with my own eyes.’

Her husband, who was of an unbelieving nature, was at first disinclined to put faith in his wife’s words, and treated her speech as a
subject for laughter and ridicule, but she went on plying him without
ceasing with accounts of what she had witnessed, so that he determined to see for himself how the matter really stood.   Then, having
made them bring his daughter into his presence, he found about her
even more marvellous things than his wife had described, and on
account of what he saw he rejoiced exceedingly, and in his pride
swore a great oath that there was in the whole world no man worthy
to be united to her in wedlock.

Very soon the fame and glory of the supreme and immortal
beauty of Biancabella began to spread itself through the whole world,
and many kings and princes and nobles came together from all parts
in order to win her love and favour and have her to wife, but not
one of all these suitors was counted worthy to enjoy her, inasmuch
as each one of them proved to be lacking in respect of one thing or
another.   But at last one day there came a-wooing Ferrandino, King
of Naples, who by his prowess and by his illustrious name blazed
out resplendent like the sun in the midst of the smaller luminaries,
and, having presented himself to the marquis, demanded of him the
hand of his daughter in marriage.   The marquis, seeing that the
suitor was seemly of countenance, and well knit in person, and full of
grace, besides being a prince of great power and possessions and
wealth, gave his consent to the nuptials at once, and, having summoned his daughter, without further parleying the two were betrothed
by joining of hands and by kissing one another.

Scarcely were the rites of betrothal completed, when Biancabella called back to mind the words which her sister Samaritana had so lovingly spoken to her, wherefore she withdrew herself from the presence of her spouse under the pretext that she had certain business of her own to see to, and, having gone to her own chamber, made fast the door thereof from within, and then passed by a secret thoroughfare into the garden. When she had come into the garden, she began to call upon Samaritana in a low voice. But the serpent no more manifested herself as heretofore, and Biancabella, when she perceived this, was mightily astonished, and, after she had searched through every part of the garden without finding a trace of Samaritana, a deep grief fell upon her, for she knew that this thing had happened to her because she had not given due attention and obedience to the commands which her sister had laid upon her. Wherefore, grieving and bewailing heavily on account of the mischance that had befallen her, she returned into her chamber, and having opened the door, she went to rejoin her spouse, who had been waiting a long time for her, and sat down beside him. When the marriage ceremonies were completed, Ferrandino led his bride away with him to Naples, where, with sumptuous state and magnificent festivities and the sound of trumpets, they were welcomed by the whole city with the highest honour.

It happened that there was living at Naples Ferrandino's stepmother, who had two daughters of her own, both of them deformed and ugly ; but, notwithstanding this, she had set her heart on marrying one of them to the king. But now, when all hope was taken from her of ever accomplishing this design of hers, her rage and anger against Biancabella became so savage that she could scarcely endure to look upon her. But she was careful to conceal her animosity, feigning the while to hold Biancabella in all love and affection. Now by a certain freak of fortune the King of Tunis at this time began to set in array a mighty force of armed men for service by land and likewise on sea, in order that he might incite Ferrandino to make war (whether he did this because Ferrandino had won Biancabella to wife, or for some other reason I know not), and at the head of a very powerful army he had already passed the bounds of the kingdom of Naples. On this account it was necessary that Ferrandino should straightway take up arms for the defence of his realm, and hurry to the field to confront his foe. Therefore, having

settled his affairs, and made provision of all things necessary for
Biancabella (she being now with child), he gave her over to the care
of his stepmother and set forth with his army.

Ferrandino had not long departed when this malevolent and
froward-minded woman made a wicked design on Biancabella's life,
and, having summoned into her presence certain retainers who were
entirely devoted to her, she charged them to conduct Biancabella
with them to some place or other—feigning that what they were
doing was done for her recreation—and that they should not leave
her until they had taken her life. Moreover, in order that she
might be fully assured that they had discharged their duty, they
were to bring back to her some sign of Biancabella's death. These
ruffians, prompt for any sort of ill-doing, at once prepared to carry
out the commands of their mistress, and making pretence of conducting
Biancabella to some place where she might recreate herself, they carried
her away into a wood, and forthwith began to make preparation to
kill her. But when they perceived how lovely she was, and gracious,
they were moved to pity and had not the heart to take her life. So
they cut off both her hands and tore her eyes out of her head, and
these they carried back to the stepmother as certain proofs that
Biancabella had been killed by them. When this impious and cruel
woman saw what they brought in their hands, her joy and satisfaction
were unbounded, and, scheming still in her wicked heart to carry out
her nefarious designs, she spread through all the kingdom a report
that both her own daughters were dead, the one of a continued fever,
and the other of an imposthume of the heart, which had caused her
death by suffocation. Moreover, she went on to declare that Biancabella, disordered by grief at the king's departure, had miscarried of
a child, and had likewise been seized with a tertian fever which had
wasted her so cruelly that there was more cause to fear her death
than to hope for her recovery. But the scheme of this wicked
cunning woman was to keep one of her own daughters in the king's
bed, maintaining the while that she was Biancabella, shrunken and
distempered by the fever.

Ferrandino, after he had attacked and put to rout the army of
his foe, marched homeward in all the triumph of victory, hoping to
find his beloved Biancabella full of joy and happiness, but in lieu of
this he found her (as he believed) lying in bed shrivelled, pale, and
disfigured. Then he went up to the bed and gazed closely at her

face, and was overcome with astonishment when he looked upon the
wreck she had become, and could hardly persuade himself that the
woman he saw there could really be Biancabella. Afterwards he
bade her attendants comb her hair, and, in place of the gems and the
precious jewels which were wont to fall from the fair locks of his
wife, there came forth great worms which had been feeding on the
wretched woman's flesh, and from the hands there came forth, not
the roses and the sweet-smelling flowers which ever sprang up around
Biancabella's, but a foulness and filth which caused a nauseous sickness to all who came near her. But the wicked old stepmother kept
on speaking words of consolation to him, declaring that all this distemper sprang from nothing else than the lengthened course of the
ailment which possessed her.

In the meantime the ill-fated Biancabella, bereft of her hands and
blind in both her eyes, was left alone in that solitary place, and,
finding herself in such cruel affliction, she called over and over again
upon her sister Samaritana, beseeching her to come to her rescue;
but no answer came to her except from the resounding voice of
Echo, who cried aloud through all the place. And while the unhappy
Biancabella was left in the agony of despair, conscious that she was
cut off from all human aid, there came into the wood a venerable old
man, kindly of aspect and no less kindly in his heart. And he, when
he listened to the sad and mournful voice which smote upon his
hearing, made his way step by step towards the place whence it came,
and stopped when he found there a blind lady with her hands cut off
who was bitterly mourning the sad fate which had overtaken her.
When the good old man looked upon her, and saw how sad was her
condition, he could not bear to leave her thus in this wilderness of
broken trees and thorns and brambles, but, overcome by the fatherly
pity within him, he led her home with him to his house, and gave
her into the charge of his wife, commanding her very strictly to take
good care of the sufferer. Then he turned towards his three
daughters, who verily were as beautiful as three of the brightest
stars of heaven, and exhorted them earnestly to keep her company,
and to render to her continually any loving service she might require,
and to take care that she wanted for nothing. But the wife, who had
a hard heart, and none of the old man's pity, was violently moved
to anger by these words of her husband, and, turning towards him,
cried out : 'Husband, what is this you would have us do with this

woman, all blind and maimed as she is? Doubtless she has been thus treated as a punishment for her sins, and for no good behaviour.' In reply to this speech the old man spake in an angry tone: 'You will carry out all the commands I give you. If you should do aught else, you need not look to see me here again.'

It happened that while the unhappy Biancabella was left in charge of the wife and the three daughters, conversing with them of various things, and meditating over her own great misfortunes, she besought one of the maidens to do her a favour and comb her hair a little. But when the mother heard this she was much angered, forasmuch as she would not allow either of her children to minister in any way to the unfortunate sufferer. But the daughter's heart was more given to pity than was her mother's, and moreover she called to mind what her father's commands had been, and was conscious of some subtle air of dignity and high breeding which seemed to emanate from Biancabella as a token of her lofty estate. So she straightway unfastened the apron from her waist, and, having spread it on the floor beside Biancabella, began to comb her hair softly and carefully. Scarcely had she passed the comb thrice through the blond tresses before there fell out of them pearls and rubies and diamonds and all sorts of precious stones. Now the mother, when she saw what had happened, was seized with dread, and stood as one struck with amazement; moreover, the great dislike which at first she had harboured towards Biancabella, now gave way to a feeling of kindly affection. And when the old man had come back to the house they all ran to embrace him, rejoicing with him greatly over the stroke of good fortune which had come to deliver them from the bitter poverty which had hitherto oppressed them. Then Biancabella asked them to bring her a bucket of clear water, and bade them wash therewith her face and her maimed arms, and from these, while all were standing by, roses and violets and other flowers in great plenty fell down; whereupon they all deemed she must be some divine personage, and no mortal woman.

Now after a season it came to pass that Biancabella felt a desire to return to the spot where first the old man had found her. But he and his wife and his daughters, seeing how great were the benefits they gathered from her presence, loaded her with endearments, and besought her very earnestly that she would on no account depart from them, bringing forward many reasons why she should not carry out her wish. But she, having resolutely made up her mind on this point, determined at all hazards to go away, promising at the same time to return to them hereafter. The old man, when he saw how firmly she was set on her departure, took her with him without any further delay back to the place where he had come upon her. And when they had reached this spot she gave directions to the old man that he should depart and leave her, bidding him also to come back there when evening should have fallen, in order that she might return with him to his house.

As soon as the old man had gone his way the ill-fated Biancabella began to wander up and down the gloomy wood, calling loudly upon Samaritana, so that her cries and lamentations rose up even to the high heavens. But Samaritana, though she was all the while nigh to her sister, and had never for one moment abandoned her, refused as yet to answer to her call. Whereupon the wretched Biancabella, deeming that she was scattering her words upon the heedless winds, cried out, 'Alas! what further concern have I in this world, seeing that I have been bereft of my eyes and of my hands, and now at last all human help is denied to me.' And as she thus spoke there came upon her a sort of frenzy, which took away from her all hope of deliverance from her present evil case, and urged her, in despair, to lay hands upon her own life. But because there was at hand no means by which she could put an end to her miserable being, she found her way to a pool of water, which lay not far distant, in the mind there to drown herself. But when she had come to the shore of the pool, and stood thereon ready to cast herself down into the water, there sounded in her ears a voice like thunder, saying: 'Alas, alas, wretched one! keep back from self-murder, nor desire to take your own life, which you ought to preserve for some better end.' Whereupon Biancabella, alarmed by this mighty voice, felt as it were every one of her hairs standing erect on her head, but after a moment it seemed to her that she knew the voice; so, having plucked up a little courage, she said : 'Who are you who wander about these woods, proclaiming your presence to me by your kindly and pitiful words?' Then the same voice replied: 'I am Samaritana, your sister, for whom you have been calling so long and painfully.' And Biancabella, when she listened to these words, answered in a voice all broken by agonized sobs, and said : 'Alas, my sister! come to my aid, I beseech you; and if at any past time I have shown myself disregardful of your counsel, I pray you to pardon me. Indeed I have erred, and I confess my fault, but my misdeed was the fruit of my ignorance, and not of my wickedness; for be sure, if it had come from wickedness, divine justice would not have suffered me, as the author of it, so long to cumber the earth.' Samaritana, when she heard her sister's woes set forth in this pitiful story, and witnessed the cruel wrongs that had been done her, spake some comforting words, and then, having gathered divers medicinal herbs of wonderful power and virtue, she spread these over the places where Biancabella's eyes had been. Then she brought to her sister two hands, and having joined these on to the wounded wrists, at once made them whole and sound again. And when she had wrought this marvellous feat Samaritana threw off from herself the scaly skin of the serpent, and stood revealed as a maiden of lovely aspect.

The sun had already begun to veil its glittering rays, and the evening shadows were creeping around, when the old man with anxious hasty steps returned to the wood, where he found Biancabella sitting beside a maiden wellnigh as lovely as herself. And he gazed steadily into her beauteous face, standing the while like to a man struck with wonder, and could scarcely believe it was Biancabella he looked upon. But when he was sure it was really she, he cried: 'My daughter, were you not this morning blind and bereft of your hands? How comes it that you have been thus speedily made whole again?' Biancabella answered him : 'My cure has been worked, not by anything I myself have done, but by the virtue and the kind ministering of this my dear sister who sits here beside me.' Whereupon both the sisters arose from the place where they were seated, and rejoicing greatly they went together with the old man to his house, where the wife and the three daughters gave them a most loving and hospitable welcome.

It came to pass after the lapse of many days that Samaritana and Biancabella, and the old man with his wife and his three daughters, left their cottage and betook themselves to the city of Naples, purposing to dwell there, and, when they had entered the city, they chanced to come upon a vacant space hard by the palace of the king, where they determined to make their resting-place. And when the dark night had fallen around them, Samaritana took in her hand a twig of laurel and thrice struck the earth therewith, uttering certain mystic words the while, and almost before the sound of these

words had ceased there sprang up forthwith before them a palace, the
most beautiful and sumptuous that ever was seen. The next morning
Ferrandino the king went early to look out of the window, and when
he beheld the rich and marvellous palace standing where there had
been nothing the night before, he was altogether overcome with
amazement, and called his wife and his stepmother to come and see
it; but these were greatly disturbed in mind at the sight thereof, for
a boding came upon them that some ill was about to befall them.

While Ferrandino was standing, scanning closely the palace before
him, and examining it in all parts, he lifted his eyes to a certain
window, and there, in the chamber inside, he beheld two ladies of a
beauty more rich and dazzling than the sun. And no sooner had
his eyes fallen upon them than he felt a tempest of passion rising in
his heart, for he assuredly recognized in one of them some similitude
of that loveliness which had once been Biancabella's. And when he
asked who they were, and from what land they had come, the answer
which was given him was that they were two ladies who had been
exiled from their home, and that they had journeyed from Persia,
with all their possessions, to take up their abode in the noble city of
Naples. When he heard this, Ferrandino sent a messenger to inquire
whether he would be doing them any pleasure in waiting upon them,
accompanied by the ladies of his court, to pay them a visit of
welcome, and to this gracious message they sent an answer, saying
that it would indeed be a very precious honour to be thus visited by
him, but that it would be more decorous and respectful if they, as
subjects, should pay this duty to him, than that he, as lord and king,
should visit them.

Hereupon Ferrandino bade them summon the queen and the
other ladies of the court, and with these (although at first they
refused to go, being so greatly in fear of their impending ruin)
he betook himself to the palace of the two ladies, who, with all
friendly signs of welcome and with modest bearing, gave him the
reception due to a highly honoured guest, showing him the wide
loggias, and the roomy halls, and the richly ornamented chambers,
the walls of which were lined with alabaster and fine porphyry, while
about them were to be seen on all sides carven figures which looked
like life. And when they had exhibited to the king all parts of the
sumptuous palace, the two fair young women approached Ferrandino
and besought him most gracefully that he would deign to come one

day with his queen and dine at their table. The king, whose heart
was not hard enough to remain unaffected by all he had seen, and
who was gifted moreover with a magnanimous and liberal spirit,
graciously accepted the invitation. And when he had tendered his
thanks to the two ladies for the noble welcome they had given him,
he and the queen departed together and returned to their own palace.
When the day fixed for the banquet had come, the king and the
queen and the stepmother, clad in their royal robes and accompanied
by some of the ladies of the court, went to do honour to the magnificent feast set out in the most sumptuous fashion. And after he
had given them water to wash their hands, the seneschal bade them
conduct the king and the queen to a table apart, set somewhat higher,
but at the same time near to the others, and having done this,
he caused all the rest of the guests to seat themselves according to
their rank, and in this fashion they all feasted merrily and joyfully
together.

When the stately feast had come to an end and the tables had
been cleared, Samaritana rose from her seat, and turning towards the
king and the queen, spake thus: 'Your majesties, in order that the
time may not be irksome to us, as it may if we sit here idle, let one
or other of us propose something in the way of diversion which will
let us pass the day pleasantly.' And when the guests heard what
Samaritana said, they all agreed that she had spoken well, but yet
there was found no one bold enough to make such a proposition as
she had called for. Whereupon Samaritana, when she perceived they
were all silent, went on: 'Since it appears that no one of this company is prepared to put forward anything, I, with your majesty's
leave, will bid come hither one of our own maidens, whose singing
perchance will give you no little pleasure.' And having summoned the
damsel, whose name was Silveria, into the banqueting-room, Samaritana commanded her to take a lyre in her hand and to sing thereto
something in honour of the king which should be worthy of their
praise. And the damsel, obedient to her lady's command, took her
lyre, and, having placed herself before the king, sang in a soft and
pleasant voice while she touched the resounding strings with the
plectrum, telling in her chant the story of Biancabella from beginning
to end, but not mentioning her by name. When the whole of the
story had been set forth, Samaritana again rose to her feet, and
demanded of the king what would be the fitting punishment, what

T

torture would be cruel enough for those who had put their hands to
such an execrable crime.   Then the stepmother, who deemed that
she might perchance get a release for her misdeeds by a prompt and
ready reply, did not wait for the king to give his answer, but cried
out in a bold and confident tone, 'Surely to be cast into a furnace
heated red hot would be but a light punishment for the offences of
such a one.'   Then Samaritana, with her countenance all afire with
vengeance and anger, made answer to her : 'Thou thyself art the
very same guilty and barbarous woman, through whose nefarious
working all these cruel wrongs have been done ; and thou, wicked
and accursed one, hast condemned thyself to a righteous penalty out
of thine own mouth.'   Then Samaritana, turning towards the king
with a look of joy upon her face, said to him, 'Behold ! this is your
Biancabella, this is the wife you loved so dearly, this is she without
whom you could not live.'   Then, to prove the truth of her words,
Samaritana gave the word to the three daughters of the old man that
they should forthwith, in the presence of the king, begin to comb
Biancabella's fair and wavy hair, and scarcely had they begun when
(as has been told before) there fell out of her tresses many very
precious and exquisite jewels, and from her hands came forth roses
exhaling the sweet scents of morning, and all manner of odoriferous
flowers.   And for yet greater certainty she pointed out to the king
how the snow-white neck of Biancabella was encircled by a fine
chain of the most delicately wrought gold, which grew naturally
between the skin and the flesh, and shone out as through the clearest
crystal.

When the king perceived by these manifest and convincing signs
that she was indeed his own Biancabella, he began to weep for the
joy he felt, and to embrace her tenderly.   But before he left that
place he caused to be heated hot a furnace, and into this he bade
them cast the stepmother and her two daughters.   Thus their repentance for their crimes came too late, and they made a miserable end
to their lives.   And after this the three daughters of the old man
were given honourably in marriage, and the King Ferrandino with
Biancabella and Samaritana lived long and happily, and when Ferrandino died his son succeeded to his kingdom.

During the telling of Lauretta's story divers of the listeners were
several times moved to tears, and, when she had brought it to
an end, the Signora bade her follow the example of those who had

gone before her, and set forth her enigma. Therefore she, not waiting for any further command, gave it in the following words :

> A proud and cruel maid I spied,
> As through the flowery meads she hied.
> Behind her trailed a lengthy train,
> Upreared her head in high disdain.
> And swiftly on her way she took,
> And sharp her touch, and eke her look.
> What though her tongue moves all around,
> She utters neither voice nor sound.
> She is long, and thin, and wise,
> He can tell her name who tries.

All the company listened attentively to the enigma which Lauretta gave to them in her sportive way, and she, when she saw there was little likelihood that anyone would find the solution thereof, spake thus: "Dear ladies, so as not to keep you any longer in suspense, or to weary yet more your minds, which must needs be somewhat harassed on account of the pathetic story I have just told you, I will tell you the answer straightway, if such be your pleasure. The damsel I described therein is nothing else than the serpent which, when it goes through the flowery meadows, keeps its head erect and its tail trailing on the ground behind it, and frightens with its sharp eye everyone who may happen to behold it."

As soon as Lauretta had finished her speech everyone was much astonished that the solution of the riddle had not been guessed by some one or other. And when she had resumed her seat the Signora made a sign to Alteria that she should tell them her fable, and she, having risen and made obeisance to the Signora, began it forthwith.

THE FOURTH FABLE.

Fortunio, on account of an injury done to him by his supposed father and mother, leaves them, and after much wandering, comes to a wood, where he finds three animals, who do him good service. Afterwards he goes to Polonia, where he gets to wife Doralice, the king's daughter, as a reward for his prowess.

THERE is a saying, very frequent in the mouths of common people, that it is not seemly to jest at affliction nor to make a mock at the truth ; forasmuch as he who keeps his eyes and ears open, and holds his tongue, is not likely to injure his fellows, and may hope himself to live in peace.

Once upon a time there lived in one of the remoter districts of Lombardy a man called Bernio, who, although he was not over well endowed with the gifts of fortune, was held to be in no way wanting with respect to good qualities of head and heart. This man took to wife a worthy and amiable woman named Alchia, who, though she chanced to be of low origin, was nevertheless of good parts and exemplary conduct, and loved her husband as dearly as any woman could. This married pair greatly desired to have children, but such a gift of God was not granted to them, peradventure for the reason that man often, in his ignorance, asks for those things which would not be to his advantage. Now, forasmuch as this desire for offspring still continued to possess them, and as fortune obstinately refused to grant their prayer, they determined at last to adopt a child whom they would nurture and treat in every way as if he were their own legitimate son. So one morning early they betook themselves to a certain spot where young children who had been cast off by their parents were often left, and, having seen there one who appeared to them more seemly and attractive than the rest, they took him home with them, and brought him up with the utmost care and good governance. Now after a time it came to pass (according to the good pleasure of Him who rules the universe and tempers and modifies everything according to His will) that Alchia became with child, and when her time of delivery was come, was brought to bed with a boy who resembled his father exactly. On this account both father and mother rejoiced exceedingly, and called their son by the name of Valentino.

The infant was well nurtured, and grew up strong and healthy and well-mannered; moreover, he loved so dearly his brother—to whom the name of Fortunio had been given—that he was inclined almost to fret himself to death whenever they chanced to be separated the one from the other. But the genius of discord, the foe of everything that is good, becoming aware of their warm and loving friendship, and being able no longer to suffer their good understanding to continue, one day interposed between them, and worked her evil will so effectively that before long the two friends began to taste her bitter fruits. Wherefore as they were sporting together one day (after the manner of boys) they grew somewhat excited over their game, and Valentino, who could not bear that Fortunio should get any advantage over him in their play, became inflamed with violent anger, and more than once called his companion a bastard and the son of a vile woman. Fortunio, when he heard these words, was much astonished, and perturbed as well, and turning to Valentino, he said to him, 'And why am I a bastard?' In reply, Valentino, muttering angrily between his teeth, repeated what he had already said, and even more. Whereupon Fortunio, greatly grieved and disturbed in mind, gave over playing and went forthwith to his so-called mother, and asked her whether he was in sooth the son of Bernio and herself. Alchia answered that he was, and, having learned that Fortunio had been insulted by Valentino, she rated the latter soundly, and declared that she would give him heavy chastisement if he should repeat his offence. But the words which Alchia had spoken roused fresh suspicion in Fortunio, and made him wellnigh certain that he was not her legitimate son; indeed, there often came upon him the desire to put her to the test, to see whether she really was his mother or not, and thus discover the truth. In the end he questioned and importuned her so closely that she acknowledged he was not born of her, but that he had been adopted and brought up in their house for the love of God and for the alleviation of the misfortune which had been sent upon herself and her husband. These words were as so many dagger-thrusts in the young man's heart, piling up one sorrow upon another, and at last his grief grew beyond endurance; but, seeing that he could not bring himself to seek refuge from his trouble by a violent death, he determined to depart from Bernio's roof, and, in wandering up and down the world, to seek a better fortune.

Alchia, when she perceived that Fortunio's desire to quit the house grew stronger every day, was greatly incensed against him, and, as she found herself powerless to dissuade him from his purpose, she heaped all sorts of curses upon him, praying that if ever he should venture upon the sea he might be engulfed in the waves and swallowed up by the sirens, as ships are often swallowed up by storms. Fortunio, driven on by a headlong access of rage, took no heed of Alchia's malediction, and, without saying any further words of farewell, either to her or to Bernio, departed, and took his way towards the east. He journeyed on, passing by marshes, by valleys, by rocks, and all kinds of wild and desert spots, and at last, one day between sext and none, he came upon a thick and densely-tangled forest, in the midst of which, by strange chance, he found a wolf and an eagle and an ant, who were engaged in a long and sharp contention over the body of a stag which they had lately captured, without being able to agree as to how the venison should be divided amongst themselves. When Fortunio came upon the three animals they were in the midst of their stubborn dispute, and not one was disposed in any way to yield to the others; but after a while they agreed that this young man, who had thus unexpectedly come amongst them, should adjudicate the matter in question, and assign to each one of them such part of the spoil as he might deem most fitting. Then, when they had assented to these preliminaries, and had promised that they would be satisfied with and observe the terms of any award he might make, even though it might seem to be unjust, Fortunio readily undertook the task, and after he had carefully considered the case, he divided the prey amongst them in the following manner. To the wolf, as to a voracious animal and one very handy with his sharp teeth, he gave, as the guerdon of his toil in the chase, all the bones of the deer and all the lean flesh. To the eagle, a rapacious fowl, but furnished with no teeth, he gave the entrails, and all the fat lying round the lean parts and the bones. To the provident and industrious ant, which had none of that strength which nature had bestowed upon the wolf and the eagle, he gave the soft brains as her share of reward for the labour she had undergone. When the three animals understood the terms of this just and carefully-considered decision, they were fully satisfied, and thanked

Fortunio as well as they could for the courtesy he had shown them.

Now these three animals held—and with justice—that, of all the vices, ingratitude was the most reprehensible; so with one accord they insisted that the young man should not depart until they should have fully rewarded him for the great service he had done them. Wherefore the wolf, speaking first, said: 'My brother, I give you the power, if at any time the desire should come upon you to be a wolf instead of a man, to become one forthwith, merely by saying the words, "Would that I were a wolf!" At the same time you will be able to return to your former shape whenever you may desire.' And in like manner both the eagle and the ant endowed him with power to take upon him their form and similitude.

Then Fortunio, rejoicing greatly at the potent virtues thus given to him, and rendering to all three of the animals the warmest gratitude for their boon, took his leave and wandered far abroad, until at last he came to Polonia, a populous city of great renown, which was at that time under the rule of Odescalco, a powerful and valorous sovereign, who had but one child, a daughter called Doralice. Now the king was ambitious to find a noble mate for this princess, and it chanced that, at the time when Fortunio arrived in Polonia, he had proclaimed throughout his kingdom that a grand tournament should be held in the city, and that the Princess Doralice should be given in marriage to the man who should be the victor in the jousts. And already many dukes and marquises and other powerful nobles had come together from all parts to contend for this noble prize, and on the first day of the tournament, which had already passed, the honours of the tilting were borne off by a foul Saracen of hideous aspect and ungainly form, and with a face as black as pitch. The king's daughter, when she viewed the deformed and unseemly figure of the conqueror of the day, was overwhelmed with grief that fate should have awarded to such a one the victory in the joust, and, burying her face, which was crimson with shame, in her tender delicate hands, she wept and lamented sore, execrating her cruel and malignant destiny, and begging that death might take her rather than that she should become the wife of this misshapen barbarian. Fortunio, when he entered the city gate, noted the festal array on all sides and the great concourse of people about the streets, and when he learned the cause of all this magnificent display he was straightway possessed with an ardent desire to prove his

valour by contending in the tournament, but when he came to consider that he was lacking in all the apparel needful in such honourable
contests, his heart fell and heavy sorrow came over him.   While he
was in this doleful mood it chanced that his steps led him past the
palace of the king, and raising his eyes from the ground he espied
Doralice, the daughter of the king, who was leaning out of one of the
windows of her apartment.   She was surrounded by a group of lovely
and highborn dames and maidens, but she shone out amongst them
all on account of her beauty, as the radiant glorious sun shines out
amidst the lesser lights of heaven.

By-and-by, when the dark night had fallen, and all the ladies of
the court had retired to their apartments, Doralice, restless and sad
at heart, betook herself alone to a small and exquisitely ornamented
chamber and gazed once more out into the night, and there below, as
luck would have it, was Fortunio.   When the youth saw her standing
solitary at the open window, he was so overcome by the charms of her
beauty that he forthwith whispered to himself in an amorous sigh:
' Ah! wherefore am I not an eagle?' Scarcely had these words issued
from his lips when he found himself transformed into an eagle, whereupon he flew at once into the window of the chamber, and, having
willed to become a man again, was restored to his own shape.   He
went forward with a light and joyful air to greet the princess, but she,
as soon as she saw him, was filled with terror and began to cry out in
a loud voice, just as if she were being attacked and torn by savage dogs.
The king, who happened to be in an apartment not far distant from
his daughter's, heard her cries of alarm and ran immediately to seek
the cause thereof, and, having heard from her that there was a young
man in the room, he at once ordered it to be searched in every part.
But nothing of the sort was found, because Fortunio had once more
changed himself into an eagle and had flown out of the window.
Hardly, however, had the father gone back to his chamber when the
maiden began to cry aloud just the same as before, because, forsooth,
Fortunio had once more come into her presence.

But Fortunio, when he again heard the terrified cries of the maiden,
began to fear for his life, and straightway changed himself into an ant,
and crept into hiding beneath the blond tresses of the lovely damsel's
hair.   Odescalco, hearing the loud outcries of his daughter, ran to her
succour, but when he found nothing more this second time than he
had found before, he was greatly incensed against her, and threatened

her harshly that if she should cry out again and disturb him he would play her some trick which would not please her, and thus he left her with angry words, suspecting that what had caused her trouble was some vision of one or other of the youths who for love of her had met their deaths in the tournament. Fortunio listened attentively to what the king said to his daughter, and, as soon as he had left the apartment, once more put off the shape of an ant and stood revealed in his own form. Doralice, who in the meanwhile had gone to bed, was so terror-stricken when she saw him that she tried to spring from her couch and to give the alarm, but she was not able to do this, because Fortunio placed one of his hands on her lips, and thus spake : 'Signora, fear not that I have come here to despoil you of your honour, or to steal aught that belongs to you. I am come rather to succour you to the best of my power, and to proclaim myself your most humble servant. If you cry out, one or other of two misfortunes will befall us, either your honour and fair name will be tarnished, or you will be the cause of your death and of my own. Therefore, dear lady of my heart, take care lest at the same time you cast a stain upon your reputation and imperil the lives of us both.'

While Fortunio was thus speaking, Doralice was weeping bitterly, her presence of mind being completely overthrown by this unexpected declaration on his part, and the young man, when he perceived how powerfully agitated she was, went on addressing her in words gentle and persuasive enough to have melted the heart of a stone. At last, conquered by his words and tender manner, she softened towards him, and consented to let him make his peace with her. And after a little, when she saw how handsome the youth was in face, and how strong and well knit in body and limb, she fell a-thinking about the ugliness and deformity of the Saracen, who, as the conqueror in the jousts, must before long be the master of her person. While these thoughts were passing through her mind the young man said to her : 'Dear lady, if I had the fitting equipment, how willingly would I enter the jousts to tilt on your behalf, and my heart tells me that, were I to contend, I should surely conquer.' Whereupon the damsel in reply said : 'If this, indeed, were to come to pass, if you should prove victorious in the lists, I would give myself to you alone.' And when she saw what a well-disposed youth he was, and how ardent in her cause, she brought forth a great quantity of gems and a heavy purse of gold, and bade him take them. Fortunio accepted them with his

U

heart full of joy, and inquired of her what garb she wished him to wear in the lists to-morrow. And she bade him array himself in white satin, and in this matter he did as she commanded him.

On the following day Fortunio, encased in polished armour, over which he wore a surcoat of white satin richly embroidered with the finest gold, and studded with jewels most delicately carven, rode into the piazza unknown to anybody there present. He was mounted on a powerful and fiery charger, which was caparisoned and decked in the same colours as its rider. The crowd, which had already come together to witness the grand spectacle of the tournament, no sooner caught sight of the gallant unknown champion, with lance in hand all ready for the fray, than every person was lost in wonderment at so brave a sight, and each one, gazing fixedly at Fortunio, and astonished at his grace, began to inquire of his neighbour: 'Ah! who can this knight be who rides so gallantly and splendidly arrayed into the lists? Know you not what is his name?' In the meantime Fortunio, having entered the lists, called upon some rival to advance, and for the first course the Saracen presented himself, whereupon the two champions, keeping low the points of their trusty lances, rushed one upon the other like two lions loosened from their bonds, and so shrewd was the stroke dealt by Fortunio upon the head of the Saracen, that the latter was driven right over the crupper of his horse, and fell dead upon the bare earth, mangled and broken up as a fragile glass is broken when it is thrown against a wall. And Fortunio ran his course just as victoriously in encountering every other champion who ventured to oppose him in the lists. The damsel, when she saw how the fortune of the day was going, was greatly rejoiced, and kept her eyes steadily fixed on Fortunio in deepest admiration, and, thanking God in her heart for having thus graciously delivered her from the bondage of the Saracen, prayed to Him that this brave youth might be the final victor.

When the night had come they bade Doralice come to supper with the rest of the court; but to this bidding she made demur, and commanded them bring her certain rich viands and delicate wines to her chamber, feigning that she had not yet any desire for food, but would eat, perchance, later on if any appetite should come upon her. Then, having locked herself in her chamber and opened the window thereof, she watched with ardent desire for the coming of her lover, and when he had gained admittance to the chamber by the same means as he had used the previous day, they supped joyfully together. Then Fortunio demanded of her in what fashion she would that he should array himself for the morrow, and she made answer that he must bear a badge of green satin all embroidered with the finest thread of silver and gold, and that his horse should be caparisoned in like manner. On the following morning Fortunio appeared, attired as Doralice had directed, and, having duly presented himself in the piazza at the appointed time, he entered the lists and proved himself again as valiant a champion as he had proved to be on the day before. So great was the admiration of the people of his prowess, that the shout went up with one voice that he had worthily won the gracious princess for his bride.

On the evening of that day the princess, full of merriment and happiness and joyous expectations, made the same pretext for absenting herself from supper as she had made the day before, and, having locked the door of her chamber, awaited there the coming of her lover, and supped pleasantly with him. And when he asked her once more with what vestments he should clothe himself on the following day, she answered that she wished him to wear a surcoat of crimson satin, all worked and embroidered with gold and pearls, and to see that the trappings of his horse were made in the same fashion ; adding that she herself would, on the morrow, be clad in similar wise. ' Lady,' replied Fortunio, ' if by any chance I should tarry somewhat in making my entry into the lists, be not astonished, for I shall not be late without good cause.'

When the morning of the third day had come, the spectators awaited the issue of the momentous strife with the most earnest expectation, but, on account of the inexhaustible valour of the gallant unknown champion, there was no opponent found who dared to enter the lists against him, and he himself for some hidden reason did not appear. After a time the spectators began to grow impatient at his non-appearance, and injurious words were dropped. Even Doralice herself was assailed by suspicions as to his worth, although she had been warned by Fortunio himself that probably his coming would be delayed; so, overcome by this hidden trouble of hers—concerning which no one else knew anything—she wellnigh swooned with grief. At last, when it was told to her that the unknown knight was advancing into the piazza, her failing senses began to revive. Fortunio was clad in a rich and sumptuous dress, and the trappings of his horse were of the finest cloth of gold, all embroidered with shining rubies and emeralds and sapphires and great pearls. When the people saw these they affirmed that the price of them would be equal to a great kingdom, and when Fortunio came into the piazza, every one cried out in a loud voice : 'Long live the unknown knight!' and after this they all applauded vigorously and clapped their hands. Then the jousting began, and Fortunio once more carried himself so valiantly that he bore to earth all those who dared to oppose him, and in the end was hailed as the victor in the tournament. And when he had dismounted from his noble horse, the chief magnates and the wealthy citizens of the town bore him aloft on their shoulders, and to the sound of trumpets and all other kinds of musical instruments, and with loud shouts which went up to the heavens, they carried him into the presence of the king. When they had taken off his helmet and his shining armour the king perceived what a seemly graceful youth he was, and, having called his daughter into his presence, he betrothed them forthwith, and celebrated the nuptials with the greatest pomp, keeping open table at the court for the space of a month.

After Fortunio had lived for a certain space of time in loving dalliance with his fair wife, he was seized one day with the thought that he was playing the part of an unworthy sluggard in thus passing the days in indolence, merely counting the hours as they sped by, after the manner of foolish folk, and of those who consider not the duties of a man. Wherefore he made up his mind to go afield into certain regions, where there might be found due scope and recognition for his valour and enterprise ; so, having got ready a galley and taken a large treasure which his father-in-law had given him, he embarked after taking leave of his wife and of King Odes-calco. He sailed away, wafted on by gentle and favourable breezes, until he came into the Atlantic Ocean, but before he had gone more than ten miles thereon, there arose from the waves the most beautiful Siren that ever was seen, and singing softly, she began to swim towards the ship. Fortunio, who was reclining by the side of the galley, bent his head low down over the water to listen to her song, and straightway fell asleep, and, while he thus slept, the Siren drew him gently from where he lay, and, bearing him in her arms, sank with him headlong into the depths of the sea. The mariners, after having vainly essayed to save him, broke out into loud lamentations

over his sad fate, and, weeping and mourning, they decked the galley
with black ensigns of grief, and returned to the unfortunate Odescalco
to tell him of the terrible mischance which had befallen them during
their voyage. The king and Doralice, when the sad news was brought
to them, were overwhelmed with the deepest grief—as indeed was
everyone else in the city—and all put on garments of mourning
black.

Now at the time of Fortunio's departure Doralice was with child,
and when the season of her delivery had come she gave birth to a
beautiful boy, who was delicately and carefully nurtured until he
came to be two years of age. At this time the sad and despairing
Doralice, who had always brooded over her unhappy fate in losing
the company of her beloved husband, began to abandon all hope of
ever seeing him again; so she, like a brave and great-souled woman,
resolved to put her fortune to the test and go to seek for him upon
the deep, even though the king her father should not consent to let her
depart. So she caused to be set in order for her voyage an armed galley,
well fitted for such a purpose, and she took with her three apples,
each one a masterpiece of handicraft, of which one was fashioned out
of golden bronze, another of silver, and the last of the finest gold.
Then, having taken leave of her father the king, she embarked with
her child on board the galley, and sailed away before a prosperous
wind into the open sea.

After the sad and woe-stricken lady had sailed a certain time over
the calm sea, she bade the sailors steer the ship forthwith towards the
spot where her husband had been carried off by the Siren, and this
command they immediately obeyed. And when the vessel had been
brought to the aforesaid spot, the child began to cry fretfully, and
would in no wise be pacified by his mother's endearments; so she gave
him the apple which was made of golden bronze to appease him.
While the child was thus sporting with the apple, he was espied by
the Siren, who, having come near to the galley and lifted her head a
little space out of the foaming waves, thus spake to Doralice : 'Lady,
give me that apple, for I desire greatly to have it.' But the princess answered her that this thing could not be done, inasmuch as the apple was
her child's plaything. 'If you will consent to give it to me,' the Siren
went on, 'I will show you the husband you have lost as far as his breast.'
Doralice, when she heard these words, at once took the apple from the
child and handed it courteously to the Siren, for she longed above all

things else to get sight of her beloved husband.   The Siren was faithful to her promise, and after a little time brought Fortunio to the
surface of the sea and showed him as far as the breast to Doralice, as
a reward for the gift of the apple, and then plunged with him once
more into the depths of the ocean, and disappeared from sight.

Doralice, who had naturally feasted her eyes upon the form of her
husband what time he was above the water, only felt the desire to see
him once more grow stronger after he was gone under again, and, not
knowing what to do or to say, she sought comfort in the caresses of
her child, and when the little one began to cry once more, the mother
gave to it the silver apple to soothe its fancy.   Again the Siren was
on the watch and espied the silver apple in the child's hand, and having
raised her head above the waves, begged Doralice to give her the apple,
but the latter, shrugging her shoulders, said that the apple served to
divert the child, and could not be spared.   Whereupon the Siren said :
' If only you will give me this apple, which is far more beautiful than
the other, I promise I will show you your husband as far as his knees.'
Poor Doralice, who was now consumed with desire to see her beloved
husband again, put aside the satisfaction of the child's fancy, and,
having taken away from him the silver apple, handed it eagerly to the
Siren, who, after she had once more brought Fortunio to the surface and
exhibited him to Doralice as far as his knees (according to her promise),
plunged again beneath the waves.

For a while the princess sat brooding in silent grief and suspense,
trying in va... to hit upon some plan by which she might rescue her
husband from his piteous fate, and at last she caught up her child in
her arms and tried to comfort herself with him and to still his weeping.
The child, mindful of the fair apple he had been playing with, continued to cry ; so the mother, to appease him, gave him at last the apple
of fine gold.   When the covetous Siren, who was still watching the
galley, saw this apple, and perceived that it was much fairer than either
of the others, she at once demanded it as a gift from Doralice, and she
begged so long and persistently, and at last made a promise to the
princess that, in return for the gift of this apple, she would bring
Fortunio once more into the light, and show him from head to foot ; so
Doralice took the apple from the boy, in spite of his chiding, and gave
it to the Siren.   Whereupon the latter, in order to carry out her
promise, came quite close to the galley, bearing Fortunio upon her
back, and having raised herself somewhat above the surface of the

water, showed the person of Fortunio from head to foot. Now, as soon as Fortunio felt that he was quite clear of the water, and resting free upon the back of the Siren, he was filled with great joy in his heart, and, without hesitating for a moment, he cried out, ' Ah ! would that I were an eagle,' and scarcely had he ceased speaking when he was forthwith transformed into an eagle, and, having poised himself for flight, he flew high above the sail yards of the galley, from whence —all the shipmen looking on the while in wonder—he descended into the ship and returned to his proper shape, and kissed and embraced his wife and his child and all the sailors on the galley.

Then, all of them rejoicing at the rescue of Fortunio, they sailed back to King Odescalco's kingdom, and as soon as they entered the port they began to play upon the trumpets and tabors and drums and all the other musical instruments they had with them, so that the king, when he heard the sound of these, was much astonished, and in the greatest suspense waited to learn what might be the meaning thereof. And before very long time had elapsed the herald came before him, and announced to the king how his dear daughter, having rescued her husband from the Siren, had come back. When they were disembarked from the galley, they all repaired to the royal palace, where their return was celebrated by sumptuous banquets and rejoicings. But after some days had passed, Fortunio betook himself for a while to his old home, and there, after having transformed himself into a wolf, he devoured Alchia, his adoptive mother, and Valentino her son, in revenge for the injuries they had worked him. Then, after he had returned to his rightful shape, he mounted his horse and rode back to his father-in-law's kingdom, where, with Doralice his dear wife, he lived in peace for many years to the great delight of both of them.

As soon as Alteria had brought to an end her long and interesting story the Signora bade her at once to set forth her enigma, and she, smiling pleasantly, obeyed the command.

Far from this our land doth dwell
One who by turns is fair or fell ;
Springing from a twofold root,
One part woman, one part brute.
Now like beauty's fairest jewel,
Now a monster fierce and cruel.
Sweetest song on vocal breath,
To lead men down to shameful death.

Alteria's most fitting and noteworthy enigma was answered in divers fashion by the listeners, some giving one interpretation of it and some another, but not one of them came upon its exact meaning. Therefore, when the fair Alteria saw there was little chance of anyone finding the true answer, she said : " Ladies and gentlemen, the real subject of my enigma is the fascinating Siren who is fabled to dwell in the deep sea. She is very fair to look upon, for her head and breast and body and arms are those of a beautiful damsel, but all the rest of her form is scaly like a fish, and in her nature she is cunning and cruel. She sings so sweetly that the mariners, when they hear her song, are soothed to slumber, and while they sleep she drowns them in the sea." When the listeners heard this clever and subtle solution given by Alteria, they praised it warmly with one accord, declaring the while that it was most ingenious. And she, smiling with pleasure and gratitude, rose from her chair and thanked them for their kindness in thus lending their attention to her story. As soon as she had taken her seat, the Signora made a sign to Eritrea to follow in the due order with her story, and she, blushing like a morning rose, began it in these words.

THE FIFTH FABLE.

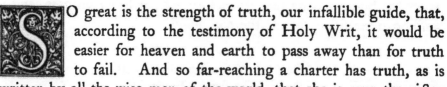

Isotta, the wife of Lucaferro Albani of Bergamo, devises how she may trick Trabaglino the cowherd of her brother Emilliano and thereby show him to be a liar, but she loses her husband's farm and returns home worsted in her attempt, and bringing with her a bull's head with gilded horns.

O great is the strength of truth, our infallible guide, that, according to the testimony of Holy Writ, it would be easier for heaven and earth to pass away than for truth to fail. And so far-reaching a charter has truth, as is written by all the wise men of the world, that she is ever the victor of time, and time never victor over her. Like as oil, if it be poured in a vessel together with water, will always rise to the top, so will truth always assert herself over falsehood. Wherefore on this account let no one be amazed over this prologue of mine, seeing that I have set it down, moved thereto by the malignity of a wicked woman, who, deeming that she might, by the means of her false allurements, lead on a young fellow to tell a lie, only induced him to speak the plain truth to her own confusion, the which, wicked woman as she was, she well merited. All this I propose to set before you in this story of mine, which I hope, both as to time and place, will prove more profitable than hurtful to all of you.

I will first tell my worthy hearers that in Bergamo, an ancient city of Lombardy, there lived not a great time ago a man of wealth and standing whose name was Pietromaria di Albani. To this man were born two sons, of whom one was called Emilliano, and the other Lucaferro. He possessed also two farms in a township not far removed, one of them known by the name of Ghorem, and the other by that of Pedrench. The two brothers, that is to say, Emilliano and Lucaferro, divided the farms between them by lot after the death of Pietromaria their father, and Pedrench fell to the share of Emilliano, and Ghorem to Lucaferro. Now Emilliano owned a very fine flock of sheep, and a herd of lusty young bullocks, and likewise a second herd of productive cows, and over the whole of these cattle one Travaglino had charge as herdsman, a man of the most approved truth and loyalty, who, however dear he held his life, would not have told a lie to save it, and who, moreover, as a herdsman had not his equal in all the world. With his herd of cows Travaglino kept several very fine bulls, amongst which there was one especially beautiful in appearance, and so great a favourite was this bull with Emilliano that he caused its horns to be gilded over with the finest gold. And as often as Travaglino might go to Bergamo after his affairs, Emilliano would never fail to question him as to the welfare of his favourite bull with the gilded horns.

It happened one day that while Emilliano was entertaining and holding converse with his brother Lucaferro and with divers other of his friends, Travaglino came anigh the company and made a sign to Emilliano his master that he wanted to speak with him. Whereupon the latter forthwith withdrew from the presence of his brother and his friends, and, having gone apart with Travaglino, held him there some long time in conversation. And after this it would happen full often that Emilliano would do the like, and leave his friends and family who might be about him, and betake himself aside to confer with his herdsman; so that at last Lucaferro, his brother,

x

lost patience at such doings, and could endure them no longer.   On
one occasion, therefore, hot with wrath and indignation, he spake to
Emilliano in these words: 'Emilliano, I am astonished beyond
measure at your behaviour, that you make more account of this
rascally cowherd of yours than you make of your own brother and
of your many trusted friends; because, forsooth, not once, but a
thousand times, if I may so express myself, you have gone away from
us when we were together in the piazza, or over our games, as if we
had been so many beasts only fit to be driven to the shambles, to go
and foregather with this lubberly ruffian of a Travaglino, your hireling, and to have long converse with him, making believe that the
affairs you had to discuss with him were of the highest importance,
while in fact nothing you talked about mattered a single straw.' To
this Emilliano made answer : 'Lucaferro, my good brother, there is
surely no need for you to fly into so hot a passion with me, while you
heap all these injurious words upon poor Travaglino, who, after all, is
a very worthy young fellow, and one on whom I set great store, both
on account of his efficiency in his calling and for his staunch loyalty
towards myself; moreover, he has yet another and special good quality,
inasmuch as he would not, to gain all the wealth there is in the world,
speak a word which was not the truth.   And furthermore he has
many other excellent traits on account of which I hold him in high
esteem ; therefore there is no reason why you should be astonished at
my fondness for him, or that I should treat him kindly.'

This answer given by Emilliano only served to stir yet deeper
his brother's bile, and they straightway began to bandy angry words
from one to the other, so that they narrowly escaped coming to
blows.   In the end Lucaferro, on account of the high commendation
pronounced by Emilliano over Travaglino's good qualities—the which
is written above—thus spake : 'You speak loud enough to-day of
the efficiency, and the good faith, and the truthfulness of this cowherd of yours, but I tell you that he is the most bungling, the most
disloyal loon in the world, as well as the biggest liar that nature ever
made.   And moreover I will pledge myself to bring all this to your
notice, and to let you hear him tell a falsehood before your very face.'
After they had spent much time in wrangling, they ended by wager-
ing their respective farms over the question, settling the affair in this
fashion, namely, that if Travaglino should be proved to be a liar, the
farm of Emilliano should pass to Lucaferro; but if, on the other

hand, he should be found truthful, Emilliano should become the owner of Lucaferro's. And over this matter, having called in a notary, they caused to be drawn up a legal instrument ratified by all the forms which are required in such cases.

After the brothers had parted one from the other, and after their wrath and indignation had gone down somewhat, Lucaferro began to be sore repentant of the wager he had made, and of the legal instrument he had requested to be enacted under the seal of the notary. Wherefore he found himself mightily troubled over the affair, and haunted by the fear lest at the end of it he might find himself deprived of his farm, out of which alone he had to find sustenance for himself and for his family. One day, when he was in his house, his wife, whose name was Isotta, remarked that he was in a very melancholy mood, and, not knowing the reason thereof, she said to him: 'Heigho, my good husband! what can be the matter with you that you are so dismal and woebegone?' And Lucaferro made answer to her: 'Wife, hold your tongue, for goodness sake, and do not heap any fresh trouble upon me in addition to what I am plagued with already.' Whereupon Isotta began to be very curious to know what this trouble might be, and she plied her husband so skilfully with questions that in the end he told her everything. Then she said to him, with her face all radiant with joy and satisfaction: 'And is it really on account of this apprehension that you have got into such a taking of fear and agitation? Keep up a good heart, for you will see that I have wit enough in me to make this lout Travaglino tell to his master's face, not one lie, but a thousand.' And Lucaferro, when he heard these words, was much comforted.

Isotta, knowing perfectly well that the beautiful bull with the gilded horns was an especial favourite of Emilliano, her brother-in-law, determined, first of all, to lay out her lures in that direction. So, having dressed herself after a fashion calculated to kindle a man's desire, and daintily painted her face, she took her way by herself out of Bergamo and went to Pedrench, where was situated the farm of Emilliano, and, having gone into the farmhouse, she found therein Travaglino, who was busy making cheese and curds of butter-milk, and greeted him, saying: 'Travaglino, my good fellow, you see I am come to pay you a visit, to take a draught of milk and to eat some of your fine curds.' 'Indeed, I am very glad to see you, my mistress,' Travaglino replied, and, having made her sit down, he began to get ready the table, and to place thereon his cheese of ewe's milk and divers other good cheer, to do the lady honour. And after a while the youth, seeing her there all alone and very fair to look upon, was somewhat taken aback, forasmuch as it was in no way her wont thus to visit him, and could hardly persuade himself that she could be in truth Isotta, the wife of his master's brother. However, because he had often before seen her, he did his best to please her and to pay her such honour as would have been due to any lady, let her be whosoever she might.

After the meal was despatched and the table cleared, Isotta, observing that Travaglino was about to go to his cheese-making and to strain his whey, said to him : 'Travaglino, my good fellow, I would fain lend you a hand in making your cheese.' And he answered her : 'Yes, if it would please you, signora.' Then, without saying another word, she tucked up her sleeves as far as her elbows, thus laying bare her fair, wanton, well-rounded arms, which shone out as white as snow, and set to work with a will to help Travaglino to make his cheese, letting him now and again get a peep at her swelling bosom, where he might also see her breasts, which seemed as round and firm as two fair globes. And, besides this, she artfully brought her own rosy cheek mighty close to Travaglino's face, so that occasionally one touched the other. Now Travaglino, notwithstanding that he was only a simple countryman and a cowherd, was by no means wanting in wit, and, although he understood well enough from the looks and the demeanour of the lady that she was fired by lecherous passion, he did nothing more in the way of a return than beguile her by ordinary speech and glances, making believe the while to wot nothing of making love. But Isotta, who began to persuade herself that the young man was all on fire with love for her, felt herself straightway so mightily inflamed with amorous desire towards him that she could with difficulty hold herself within bounds. Although Travaglino perceived well enough what was the drift of the lady's lascivious wishes, he did not dare to say a word to her thereanent, fearing lest he might unduly trouble her and perhaps give offence. Wherefore the lovesick dame, by way of making an end of Travaglino's bashful dallying, said to him : 'Travaglino, what is the reason that you stand there so mum and thoughtful, and do not venture to say a word to me ? Peradventure there has come into your head the wish to ask some favour of me. Take good care and do not keep your desire a secret, whatever it

may be, since by so doing you will work an injury to yourself, and not me, seeing that I am completely at your pleasure and wish.' Travaglino, when he heard these words, put on a more sprightly manner and made a pretence of being greatly wishful to enjoy her. The besotted dame, when she saw that the young man at last gave signs of being moved to amorous intent, determined that the time had come to set about the business on which she was bent, so she spake to him thus: 'Travaglino, I am going to ask you to do me a great favour, and, if you should be churlish enough to refuse to grant it, I tell you plainly that it will look as if you held very light the love I bear you; moreover, your refusal will perchance be the cause of my ruin, or even of my death.'

To this speech Travaglino answered: 'Signora, for the love I have for you I am ready to devote my life and all I possess in the world to your service, and if it should chance that you demand of me to carry out some enterprise of great difficulty, nevertheless, on account of my own love and of the love which you have shown for me, I will easily accomplish it.' Then Isotta, taking courage from these words of Travaglino, said: 'If indeed you are my friend, as I well believe you to be, I shall know full soon.' 'Lay what command on me you will, signora,' replied Travaglino, 'and you will see clearly enough whether I am your friend or not.' 'All that I want of you,' said Isotta, 'is the head of that bull of yours which has his horns gilded. Give me this, and you may do with me what you please.' Travaglino, when he heard this request, was wellnigh overcome with amazement; but, inflamed by the pricks of fleshly desire, and by the allurements of the lustful woman before him, he made answer to her: 'Signora, can it be that this is all you want of me? You shall have, not only the head of the bull, but the body as well; nay, I will hand over my own self into your keeping.' And after he had thus spoken, Travaglino plucked up heart and folded the lady in his arms, and they together took part in the sweetest delights of love. When this was done, Travaglino cut off the bull's head, and, having put it in a sack, handed it over to Isotta, who, well satisfied that she had accomplished her purpose and got much pleasure and delight besides, made her way back to her house, bearing with her more horns than farms in her sack.

Now Travaglino, as soon as the lady had taken her departure, began to feel somewhat troubled in mind and to cast about for some

excuse which he might bring forward to his master when he should
be called upon to account for the death of the bull with the gilded
horns, which was so greatly beloved by Emilliano.   While the
wretched Travaglino was held by these torments of his mind, knowing neither what to say or to do, it came into his head at last to take
a branch of one of the pruned trees which grew about, and to dress
this up with some of his own poor garments, and to make believe
that it was Emilliano.   Then, standing before this scarecrow, he
proposed to make trial of what he should do and say when he should
be brought face to face with his master.   Wherefore, after he had
set up the tree branch thus bedizened in a chamber of the house with
his own cap on its head and with certain of his garments upon
its back, Travaglino went out from the chamber for a short space of
time, and then came back and entered, saluting the branch as he went
in, and saying, 'Good day, my master!' and then, making answer out
of his own mouth, he replied, 'I am glad to see you, Travaglino.
How do you find yourself, and how are things going on at the farm?
It is a long time since I have seen anything of you.'   'I am very
well,' replied Travaglino, 'but I have been so busy of late that
I have not been able to find time to come and see you.'   'How did
you leave the bull with the gilded horns?' asked Emilliano, and
then Travaglino made as if he would answer: 'Master, I have to
tell you that your favourite bull has been eaten of wolves while
he was straying in the woods.'   'Then where are his skin and his
gilded horns?' Emilliano inquired.   And when he had come to this
point poor Travaglino could not hit upon any answer he could possibly give; so, wellnigh overcome with grief, he left the chamber.
After a little he came in again and recommenced his discourse by
saying, 'God keep us all, good master!'   'And you also, Travaglino,'
said Emilliano, 'and how prosper things at the farm? how is the bull
with the gilded horns?'   'I am very well,' said Travaglino, 'but
one day lately the bull broke out of the yard, and having fallen
a-fighting with some of the other bulls, was so heavily mauled by
them that he died of his injuries straightway.'   'Then where are
his skin and his gilded horns?' asked Emilliano.   Whereupon Travaglino knew no better what answer he should give to this question
than before.   Finally, having gone through the same discourse several
times, he had to give up the matter in despair, through not being
able to devise any reply which sounded at all reasonable.

Now Isotta, as soon as she had returned to her house, said to her husband: 'What will that poor lout Travaglino do when he shall set about excusing himself to Emilliano with regard to the death of that bull with the gilded horns which was such a pet with his master? How will he clear himself of such a trouble as this without telling a lie or two? See, here is the head of the bull, which I have brought back with me to use as a testimony against him when he shall begin with his false tales.' But the dame said not a word to her husband as to how she had made for his own benefit two fine horns, bigger than those of a hart royal. Lucaferro, when he saw the bull's head, was overjoyed and could hardly contain himself for glee, making sure that he would now win his wager, but the issue of the affair fell out in mighty different fashion, as you will learn later on.

Travaglino, after he had essayed divers bouts of questions and answers with his scarecrow man, discoursing just as if he were in conversation with the master himself, and finding in the end that they none of them would serve the end he had in view, made up his mind without further ado to go and seek his master forthwith, no matter what might happen. Wherefore, having set forth towards Bergamo, he presented himself before his master, to whom he gave a hearty salute. Emilliano, after he had greeted his herdsman in return, said to him, 'And what business has been taking up all your time and thoughts of late, Travaglino, that you have let so many days pass without coming here or without letting us have any news of you?' Travaglino replied, 'Master, the many jobs I have had in hand have kept me fully occupied.' Then said Emilliano, 'And how goes on my bull with the gilded horns?'

When he heard these words, poor Travaglino was overcome with the direst confusion, and his face flushed with shame as red as a burning furnace, and he was fain to find some excuse for his fault and to hide the truth. But in the end the fear of saying aught which might sully his honour stood him in good stead, and made him take heart of grace and tell his master the whole story from beginning to end: how Isotta had beguiled him, and how his dealings with her had ensued in the death of the bull. Emilliano was amazed beyond measure as he listened to this story, which, however great his fault might have been, at least proved Travaglino to be a truthful fellow and one of good character. So in the end Emilliano won the wager with regard to the farm, and Lucaferro gained nothing but a pair of horns for his own head, while his good-for-nothing wife Isotta, in trying to dupe another, was finely duped herself, and got nothing but shame for her trouble.

When this instructive fable was finished, every one of the worthy company of listeners was loud in blame of the dissolute Isotta, and equally loud in commendation of Travaglino, holding up to ridicule the silly loose-minded woman, who had in such vile manner given herself away to a herdsman, of which ill-doing the real cause was her innate and pestilential avarice. And seeing that Eritrea had not as yet propounded her enigma, the Signora, glancing at her, made a sign that she must not interrupt the procedure they had followed so far. Whereupon Eritrea, without any farther delay, gave her enigma:

> I saw one day in fine spring weather,
> A head and a breech full close together.
> Another breech I likewise found
> Squatting at ease upon the ground.
> And one, as strong as any mule,
> Stood quiet, subject to the rule
> Of two, who in the head shone bright,
> And looked with pleasure on the sight.
> Meantime the head pressed closer still,
> And ten there were who worked with will,
> With dexterous grasp, now up, now down.
> No prettier sight in all the town.

Though the ladies made merry enough over the fable, they held the enigma to be no less of a jest. And, because there was not one of them who seemed likely to be able to solve it, Eritrea spake as follows: "My enigma, ladies and gentlemen, is intended to describe one who sits down under a cow and sets to work to milk her. And for the same reason he who milks the cow must keep his head close to the cow's breech, and the milker, for his good convenience, sits with his breech on the ground. She is very patient, and is kept in restraint by one, namely, he who milks her, and is watched by two eyes, and is stroked by two hands and the ten fingers, which draw from her the milk." This very clever enigma pleased them all mightily, as well as the interpretation thereof; but, seeing that every star had now disappeared from the heaven, save only a certain one which still shone in the whitening dawn, the Signora gave order that every one of the company should depart whithersoever he would, and take rest until the coming evening, commanding at the same time that each one should duly appear again at the appointed place under pain of her displeasure.

The End of the Third Night.

Night the Fourth.

The Fables and Enigmas of Messer Giovanni Francesco Straparola da Caravaggio.

Night the Fourth.

LREADY the golden-haired Apollo in his radiant chariot had sped away from this hemisphere of ours, and, having sunk beyond the distant line of sea, had betaken himself to the antipodes, and all those who had been labouring in the fields, now weary with their hard toil, felt no desire for aught save to repose quietly in their beds, when the worshipful and highborn company assembled themselves joyfully once more in the accustomed spot. And after the ladies and gentlemen had spent a short time in mirthful converse, the Signora Lucretia, when silence had been restored, bade them bring forth the golden vase. Then, having written with her own hand the names of five of the ladies and cast them into the vase, she called to the Signor Vangelista and directed him to draw out of the vase the names one by one, in order that they might clearly know to which of their companions the duty of story-telling on that same night would be assigned. Then Signor Vangelista, rising from his seat and breaking off the pleasant discourse he was holding with Lodovica, went obediently towards the Signora, and, having sunk down upon his knees reverently at her feet, he put his hand in the vase and drew out first the name of Fiordiana, then that of Vicenza, then that of Lodovica, next that of Isabella, and last the name of Lionora. But before they made a beginning of their story-

telling the Signora gave the word to Molino and to the Trevisan that they should take their lutes and sing a ballad. The two gentlemen did not wait for any further command, but forthwith tuned their instruments and sang to a joyous strain the following verse :

SONG.

There is a face which is my sun of love,
　In whose kind warmth I breathe and move,
　Or faint beneath its scorching ray ;
And when it shines amongst the fairest fair,
　My lady reigns beyond compare,
And all around her bend beneath her sway.

Happy, thrice happy, is that favoured one,
　Who sees no face but hers alone,
　And passion's nectar eager sips,
Who listens to the music of her tongue,
　More sweet than lay by seraphs sung,
In words that fall like jewels from her lips.

But happier still were I if she benign
　Would place her lily hand in mine,
And mark me worthy such a prize to claim.
　Dull clod of earth although I be,
　Then should I full fruition see
Of every hope, and end of every aim.

The song was attentively listened to and warmly commended by every one of the company. And when the Signora saw that it had come to an end she directed Fiordiana, to whom had been assigned the first turn of story-telling on this the fourth night, that she should begin hers straightway, and follow the order which had been observed since the beginning of their entertainment ; and the damsel, who was no less eager to speak than the rest of the company were to listen, thus began her fable.

THE FIRST FABLE.

Ricardo, King of Thebes, had four daughters, one of whom, having become a wanderer and altered her name of Costanza to Costanzo, arrived at the court of Cacco, King of Bettinia, who took her to wife on account of the many worthy deeds wrought by her.

I MUST first tell you, fair and gracious ladies, that the fable which Eritrea told to us on the evening last past has brought me into so bashful a mood that I feel but little in the humour to act the story-teller to-night. Nevertheless, the sense of obedience I have for every command of the Signora, and the respect I feel for the whole of this honourable and gracious company, compels and encourages me to make trial with a certain story which, though it assuredly will not be found as pleasing as the one recently related by Eritrea, I will give you for what it is worth. You shall hear how a certain damsel, endowed with a noble soul and high courage, one who in the course of her noteworthy adventures was far better served by fortune than by reason, held it preferable to become a servant than to fall into a base manner of life; how, after enduring servitude for some time, she became the wife of King Cacco, and lived content with her reward. All this will be set forth to you in the story I am about to tell you.

In Egypt is situated the great and splendid city of Thebes, a place richly ornamented with noble buildings, public as well as private, situated in a country rich in cornfields growing white for the sickle, and favoured with fresh water in abundance; abounding, moreover, in all those things which go to make up a glorious city. In times long past this city was under the rule of a king called by name Ricardo, a man profoundly wise, of great knowledge, and of the highest valour. Now this monarch, desiring greatly to have an heir to his kingdom, took to wife Valeriana, the daughter of Marliano, King of Scotland, a lady who was, in truth, perfection itself, very fair to look upon, and exceedingly gracious. Of her he begot three daughters, who were gentle in their manners, full of grace, and fair as rosebuds in the morning. Of these one was called Valentia, another Dorothea, and the third Spinella. In the course of time it became manifest to Ricardo that Valeriana his wife had come to that season of life when women commonly cease from child-bearing, and that his three daughters were all of them ripe for marriage, wherefore he determined forthwith to dispose of the three princesses in honourable wedlock, and at the same time to divide his kingdom into three parts, whereof he proposed to give one to each of his daughters, only keeping for himself so much as he judged would suffice for the entertainment of himself, and of his family, and of his court. And all these plans he carried out as he had deliberated with himself, so that the result of his project proved to be exactly what he had wished it to be.

In due time the three maidens were given in marriage to three powerful kings, one to the King of Scardona, another to the King of the Goths, and the third to the King of Scythia; and to each one of them was assigned, by way of dowry, a third part of their father's kingdom, Ricardo himself keeping back only a very small portion thereof to serve to satisfy his vital needs. And thus the good king, with Valeriana, his well-beloved wife, lived righteously in peace and comfort. But it happened, after a few years had passed, that the queen, of whom the king expected no further offspring, proved to be with child, and at the end of her time was brought to bed with a very beautiful little girl, whom the king welcomed with affection and caresses as warm as he had given to the other three children. But the queen was not so well pleased with this last infant, not, however, on account of any dislike for the child herself, but because, seeing that the kingdom was now divided into three parts and given away, she feared that there would be no chance of furnishing this daughter with a dowry sufficient to win her a marriage worthy of their state. She desired at the same time that the child should receive the share due to a daughter of hers. But, having handed over the child to the care of a very competent nurse, she gave strict command to her to use the greatest care in her charge, to give the child good instruction, and to train her in the gentle and praiseworthy manners and carriage which become a fair and graceful maiden. The child, to whom the name of Costanza was given, grew day by day more lovely and her manners more engaging, nor could any subject from the most learned masters be brought forward which she would not at once apprehend most readily. By the time Costanza was twelve years of age she had already learned to embroider, to sing, to dance, to play the lute, and to do every one of those feats which are rightly held to mark a princess of rank. But, not content with these graces, she gave herself also to the study of polite letters, which proved to be to her so great a source of pleasure and delight that she would spend over them not merely the day, but the night as well, striving always to find out the exquisite beauties of the books she studied. And over and above all these excellencies she mastered completely the art of war in learning how to gentle horses, and to handle arms, and to run in the lists as if she had been a strong and well-trained man-at-arms and not a damsel. In jousting, indeed, she was so skilled that she ofttimes came out of the contest victorious, just as if she had been one of those valorous knights who are held worthy of the highest honour. Wherefore, on account of all these virtues, and on her own account as well, Costanza was greatly loved by the king and the queen and by all those around them, so that there seemed to be no limit to their affection.

When Costanza had come to a marriageable age, the king her father, finding that he had now neither the state nor the gold required to secure for her a match with some potent sovereign equal to her merits, was greatly troubled thereanent, and often took counsel with the queen concerning the matter; but the prudent Valeriana, in whose sight the good qualities of their child appeared to be so many and so great that no other lady in the land could in any way be put on a level with her, was not disquieted at all, and consoled the king with gentle and loving words, bidding him keep a light heart, and not to doubt at all but that in the end some powerful sovereign, fired with love by the many virtues of their daughter, would not disdain to take her to wife, even though they might not be able to give her a dowry.

Before many months had passed the damsel was sought in marriage by divers gallant gentlemen, amongst whom was Brunello, the son of the Marquis of Vivien, whereupon the king and the queen called their daughter to them into their chamber, and when they were all seated, the king spake thus: 'Costanza, my well-beloved child, the time is now come when it is meet that you should be married, and we have found for you as a husband a youth who ought to please your taste. He is no other than the son of the Marquis of Vivien, our good friend and neighbour; his name is Brunello, and he is a graceful seemly youth, the report of his valorous deeds having spread already throughout the world. And moreover he asks of us nought besides our own goodwill and your fair sweet self, upon which I put a value exceeding that of all the pomp and treasure of the world. You must know that, though you are the daughter of a king, yet I cannot, on account of my poverty, find for you a more exalted alliance. Wherefore you must be content with this establishment and conform to our wishes.' The damsel, who was very prudent and conscious that she was sprung from high lineage, listened attentively to her father's words, and, without wasting any time over the matter, answered him as follows: 'Sacred majesty, there is no need that I should spend many words in replying to your honourable proposal, but simply that I should speak as the question between us demands. And first I desire to testify to you my gratitude, the warmest I can express, for all the affection and benevolence you exhibit towards me in seeking to provide me with a husband without any request from me. Next—speaking with all submission and reverence—I do not purpose to let myself fall below the race of my ancestors, who from all time have been famous and illustrious, nor do I wish to debase the crown you wear by taking for a husband one who is our inferior. You, my beloved father, have begotten four daughters, of whom you have married three in the most honourable fashion to three mighty kings, giving with them great store of gold and wide domains, but you wish to dispose of me, who have ever been obedient to you and observant of your precepts, in an ignoble alliance. Wherefore I tell you, to end my speech, that I will never take a husband unless I can be mated, like my three sisters, to a king of a rank that is my due.' Shortly after this, Costanza, shedding many tears the while, took leave of the king and queen, and, having mounted a gallant horse, set forth from Thebes alone, and determined to follow whatever road fortune might lay open to her feet.

While she was thus journeying at hazard she deemed it wise to change her name, so in lieu of Costanza she called herself Costanzo, and donned a man's attire. She passed over many mountain ranges, and lakes, and marshes, and saw many lands, and heard the tongues and took heed of the ways and manners of certain races who live their lives after the fashion of brutes rather than of men. At last, one day at the set of sun, she arrived at a famed and celebrated city called Costanza, the capital of all the country round, and at that time under the rule of Cacco, King of Bettinia. And, having entered therein, she forthwith began to admire the superb palaces, the straight roomy streets, the running water, the broad rivers, and the clear, soft, trickling fountains. Then, when she had come near to the piazza,

she saw the spacious and lofty palace of the king, adorned with columns
of the finest marble and porphyry, and, having raised her eyes somewhat, she saw the king, who was standing upon a gallery which commanded a view of the whole piazza, and taking off her cap from her
head she made him a profound reverence. The king, when he perceived the fair and graceful youth down below, had him called and
brought into his presence, and as soon as Costanzo stood before him
he demanded from what country he had come, and by what name he
was called. The youth, with a smiling face, gave answer that he had
journeyed from Thebes, driven thence by envious and deceitful fortune,
and that Costanzo was his name. He declared, moreover, that he
desired greatly to attach himself to the service of some gentleman of
worth, pledging himself to serve any such lord with all the faith and
affection that good service merited. The king, who meantime was
mightily pleased with the appearance of the youth, said to him:
'Seeing that you bear the name of this my city, it is my pleasure that
you tarry here in my court with no other duty laid upon you than to
attend to my person.' The youth, who desired no better office than
this, first rendered to the king his gratitude, and then joyfully accepted
service under him as lord, offering at the same time to hold himself
ready to discharge any duty which might be assigned to him.

So Costanza, in the guise of a man, entered into the service of
the king, and served him so well and gracefully that every one who
came near him was astonished beyond measure at his talents. And
it chanced that the queen, when she had well observed and considered
the graceful bearing, the pleasant manners, and the discreet behaviour
of Costanzo, began to cast her eyes more diligently upon him, until
at last, so hotly did she grow inflamed with love of him, neither by
day nor by night did she turn her thoughts upon any other. And
so soft and so loving were the glances that she would continually dart
towards him, that not only a youth, but even the hardest rock, or the
unyielding diamond even, might well have been softened. Wherefore the queen, being thus consumed with passion for Costanzo,
yearned for nothing else than that she might some day find occasion
to foregather with him alone. And before long it came to pass that
chance gave her the opportunity of conversing with him, so she
straightway inquired of him whether it would be agreeable to him to
enter into her service, making it known to him likewise that by
serving her he would gain, over and above the guerdon which she would

give him, the approbation or even the reverence and respect of all the court.

Costanzo perceived clearly enough that these words which came out of the queen's mouth sprang from no goodwill of hers for his advancement, but from amorous passion. Knowing moreover that, being a woman like herself, he could in no way satisfy the hot un-bridled lust which prompted them, with unclouded face he humbly made answer to her in these words : 'Signora, so strong is the obli-gation of service which binds me to my lord your husband, that it seems to me I should be working him a base injury were I to with-draw myself from my obedience to his will. Therefore I pray you to hold me excused, and to pardon me that I am not ready and willing at once to take service with you, and to accept, as the reason of this my refusal of your gracious offer, my resolve to serve my lord even unto death, provided that it pleases him to retain me as his man.' And, having taken leave of the queen, he withdrew from her presence. The queen, who was well aware that men do not fell to earth a hard oak-tree with a single stroke, many and many a time after this made trial, with the deepest cunning and art, to entice the youth to take service under her, but he, as constant and as strong as a lofty tower beaten by the winds, was not to be moved. As soon as the queen became conscious of this, the ardent burning love in her was turned to mortal bitter hatred, so that she could no longer bear the sight of him. And, having now grown anxious to work his destruction, she pondered day and night how she might best set to work to clear him out of her path, but she was in great dread of the king, for that he continued to hold the youth in high favour.

In a certain district of the province of Bettinia there was to be found a strange race of beings, in whom one half of the body, that is to say, the upper part, was made after the fashion of a man, though they had ears like those of animals, and horns as well. But in their lower parts they had members resembling those of a rough shaggy goat, with a little tail, twisted and curling, of the sort one sees upon a pig. These creatures were called satyrs, and by their depredations they caused great loss and damage to the villages and the farms and the people living in the country thereabout. Wherefore the king desired greatly to have one of these satyrs taken alive and delivered over into his keeping, but there was found no one about the court with heart stout enough to undertake this adventure and capture a satyr for the

king. By sending him on an errand of this sort the queen hoped to
work Costanzo's destruction, but the issue of the matter was not at
all what she desired, for in this case, as in many others, the would-be
deceiver, by the workings of divine providence and supreme justice,
was cast under the feet of the one she purposed to beguile.

The treacherous queen, being well aware of the king's longing,
happened to be one day in converse with him concerning divers
matters, and, while they were thus debating, she said to him: 'My
lord, have you never considered that Costanzo, your faithful and devoted servant, is strong and vigorous enough in body, and daring and
courageous enough in soul, to go and capture for you one of these
satyrs, and to bring him back to you alive, without calling on anyone else to aid him. If the matter should fall out in this wise, as I
believe it would, you might easily make trial of it, and in the course
of an hour attain the wish of your heart, and Costanzo, as a brave
and valiant knight, would enjoy the honour of the deed, which would
be accounted to him for glory for ever.' This speech of the cunning
queen pleased the king greatly, and he straightway bade them summon
Costanzo into his presence. When the youth appeared the king thus
addressed him: 'Costanzo, if indeed you love me, as you make
show of doing, and as all people believe, you will now carry out fully
the wish I have in my heart, and you yourself shall possess the glory
of the fulfilling thereof. You are surely aware that what I desire
more than aught else in the world is to have a satyr alive in my own
keeping. Wherefore, seeing how strong and active you are, I reckon
there is no other man in all my kingdom so well fitted to work my will
in this affair as you; so, loving me as you do, you will not refuse to
carry out my will.' The youth, who suspected not that this demand
sprang from aught else than the king's desire, was anxious to give no
cause of vexation to the king, and with a cheerful and amiable face
thus made answer: 'My lord, in this and in everything else you
may command me. However weak and imperfect my faculties may
be, I will on no account draw back from striving to fulfil your wishes,
even though in the task I should meet with my death. But, before I commit myself to this perilous adventure, I beg you, my lord,
that you will cause to be taken into the wood where the satyrs abide
a large vessel with a wide mouth of the same size as those which the
servants use in dressing smooth the shifts and other kinds of body
linen. And besides this I would have taken thither a large cask of

good white wine, the best that can be had and the strongest, together
with two bags full of the finest white bread.'   The king forthwith bade
them get in readiness everything which Costanzo had described, and
Costanzo then journeyed towards the wood in question.   Having
arrived there he took a copper bucket and began to fill it with white
wine drawn from the cask, and this he poured into the other vessel
which stood near by.   Next he took some of the bread, and, having
broken it in pieces, he put these into the vessel full of wine.   This
being done he climbed up into a thick-leaved tree which stood hard
by, and waited to see what might happen next.

Costanzo had not been long up in the tree before the satyrs, who
had smelt the odour of the fragrant wine, began to draw near to the
vessel, and having come close to it, each one swilled therefrom a good
bellyful of wine, greedy as the hungry wolves when they fall upon a
fold of young lambs.   And after they had filled their stomachs and
had taken enough, they lay down to sleep, and so sound and deep
was their slumber that all the noise in the world would not have
roused them.   Then Costanzo, seeing that the time for action had
come, descended from the tree and went softly up to one of the
satyrs, whose hands and feet he bound fast with a cord he had
brought with him.   Next, without making any noise, he laid him
upon his horse and carried him off.   And while Costanzo was on his
way back, with the satyr tightly bound behind him, they came at the
vesper hour to a village not far from the city, and the creature, who
by this time had recovered from the effects of the wine, woke up and
began to yawn as if he were rising from his bed.   Looking around
him he perceived the father of a family, who with a crowd around
him was going to bury a dead child, weeping bitterly the while, and
the priest, who conducted the service, was singing.   When he looked
upon this spectacle the satyr began to laugh mightily.   Afterwards,
when they had entered the city and were come to the piazza, the
satyr beheld a great crowd of people who were staring open-mouthed
at a poor lad who had just mounted the gallows to be hanged by the
executioner, and the satyr laughed thereat even louder than he had
laughed before.   And afterwards, when they were come to the
palace, a great joy seized upon the people standing by, and they all
cried out ' Costanzo! Costanzo!'   And the satyr, when he heard this
shouting, laughed louder than ever.

When Costanzo was conducted into the presence of the king and of the queen and her ladies, he presented to the king the satyr, who thereupon laughed again, and so loud and long was his laughter that all those that were there present were not a little astonished. After this the king, seeing with what diligence Costanzo had fulfilled his dearest wish, held him in as high affection and esteem as ever lord extended to servant, but this humour of his only added fresh griefs to the load which already lay upon the queen's heart; for that, having schemed to ruin Costanzo, she had done nothing but exalt him to yet greater honour. Wherefore the wicked queen, not being able to endure the sight of such great prosperity as had come to Costanzo, devised yet another snare for him, which was this. She knew that the king was wont to go every morning to the cell where the satyr was kept in hold, and for his diversion would essay to make the creature talk, but as yet he had in no wise succeeded in his efforts. Wherefore, having sought out the king, she said to him: 'Sire, you have betaken yourself over and over again to the satyr's cell, and you have wearied yourself in your endeavours to induce him to talk with you in order that you might take diversion therefrom, but the creature still shows no sign of speaking a word. Why, therefore, should you further worry your brains over this affair, for you may take it for certain that, if Costanzo were only willing, he could easily make the satyr converse and answer questions.'

The king, when he listened to these words, straightway bade them summon Costanzo into his presence, and when he came the king thus addressed him: 'Costanzo, I am well assured that you know how great is the pleasure I get from the satyr you captured for me; nevertheless it irks me greatly to find that he is dumb, and will never make any answer to the words I say to him and the questions I put. If you would only do all that you might, I am sure that you would be able to make him speak.' 'Sire,' Costanzo replied, 'that the satyr is dumb is no fault of mine; it is not the office of a mortal, like me, to make him speak, but of a god. But if the reason of his muteness comes not from any natural or accidental defect, but from stubborn resolve to keep silence, I will do all that lies in my power to make him open his mouth in speech.' Then, having gone together to the satyr's prison, they gave him some dainty food, and some wine still better, and called out to him, 'Eat, Chiappino' (for this was the name they had given to the satyr). But the creature only stared at them without uttering a word. Then they went on:

'Come, Chiappino, tell us whether that capon and that wine are to your taste;' but still he was silent. Costanzo, perceiving how obstinate the humour of the creature was, said, 'So you will not answer me, Chiappino. Let me tell you you are doing a very foolish thing, seeing that I can if I will let you die of hunger here in prison.' And at these words the satyr shot a side-glance at Costanzo. After a little Costanzo went on : 'Answer me, Chiappino; for if you speak to me (as I hope you will) I will liberate you from this place.' Then Chiappino, who had listened with eagerness to all that had been said, answered, as soon as he heard speak of liberation, 'What will you of me?' Costanzo then said, 'Tell me, have you eaten and drunk well?' 'Yes,' said Chiappino. 'Now I want you, of your courtesy, to tell me,' said Costanzo, 'what thing it was that moved you to laughter in the village street when we met with the body of the child on its way to be buried?' To this Chiappino answered, 'I laughed, indeed, not at the dead child, but at the so-called father, to whom the child in the coffin was in fact no kin at all, and I laughed at the priest singing the office, who was the real father,' by which speech the satyr would have them understand that the mother of the child had carried on an intrigue with the priest. Then said Costanzo, 'And now I want to know, my Chiappino, what it was that made you laugh yet louder when we were come into the piazza?' 'I laughed then,' replied Chiappino, 'to see a thousand or more thieves, who had robbed the public purse of crowns by the million, who deserved a thousand gibbets, standing in the piazza to feast their eyes on the sight of a poor wretch led to the gallows, who, perchance, had merely pilfered ten florins wherewith to buy bread for himself and his poor children. That was why I laughed.' Then said Costanzo, 'And besides this, I beg you to tell me how it was that, when we were come into the palace, you laughed longer and louder than ever?' 'Ah, I beg you will not trouble me more at present,' said Chiappino, 'but go your way and come back to-morrow, and then I will answer you and tell you certain things of which perchance you have no inkling.' When Costanzo heard this, he said to the king, 'Let us depart and come back to-morrow, and hear what this thing may be.' Whereupon the king and Costanzo took their leave, and gave orders that Chiappino should be given to eat and drink of the best, and that he should be allowed to chatter as he would.

When the next day had come they both went to see Chiappino, and they found him puffing and blowing like a great pig, and, having gone close to him, cried out to him several times in a loud voice. But Chiappino, who had well filled his belly, answered nought. Then Costanzo gave him a sharp prick with a dart which he had with him, whereupon the satyr awoke and stood up and demanded who was there. 'Now get up, Chiappino,' said Costanzo, 'and tell us that thing which yesterday you promised we should hear, and say why you laughed so loud when we came to the palace?' To which question Chiappino made this reply : 'For a reason which you ought to understand better than I. It was, forsooth, at hearing them all shouting "Costanzo! Costanzo!" while all the time you are Costanza.' The king when he heard this could in no wise comprehend what this saying of Chiappino's might mean ; but Costanzo, who immediately recognized its import, in order to keep him from speaking more, at once stopped the way for him [1] by saying : 'And when you had been brought into the very presence of the king and queen, what made you laugh then as if nothing could stop you?' To this Chiappino made answer : 'I laughed then so outrageously because the king, and you as well, believed that the maidens who were in service on the queen were really maidens, whereas the greater part of them were young men.' And then he was silent.

When the king heard these words he knew not what to think, but he said nothing ; and, having left the wild satyr, he went out with Costanzo, wishing to learn clearly what might be the meaning of what he had heard. And after he had made due inquiry he found that Costanzo was in truth a woman, and not a youth, and that the supposed damsels about the queen were sprightly young men, as Chiappino had said. And straightway the king bade them light a great fire in the middle of the piazza, and into it, in the presence of all the people, he caused to be cast the queen and all her paramours. And, bearing in mind the praiseworthy loyalty and the open faithfulness of Costanza, and marking moreover her exceeding beauty, the king made her his wife in the presence of all his barons and knights. When he knew who her parents were, he greatly rejoiced, and forthwith despatched ambassadors to King Ricardo and to Valeriana his wife, and to the three sisters of Costanza, to tell them how she was

---

[1] Orig., *gli troncò la strada.*

now the wife of a king; whereupon they all felt the joy due to such good news. Thus the noble Costanza, in recompense for the faithful service she rendered, became a queen and lived long with Cacco her husband.

When Fiordiana had brought her fable to an end, the Signora made a sign to her to give her enigma. The damsel, who was somewhat haughty, rather by chance than by nature, set it forth in the following words :

> Over savage lions twain
> A spirit soft and mild doth reign.
> By her side four damsels move,
> Prudence, Valour, Faith, and Love.
> She bears a sword in her right hand;
> Before it calm the righteous stand,
> But wicked men and souls unjust
> It smites and lays them in the dust.
> Discord nor wrong with her may rest,
> And he who loves her wins the best.

This clever enigma set forth by Fiordiana, who indeed was a damsel of subtle mind, won the praise of all, and some found its meaning to be one thing, and some another. But there was no one of all the company who rightly divined it, seeing that all their solutions were far wide of the true one. When Fiordiana saw this she said in a lively tone, " Ladies and gentlemen, I see you are troubling yourselves in vain, seeing that my enigma means nothing else than that infinite and equal justice which like a gentle spirit rules and restrains both the hungry, savage lions, and likewise the proud, unconquerable spirit of man. More than that, justice makes steadfast her faith, holding in her right hand a sharp sword, and accompanied always by four virgins, Prudence, Charity, Fortitude, and Faith. She is gentle and kind to the good, and severe and bitter to the perverse and bad." When Fiordiana ceased speaking, the listeners were greatly pleased with the interpretation of her enigma. Then the Signora bade the gracious Vicenza to follow in her turn with a fable, and she, eager to obey this command, spake as follows.

THE SECOND FABLE.

Erminione Glaucio, an Athenian, takes to wife Filenia Centurione, and, having become jealous of her, accuses her before the tribunal, but by the help of Hippolito, her lover, she is acquitted and Erminione punished.

F a truth, gracious ladies, there would be in all the world no condition more sweet, more delightful, or more happy than the service of love, were it not for that bitter fruit which springs from sudden jealousy, the foe which drives away gentle Cupid, the betrayer of kindly ladies, the foe who day and night tries to compass their death. Wherefore there comes into my recollection a fable which ought to be received by you with some satisfaction, seeing that from it you will be able readily to understand the hard and piteous fate which befell a gentleman of Athens, who, because of his impotent jealousy, sought the taking off of his wife by the sword of justice, but was instead condemned himself, and met his death thereby. Which judgment ought to please you, because, if I am not greatly in error, you are yourselves all of you more or less in love.

In Athens, the most ancient city of Greece, and one which was in times past the veritable home and resort of all learning, though now, through her flighty vanity, entirely ruined and overthrown, there resided once upon a time a gentleman named Messer Erminione Glaucio, a man of much consideration and repute in the city, rich in purse, but at the same time of mean intelligence. Now it chanced that when he was an old man, finding himself without progeny, he made up his mind to marry, and took to wife a damsel named Filenia, daughter of Messer Cesarino Centurione, of noble descent and gifted with marvellous beauty and with good qualities out of number. In short, there was in all the city no other maiden who was her equal. And, forasmuch as he was greatly in fear lest his wife, on account of her marvellous beauty, should be courted by divers of the gallants of the city, and perhaps give occasion for some disgraceful scandal, through which the finger of scorn might be pointed at him, he resolved to restrain her in a certain lofty tower of his palace, out of sight of all passers-by. And before long it happened that the wretched old dotard, without knowing why, let his jealousy rise to such a pitch that he mistrusted even himself.

There was residing in the city at this time a certain scholar of Crete, young in years, but very discreet, and greatly loved and esteemed by all who knew him on account of his amiability and grace. The name of this youth was Hippolito, and before Filenia was married he had paid suit to her, and, besides this, he was on intimate terms with Messer Erminione, who held him as dear as if he had been his own son. At a certain time during his scholar's course he found himself somewhat disinclined for study; so, desiring to recruit his spirits, he took his departure from Athens, and having gone into Crete, he sojourned there for a time, to discover on his return that Filenia was married. On this account he fell into an access of melancholy, and he grieved the more because he was now deprived of all hope of seeing her at his pleasure, nor could he endure to remember that a maiden so lovely and graceful should be bound in marriage to a toothless, slobbering old man.

Wherefore the love-stricken Hippolito, finding himself no longer able to endure the burning pricks and the sharp arrows of love, set himself to find out some method, some hidden way by which he might enjoy the fulfilment of his desires. And after he had well considered the many schemes which presented themselves to him, he fixed at last upon a certain one which appeared to him the most fitting. To put this in execution he first betook himself to the shop of a carpenter, his neighbour, where he ordered to be made two chests of the same length and breadth and width, and of the same measure and quality, so that no one would be able to distinguish the one from the other. This done, he repaired to Messer Erminione's house, and, making pretence of wanting something of him, spake in cunning wise the following words: 'Messer Erminione, you know well enough that I love and reverence you as if you were my own father, and for my part if I were not well convinced of your affection for myself, I would never dare, with such assurance as I now use, to beg any favour of you; but, seeing that I have ever found you well disposed to me, I am wellnigh certain that I shall now get from you that service which my heart so greatly desires. It happens that I am constrained to leave Athens and to go to the city of Frenna to expedite some very important matters of business, and I must remain there until such time as these shall be completed. And because I have no one about me whom I can fully trust, seeing that I am served only by menials and hirelings, of whom I am in no way well assured, I would fain that you hold in charge for me—provided that it be your pleasure so to do—a certain chest of mine full of articles of value which I happen to possess.' Messer Erminione, suspecting nought of the craft of the young scholar, made answer to him that he was well content to grant this favour, and that for greater security the chest should be deposited and kept in the same chamber in which he slept. On hearing this reply the scholar returned to Messer Erminione his thanks, the warmest he knew how to render, promising the while to keep in mind the memory of this great favour done to him as long as he should live. Then he begged the old man to do him the honour to go with him as far as his own dwelling, in order that he might exhibit to him the various articles which he had stored in the chest. Wherefore the two, having gone together to the house of Hippolito, the latter pointed out a chest filled with rich garments and jewels and necklaces of no small value, and then, having summoned a certain one of his servants and presented him to Messer Erminione, he said: 'If at any time, Messer Erminione, this my servant should be seeing after the removal of my chest, you can trust him to the full as if he were my own self.' And when Messer Erminione had taken his departure Hippolito hid himself in the other chest, which was exactly like the one filled with garments and jewels, and having fastened it from the inside, he bade his servant carry it to a certain place he knew of. The servant, who was privy to the affair, obedient to his master's order called a porter, and having lifted the burden on the man's back, ordered him to bear it to the tower in which was situated the chamber where Messer Erminione slept every night with his young wife.

Messer Erminione, being one of the chiefs of the city and a man of wealth and influence, it fell to his lot, on account of the worshipful state he filled, to go for a certain space of time to a place called Porto Pireo, distant about twenty stadi from the city of Athens, and there to compose certain suits and strifes which had arisen between the townsmen and the peasants round about—albeit he found this errand but little to his taste. Wherefore, when Messer Erminione had gone his way, tormented as ever by the jealousy which day and night weighed upon him, the youth, shut up in the chest which now stood in Madonna Filenia's bedroom, was waiting for the favourable moment.

More than once had he heard the fair dame weeping and sighing as she bemoaned her hard lot, and the place and the hour which had seen her given in marriage to a miserable old man who had proved to be the ruin of her life. And when it seemed to him that she was in her first sleep, he got out of the chest, and, having gone to the bedside, said in a soft voice : 'Awake, my soul! for I, your Hippolito, am here.' And when she was fully aroused, and saw him and knew who he was (for there was a candle burning in the chamber), she was inclined to cry out; but the young man, putting his hand upon her lips, would not allow this, and thus addressed her in a voice full of agitation : 'Be silent, heart of mine! do you not see that I am Hippolito, your faithful lover? Of a truth I cannot live apart from you.' The fair young woman was somewhat comforted by these words, and by the time she had found the opportunity for comparing the worth of her old husband with the youthful Hippolito, she was by no means ill-satisfied with the turn things had taken, and lay all night with her lover, spending the time in loving conversation and railing at the impotent ways of her doltish husband. Before they parted they agreed together to meet again in like manner, and when the morning began to dawn the youth got back into his chest, and every evening would issue therefrom and spend the night with the lady.

Now, after a good many days had elapsed, Messer Erminione, giving the business good speed both on account of the discomfort he himself suffered and of the rabid jealousy which never ceased to torment him, put an end to all the disputes he had been called upon to settle, and went back to his home. The servant of Hippolito, as soon as he heard the news of Messer Erminione's return, went without losing time to his house, and, according to the agreement which had been settled, demanded of him in the name of his master Hippolito the return of the chest, and this Messer Erminione gave up to him without a word of demur. Wherefore, having summoned a porter, the servant caused the chest to be conveyed home. Then Hippolito, having come out of his hiding-place, went forthwith to the piazza, where he met with Messer Erminione, and after he had embraced him, he thanked him most courteously in the warmest terms he could find for the great kindness he had received, and at the same time declared that he himself and all that he possessed should ever be ready at Messer Erminione's service.

It chanced that on a certain morning Messer Erminione remained in bed with his wife somewhat later than was his wont, and, lifting up his eyes, he remarked upon the wall and high above his head certain stains which looked as if they had been caused by someone spitting thereon.   Wherefore his inveterate jealousy began once more to trouble him, and he was mightily amazed at what he saw, and began to turn it over in his mind in such wise that, after he had well considered the matter, he could not bring himself to believe that the marks on the wall in question were any work of his.   Then, with strong apprehension as to their meaning, he turned to his wife and with an angry troubled face demanded of her: 'What have you to say about those spit marks high up on the wall there? I am well assured they were never made by me, for I never spat up there in my life.   I strongly suspect that you have betrayed my honour.'   Filenia, laughing the while at this speech, thus answered him: 'Is there no other charge you would like to bring against me?' Messer Erminione, when he saw her begin to laugh, grew more infuriated than ever, and said: 'Ah, you laugh, do you, wicked woman that you are? Now, tell me quickly what it is that makes you laugh.' 'I am laughing,' answered Filenia, 'at your own foolishness.'   At these words Messer Erminione began to chafe with rage,[1] and, being anxious to make trial of his own powers and to see whether he could spit so high, with much coughing and gasping he strained with all his might to reach the mark on the wall by his spitting, but he wearied himself in vain, for the spittle always fell down again and lighted upon his visage, plastering him thickly with filth.   And after the wretched old man had made this trial many times, he found that he only got in worse case every turn.   So, by the light of this experience, he persuaded himself that his wife had assuredly played him false, and, turning to her, he began to assail her with the most rascally words that could be applied to a guilty woman, and, if he had not been in fear of the law and of his own neck, he would surely have slain her then and there with his own hands, but he managed to restrain himself, deeming it better to deal with her by legal process than to stain his hands in her blood.   Not satisfied with the rating he had already given her, he betook himself, full of wrath and anger, to the tribunal, where he preferred before the judge a charge of adultery against his wife.   But, seeing that it lay not within the power of the judge to pronounce condemnation upon

---

[1] Orig., *tra se stesso se radeva.*

her unless the legal statutes should have been duly observed, he ordered Filenia to be brought before him in order that he might narrowly examine her.

Now, there was in Athens a law, which was held in the highest reverence, providing that any woman who might be charged by her husband with adultery should be placed at the foot of a certain red column, round which was entwined a serpent, and there make oath whether or not the accusation of adultery brought against her were true. And after she had taken the oath she was required forthwith to put her hand in the serpent's mouth, and then, if she should have sworn falsely, the serpent would at once bite off her hand; otherwise, she received no injury. Hippolito, who had already heard rumours of this charge before the tribunal, and that the judge had sent to fetch Filenia to put her on her defence, being a youth of resource at once took action to see that she should not run into the snares of ignominious death. By way of rescuing her from condemnation he first of all stripped off all his clothes and donned in their stead some rags befitting a madman, and then, without being seen by anyone, he left his own lodging and ran straight to the tribunal as if he had been someone out of his mind, acting well the part of a crazy man as he went along the streets.

Now it chanced that while the officers of the court were haling along the poor lady towards the tribunal, all the people of the city gathered themselves together to take note as to how the cause would end, and in the midst of the crowd the pretended madman, forcing his way now here, now there, worked himself so well to the front that he found opportunity to cast his arms round the neck of the woeful lady, and to press a kiss upon her lips, which caress she, seeing that her arms were bound behind her back, could in no wise escape. When the young woman had been brought into the presence of the tribunal the judge addressed her in these words: 'As you may see, Filenia, your husband Messer Erminione is here to lay complaint against you that you have committed adultery, and furthermore prays that I should deal out to you the due penalty according to the statute; wherefore you must now make oath and say whether or not the charge which your husband brings against you is true.' Then the young woman, who was very wary and keen of intellect, swore with confidence that no man had ever touched her save her husband and the madman who was now present before them all. Then, after she had sworn, the

underlings of the court led her to the place where was the serpent, which, after Filenia's hand had been placed in its mouth, did her no harm whatever, inasmuch as what she had sworn was really the truth, namely, that no man had ever given her caress of any sort except her husband and the so-called madman.

When they perceived this, the crowd, and all her kinsfolk, who had come thither to see the solemn and terrible sight, at once set her down as innocent and wrongfully accused, and cried out that Messer Erminione deserved the same death which was the penalty of the crime imputed to his wife. But, for the reason that he was a noble, a man of high lineage, and one of the chiefs of the city, the president would not permit him to be publicly burned (for so much power the law gave him), but, in order that he might duly discharge his office, he sentenced Erminione to be thrown into prison, where, after a short space of time, he expired. This is the wretched end which Messer Erminione put to his senseless jealousy, and by these means the young wife was delivered from an ignominious death. Before great length of time had passed Hippolito made her his lawful wife, and they lived many years happily together.

When the story told by the discreet and modest Vicenza had come to an end—a story which pleased all the ladies mightily—the Signora bade her to propound her enigma in due course, and she, raising her pretty smiling face, instead of one of her songs gave the following riddle:

> When hope and love and strong desire
> Are born to set the world on fire,
> That self-same hour a beast is born,
> All savage, meagre, and forlorn.
> Sometimes, with seeming soft and kind,
> Like ivy round an elm-tree twined,
> It clips us close with bine and leaf,
> But feeds on heartache, woe, and grief.
> Ever in mourning garb it goes,
> In anguish lives, in sorrow grows.
> And worse than worst the fate of him
> Who falls beneath its talons grim.

Here Vicenza brought her enigma to an end. The interpretations of its meaning were diverse, and no one of the company was found clever enough to fathom its true import. When Vicenza saw this, she sighed a little impatiently, and then, with a smiling face, spake as follows: " The enigma I have set you to guess means nothing else than chilling jealousy, which, all lean and faded, is born at the same birth with love itself, and winds itself round men and women as well, just as the gently-creeping ivy embraces the trunk so dear to it. This jealousy feeds on heartache, seeing that a jealous one always lives in anguish and moves about in sombre garb on account of the continual melancholy that torments him." This explication of the enigma gave great pleasure to all, and especially to Signora Chiara, whose husband had a temper somewhat jealous. But, to let no one say to himself that Vicenza's enigma had been framed to fit his case, the Signora bade them at once put a stop to their laughter, and signed to Lodovica, whose turn it was to tell the next story, that she should forthwith begin, and the damsel opened her fable in the following words.

THE THIRD FABLE.

Ancilotto, King of Provino, takes to wife the daughter of a baker, and has by her three children. These, after much persecution at the hands of the king's mother, are made known to their father through the strange working of certain water, and of an apple, and of a bird.

HAVE always understood, lovesome and gracious ladies, that man is the noblest and most capable of the living creatures fashioned by nature, seeing that God made him in His own image and similitude, and willed that he should rule and not be ruled. And on this account it is said that man is the perfect animal, and of greater excellence than any of the others, because all these, not even excepting woman, are subject to him. Therefore, those who by deceit and cunning compass the death of so noble a creature commit a foul crime. And there is no wonder if sometimes those who work for the bane of others run heedlessly into destruction themselves, as did four women I have to tell of, who, in trying to destroy others, were themselves cut off and made a wretched end. All this you will readily understand from the fable I purpose to tell you.

In Provino, a very famous and royal city, there lived in ancient times three sisters, fair of person, gracious in manners, and courteous

in bearing, but of base lineage, being the daughters of a certain
Messer Rigo, a baker who baked bread for other folk in his oven.
Of these one was named Brunora, another Lionella, and another
Chiaretta. It happened one day when the three sisters were in their
garden, and there taking much delight, that Ancilotto the king, who
was going to enjoy the diversion of hunting with a great company,
passed that way. Brunora, the eldest sister, when she looked upon
the fair and noble assemblage, said to her sisters Lionella and Chiaretta, 'If I had for my husband the king's majordomo, I flatter myself that I would quench the thirst of all the court with one glass of
wine.' 'And I,' said Lionella, 'flatter myself that, if the king's
private chamberlain were my husband, I would pledge myself to
make enough linen from a spindle of my yarn to provide shifts
of the strongest and finest make for all the court.' Then said Chiaretta, 'And I, if I had the king himself for my husband, I flatter
myself that I would give him three children at one birth, two sons
and a daughter. And each of these should have long hair braided
below the shoulders, and intermingled with threads of the finest gold,
and a golden necklace round the throat, and a star on the forehead
of each.'

Now it chanced that these sayings were overheard by one of the
courtiers, who hastened to the king and told him of the young girls'
discourse, and the king, when he heard the tenour thereof, at once
commanded that they should be brought before him, and this done,
he examined them one by one as to what they had said in the
garden. Whereupon each one, with the most respectful words, told
the king what she had spoken, and he was much pleased thereat.
So then and there he wedded Brunora to the majordomo and Lionella to the chamberlain, while he himself took Chiaretta to wife.
There was no hunting that day, for the whole company returned to
the city, where the marriages were celebrated with the greatest pomp.
But the mother of Ancilotto was greatly wroth at his marriage, for
however fair Chiaretta might be in face and figure, and graceful in
her person, and sweet and modest in her conversation, the queen-
mother held it to be a slight to the royal dignity that her daughter-
in-law should be of vile and common descent, nor could she endure
it that the majordomo and the chamberlain should be brothers-
in-law of the king her son. These things kindled so hotly the
rage of the queen-mother against Chiaretta that she could scarce

endure her presence; nevertheless she hid her wrath so as not to offend her son. In due time (by the good pleasure of Him who rules over all), Chiaretta became with child, to the great joy of the king, whose fancy at once busied itself with the prospect of the lovely progeny he had been promised.

Just at the time when Chiaretta was expecting to be brought to bed, Ancilotto was forced to make a journey to a distant country and to abide there some days, and he directed that, during his absence, his mother should see to the welfare of the queen and of the children who, he hoped, would soon be born. The queen-mother, though she hated her daughter-in-law, let not the king see this, and assured him that she would take the greatest care of them all, while he might be away, and before the king had been gone many days (as Chiaretta when she was a virgin had pledged) three lovely children, two boys and a girl, were born. Likewise their hair was braided below their shoulders, and they bore golden chains on their necks and golden stars on their foreheads. The queen-mother, whose hatred against Chiaretta burned as malignantly as ever, no sooner cast her eyes upon the innocent children than she determined to have them put away privily, so that no one might know they had even been, and that Chiaretta might be disgraced in the sight of the king. And besides this, Brunora and Lionella had grown to regard their sister with violent hate and jealousy since she had become their sovereign, and lost no chance to aggravate, by all sorts of cunning wiles, the spite of the queen-mother against Chiaretta.

On the very same day that the queen was delivered, it chanced that there were born in the stable-yard three black mongrel pups, two dogs and a bitch, which, by some strange freak, had white stars on their foreheads and bore round their necks traces of a gorget. This coming to the knowledge of the two sisters, they took the pups away from the dam and brought them to the queen-mother, and with humble salutations said to her : ' We know, madam, that your highness has little love for our sister, and quite justly ; for she is of humble stock, and it is not seemly that your son and our king should have mated with such an one. Hence, knowing the mind you have towards her, we have brought you here three mongrel pups, which, as you will see, were born with a star on their foreheads, and you can deal with them as you list.' At these words the queen-mother was much pleased, divining well their evil intent, and she contrived to bring to her daughter-in-law, who as yet had not seen the children she had borne, the three whelps, telling her at the same time they were her own offspring. And for the better hiding of this trick the wicked old woman bade the midwife to tell the same story to the queen. So when she herself and the two sisters and the midwife returned to the chamber, they presented to the queen the three mongrel whelps, saying, 'See, O queen, the fruit of your womb! Cherish it well, so that the king, when he comes back, may rejoice in the fair gift you have made him.' And with these words the midwife put the mongrels by her side, consoling her and telling her that such mischances as hers happened now and then to persons of high estate.

These wicked women having carried out this barbarous work, it only remained for them to contrive a cruel death for the three lovely children of the queen. But God mercifully held them back from soiling their hands with the blood of their kin. They made a box, which they waxed within, and, having put the children therein, they closed it and cast it into the river to be borne away by the stream. But God in His justice would not allow these innocents to suffer. As the box floated along it was espied by a certain miller named Marmiato, who haled it out and opened it, and found within three smiling children. Seeing how fair and graceful they were, he deemed them to be the children of some noble lady who, to hide her shame, had committed this crime. Having taken home the box he said to his wife, who was called Gordiana, 'See here, wife, what I have found in the river; it is a present for you.' Gordiana received the children joyfully, and brought them up as if they had been her own, giving to one the name of Acquirino, to another Fluvio—as they had been found in the river—and to the girl that of Serena.

Ancilotto, when he came back from his journey, was in high spirits, for he fully expected to find on his return that Chiaretta had fulfilled her pledge and given him the three fair children as she had promised; but the issue was not what he hoped, for the cunning queen-mother, when she saw her son drawing near, went to meet him, and told him that the wife he prized so highly had given him, instead of three children, three mongrel dogs. And having brought him into the chamber of the unfortunate Chiaretta, she showed him

the pups which were lying beside her.   The queen began to weep
bitterly and to deny that the dogs were her offspring, but her wicked
sisters came and declared that everything the old mother had said was
the truth.   The king when he heard this was greatly disturbed, and
fell to the ground grief-stricken.   After he had come to himself he
could scarce believe such thing could be; but at last he gave ear to
his mother's false tale.   But Chiaretta's dignity and sweetness, and
the patience with which she bore the insults of the courtiers, won
him over to spare her life, and to sentence her to be kept in a cell
under the place where the cooking pots and pans were washed, and
to be fed on the garbage which was swept off the dirty sink.

While the unhappy queen passed her life in this filthy wise, feeding upon carrion, Gordiana, the wife of the miller Marmiato, gave
birth to a son who was christened Borghino and brought up with the
three foundlings.   When Gordiana went to cut the hair of these there
often fell out of it many precious stones and great white pearls ; so with
these riches Marmiato was able to give over the humble calling of a
miller, and to live with his wife and the four children a life of ease and
delicacy.   But when the three foundlings had come to years of discretion they learned by chance that they were not the children of
Marmiato and Gordiana, but had been found floating in a box on
the river.   As soon as they knew this they became very unhappy,
and resolved to go their way and try their fortune elsewhere, much
to the chagrin of their foster-parents, who saw they would no longer
enjoy the rich harvest of jewels which was wont to fall from the
children's locks and starry foreheads.   The brothers and their sister
having left Marmiato the miller and Gordiana, they all wandered
about for some days, and at last came by chance to Provino, the
city of Ancilotto their father, where they hired a house and lived
together, maintaining themselves by selling the jewels which still fell
out of their hair. One day the king, who was riding into the country
with some of his courtiers, chanced to pass the house where the three
were living, and they, as soon as they heard the king was coming,
ran down the steps and stood bareheaded to give him a respectful
salutation. They had never seen Ancilotto, so his face was unknown
to them. The king, whose eyes were as keen as a hawk's, looked at
them steadily, and remarked that on their foreheads there was something like a golden star, and immediately his heart was filled with
strong passion, and he felt that they might prove to be his children.

He stopped and said to them : ' Who are you, and from whence do
you come ? ' And they answered humbly, ' We are poor strangers
who have come to dwell in this your city.' Then said Ancilotto,
' I am greatly pleased ; and what are you called ? ' Whereupon they
replied that one was named Acquirino, and the other Fluvio, and
the sister, Serena. The king then bade them to dinner with him
next day ; and the young people, though they were almost overcome
by his gracious invitation, did not venture to decline it. When
Ancilotto returned to the palace he said to his mother : ' Madam,
when I was abroad to-day I came by chance upon two handsome
youths and a lovely maiden, who, as they had golden stars on their
foreheads, must be I think the children promised to me by Queen
Chiaretta.'

The wicked old woman smiled at the king's words, making believe
they were but fancy, but within she felt as if a dagger had smitten
her heart. Then she bade them summon the midwife who had been
present at the birth, and said to her in private, ' Good gossip, do you
not know that the king's children, so far from being dead as we
hoped, are alive, and are grown up as beautiful as the day ? ' ' How
can this be ? ' replied the woman ; ' were they not drowned in the river ?
Who has told you this ? ' The queen-mother answered : ' From what
I gather from the words of the king I am almost sure they are alive.
We must be up and doing at once, for we are in great danger.' ' Do
not be alarmed, madam,' said the midwife, ' I have in mind a
plan by which we can now assuredly compass the destruction of all
the three.'

The midwife went out, and immediately found her way to the
house of the king's children, and, finding Serena alone, she saluted
her and talked of many things. After she had held a long discourse
with her, she said, ' My daughter, I am curious to know if you have
in your house any water which can dance.' Serena, somewhat surprised at this question, answered that she had not any. ' Ah, my
daughter,' said the gossip, ' what delights you would enjoy if you
had some of it ! and if you could bathe your face in it you would
become more beautiful even than you are now.' Said the girl, with
her curiosity aroused, ' And how can I get it ? ' ' Have you not
brothers ? ' the gossip asked. ' Send them to fetch it ; they will easily
find it, for it is to be had not far from these parts.' And with these
words she departed. After a little Acquirino and Fluvio came back,

and at once Serena began to beseech them that they would do their best, for the love they bore her, to get for her some of the wonderful dancing water ; but they laughed at her request as a silly fancy, and refused to go on a fool's errand, seeing that no one could say where it was to be found. However, persuaded at last by the petition of their sister, whom they loved very dearly, they departed together to do her bidding, taking with them a phial to hold the precious water. When they had gone several miles they came to a fountain out of which a snow-white dove was drinking, and they were amazed when the bird spoke to them these words: 'What seek ye, young men?' To this Fluvio answered, 'We seek the precious dancing water.' 'Wretched youths,' said the dove, 'who sends you on such a quest as this?' 'We want it for our sister,' said Fluvio. 'Then you will surely meet your deaths,' said the dove, 'for the water you are in search of is guarded by many fierce beasts and poisonous dragons, who will certainly devour you; but if you must needs have some of it, leave the task to me, for I will surely bring it back to you;' and having taken the phial the dove flew away out of sight.

Acquirino and Fluvio awaited her return with the greatest anxiety, and at last she came in sight, bearing the phial filled with the magic water. They took it from her, and, having thanked her for the great service she had rendered them, returned to their sister and gave her the water, exhorting her never to impose such another task upon them, because they had nearly met their deaths in attempting it. A short time after this the king again met the two brothers and said to them: 'Why did you not come to dine with me after accepting my invitation?' 'Gracious majesty,' they answered with profound respect, 'a pressing errand called us away from home.' Then said the king, 'To-morrow I shall expect to see you without fail.' The youths having made their apology, the king returned to the palace, where he met his mother and told her he had once more seen the youths with the stars on their foreheads. Again the queen-mother was greatly perplexed, and again she bade them summon the midwife, to whom she secretly told all she had heard, and at the same time begged her to find a way out of the danger. The gossip bade her take courage, for she would so plan this time that they would be seen no more. The midwife went again to seek Serena, whom she found alone, and asked her whether she had got any of the dancing water. 'I have it,' the girl replied, 'but the winning of it nearly

caused the death of my brothers.'   'The water is fair enough,' said
the woman, ' but you ought to have likewise the singing apple.   You
never saw fruit so fair to look upon, or listened to music so sweet as
that which it discourses.'   'But how shall I get it?' said Serena; 'for
my brothers will never go in search of it, seeing that in their last
venture they were more in peril of death than in hope of life.'   'But
they won the dancing water for you,' said the woman, 'and they are
still alive; they will get for you the singing apple just as harmlessly;'
and, having spoken, she went her way.

Scarcely had the midwife gone when Acquirino and Fluvio came
in, and again Serena cried out to them : 'Oh, my brothers! I hear
now of another wonder, more beautiful far than the dancing water.
It is the singing apple, and if I cannot have it I shall die of
vexation.'   When Acquirino and Fluvio heard these words they chid
her sharply, affirming that for her sake they were reluctant to brave
again the risk of death.   But she did not cease her prayers, and she
wept and sobbed so sorely that the brothers, seeing that this new
desire of hers came from her inmost soul, again gave way and agreed
to satisfy it at whatever risk.   They mounted and rode on till they
came to an inn, and demanded of the host whether he could let them
know where was to be found the apple which sang so sweetly.   He
told them he knew thereof, and warned them of the perils which lay
in the path of anyone bold enough to seek to pluck it.   'It grows,'
he said, ' in the midst of a fair garden, and is watched day and night
by a poisonous beast which kills without fail all those who come nigh
to the tree.'   'What then would you counsel us to do?' said the
youths; 'for we are set upon plucking the apple at all cost.'   'If you
will carry out my behests,' said the host, 'you may pluck the apple
without fear of the poisonous beast or of death.   You must take this
robe, which, as you see, is all covered with mirrors, and one of you
must put it on, and thus attired enter the garden, the door of which
will be found unfastened ; but the other must bide without and
be careful not to let himself be seen.   And the beast forthwith will
make for the one who enters, and, seeing an exact similitude of himself reflected by the mirrors, will fall down to the ground, and then
the adventurer may go quickly up to the tree and pluck tenderly the
singing apple and without once looking behind him quit the garden.'
The young men thanked their host courteously, and observed all his
directions so faithfully that they won the apple without mischance, and

carried it back to Serena, and again besought her no more to compel
them to run into such danger.   Thus for a second time they failed
to keep their engagement with the king, who, meeting them again a
few days afterwards, said: 'For what reason have you once more
disobeyed my commands and failed to come and dine with me?'
Fluvio answered as before that some weighty matters of business
had intervened and kept them from doing themselves the great
honour the king had proposed for them.   Then said the king, 'You
must come to-morrow, and see that you fail not.'   Acquirino promised
obedience, and the king returned to his palace, where he met his
mother and told her he had again seen the two youths, that he was
more firmly persuaded than ever that they must be the children
promised him by Chiaretta, and that he would feel no rest till they
should have eaten at his table.   The queen-mother when she heard
that they yet lived was in sore terror, doubting not that her fraud
had been discovered, and thus, struck with grief and terror, she sent for
the midwife and said to her: 'I surely thought the children were
dead by this time, and that we should hear no more of them; but
they are alive, and we stand in peril of death.   Look therefore to
our affair; otherwise we shall be lost.'   'Noble lady,' said the midwife,
'take heart.   This time I will work their bane without fail, and you
will bless me therefor, seeing that they will trouble you no longer;'
and the woman, full of rage at her failure, again repaired to the
house of Serena, where she found the girl alone.   With crafty speech
she inquired of Serena whether she had indeed got the singing apple,
and the girl made answer that she had.   Then said the cunning
woman: 'Ah, my daughter, you must think that you have nothing
at all if you do not get one thing more, the most beautiful, the most
graceful thing in the world.'   'Good mother, what may this fair
thing be?' said the girl.   The old woman replied: 'It is the beautiful green bird, my child, which talks night and day, and speaks
words of marvellous wisdom.   If you had it in your keeping you
might indeed call youself happy;' and, having thus spoken, she went
her way.

Acquirino and Fluvio came in almost directly after she was gone,
and Serena forthwith began to beg them to do her one last favour,
whereupon they asked her what might be this boon which she desired.   She answered that she wanted the beautiful green bird.
Fluvio, who had plucked the apple guarded by the venomous beast,

was still haunted by the peril of his adventure, and refused to go in quest of the bird. Acquirino, though for a long time he too turned a deaf ear, was finally moved by the brotherly love he felt and by the hot tears of grief which Serena shed, and determined to satisfy her wish. Fluvio also agreed to accompany him, and, having mounted their horses, they rode for several days, until at last they came into a flowery green meadow, in the midst of which stood a lofty tree surrounded with marble statues which mocked life by their marvellous workmanship. Through the meadow there ran a little stream, and up in the tall tree lived the beautiful green bird, which hopped about from bough to bough in lively fashion, uttering the while words which seemed rather divine than human. The young men dismounted from their palfreys, which they left to graze at will, and went close to the marble statues to examine them; but, as soon as they touched these, they themselves were turned into marble as they stood.

Now Serena, when for several months she had anxiously looked for the return of her dear brothers Acquirino and Fluvio, began to despair and to fear she would never see them more, and, over-come with grief at their unhappy fate, she resolved to try her own fortune. So she mounted a mettlesome horse, and rode on and on till she came to the fair meadow where the green bird was hopping about on the tall tree and softly talking. There the first things she saw were her brothers' horses, which were grazing on the turf, and, casting her eyes upon the statues, she saw that two of them must be Acquirino and Fluvio, for the unhappy youths, though turned into marble, retained their features exactly as in life. Serena dismounted, and going softly up to the tree she laid hands on the green bird from behind, and he, finding himself a prisoner, besought her to let him go, and promised that at the right time and place he would remember her. But Serena answered that first of all he must restore her brothers to their former state, upon which the bird replied: 'Look then under my left wing, and there you will find a feather much greener than any of the others and marked with yellow. Pluck it out and touch with it the eyes of the statues, and then your brothers will return to flesh and blood.' Serena raised the wing and found the feather, and did as the bird had directed, and the statues of Acquirino and Fluvio at once became living men and embraced their sister joyfully.

This wonder being accomplished, the bird again besought Serena to give him his liberty, promising that if she would grant his prayer

he would come to her aid whenever she might call upon him; but
Serena was not to be thus cajoled, and declared that before she would
let him go free he must help them to find their father and mother, and
that until he had accomplished this task he must be her prisoner.

There had already arisen some dispute amongst the three as to
who should have the bird in keeping, but in the end they settled that
it should be left in charge of Serena, who tended it with great care
and watched over it. The affair having come to this happy issue, they
mounted their horses and rode home. Meantime Ancilotto had often
passed by their house, and finding it empty was much astonished, and
inquired of the neighbours what had become of them; but all he
could learn was that nothing had been seen of them for many days.
They had not been back long before the king again rode by, and,
catching sight of them, asked how it was that nothing had been seen
of them for so long, and why they had disregarded his commands so
often. Acquirino answered with deep respect that some amazing
troubles and adventures had befallen them, and that if they had not
presented themselves at the palace before his majesty as he had desired
it was through no want of reverence. They were all anxious to amend
their conduct in the future.

The king, when he heard they had been in tribulation, was moved
to pity, and bade them all accompany him back to the palace to dinner;
but before they set forth Acquirino filled secretly a phial with the
dancing water, Fluvio took the singing apple, and Serena the talking
bird, and they rode back with the king and joyously entered the palace
with him and sat down at the royal table. It chanced that the queen-
mother and also the two sisters of Chiaretta marked them as they
passed, and observing the beauty of the maiden and the handsome
bright-eyed youths, they were filled with dread and suspicion as to
who they might be. When the royal banquet had come to an end,
Acquirino said to the king : ' May it please your majesty that, before
we take our leave, we should show your majesty some marvels which
may delight you;' and with these words he poured into a silver tazza
some of the dancing water, while Fluvio put his hand into his bosom
and drew therefrom the singing apple, which he placed beside the
water. Serena also brought out the talking bird, and set it on the
table. Immediately the apple began to sing most sweetly, and the
wonderful water to dance, so that the king and all the courtiers were
delighted and laughed aloud with pleasure; but the queen-mother and

the wicked sisters were smitten with dire dismay, for they felt that their doom was near.

At last, when the apple and the water had ceased to sing and dance, the bird opened its mouth and said : ' O sacred majesty ! what doom should be dealt to those who once plotted death against two brothers and a sister ? ' Then the cunning queen-mother, scheming to excuse herself, cried out : ' No lighter doom than death by burning ; ' and in this condemnation all those who were present agreed.   To answer her the singing apple and the dancing water said straightway : ' Ah, false and cruel woman ! your own tongue has doomed yourself, and those wicked and envious sisters of the queen, and the vile midwife, to this horrible death.'

When the king heard these words his heart grew cold with terror ; but before he could speak the talking bird began and said : ' O sacred majesty ! these are the three children you longed for, your children who bear the star on their foreheads ; and their innocent mother, is she not to this day kept a prisoner under the filthy scullery ? ' Then the king saw clearly how he had been tricked, and gave order that the unhappy Chiaretta should be taken out of her noisome prison and robed once more in her royal garments, and, as soon as this had been done, she was brought into the presence of the king and of his court. And though she had for so long time suffered such cruel usage, she retained all her former loveliness.   Then the talking bird related the strange history from beginning to end, and the king, when he knew it all, embraced tenderly Chiaretta and their three children ; but the dancing water and the singing apple and the talking bird, having been set at liberty, disappeared straightway.

The next day the king commanded to be lighted in the centre of the market a huge fire, into which he caused to be thrown, without pity, his mother and the two sisters of Chiaretta and the midwife, so that in the presence of everybody they might be burnt to death.   And Ancilotto lived happily many years with his beloved wife and his beautiful children, and, having chosen for Serena an honourable husband, he left his two sons the heirs of his kingdom.

Lodovica's story gave great delight to all the ladies, and the Signora, having commanded her to supplement it in due order, she propounded the following enigma :

When Sol pours down his fiercest heat,
High on Gheraldo's lofty seat,

A wight I marked, with roguish eye,
Shut fast within a closure high.
All through the day he prates and talks,
And clad in robes of emerald walks.
I've told you all except his name,
And that from your own wit I claim.

Many were the interpretations put upon this enigma, but no one came near to the mark save the charming Isabella, who, greatly pleased with herself, said in a merry tone : " There is no other possible signification of Lodovica's enigma except to name the parroquet, which lives within a cage, the closure, and has plumage green as emerald, and talks all day long." The clever solution of the riddle pleased everybody except Lodovica, who had flattered herself that no one would be clever enough to solve it, and who now became almost dumb with vexation. A little later, when the flush of anger had faded somewhat from her cheek, she turned to Isabella, whose turn it was to tell the fourth story, and said : " I am vexed, Isabella, not from envy of you, as the teller of the next story, but because I feel myself inferior to those other companions of yours who have had to give the solution of their riddles, the company not being able to solve them ; whereas mine was guessed at once. Be assured, however, that if I can give you a Roland for your Oliver, I will not be caught napping." [1] Isabella answered quickly, " You will do well, Signora Lodovica, but—" Here the Signora, who saw that the contention was like to grow warm between the two, commanded Isabella to go on at once with her story, which, with a smile, she began to tell as follows.

[1] Orig., *che se io potrò rendervi il contra cambio non starò a dormire.*

THE FOURTH FABLE.

Nerino, the son of Gallese, King of Portugal, becoming enamoured of Genobbia, wife of Messer Raimondo Brunello, a physician, has his will of her and carries her with him to Portugal, while Messer Raimondo dies of grief.

I MUST tell you, charming ladies, that there are very many men who, because they have consumed a great part of their time over the study of letters, are persuaded that they are mighty wise, whereas in truth they know little or nothing. And while men of this sort think they are marking their foreheads with lines of wisdom, they too often only scoop out their own eyes,[1] which thing happened to a certain physician, greatly skilled in his calling, for he, while he deemed he was about to put a cheat upon another, was himself most ignominiously duped, to his own great injury, all of which you will learn from the fable which I will presently tell you.

Gallese, King of Portugal, had a son whose name was Nerino, and in the bringing up of this boy he followed such a course that up to the time when he reached his eighteenth year Nerino had never once cast eyes upon a woman except his mother and the nurse who had the care of him. Wherefore when he had come to full age the king determined to send him to pursue his studies in the university of Padua, so that he might get a knowledge of Latin letters and of the tongue and manners of the Italians as well. And the plan which he had devised he duly carried out. When the young Nerino had come to Padua, he soon acquired the friendship of many of the scholars, and every day these would come to pay their respects to him, one of the above named being a certain Messer Raimondo Brunello, a physician. It chanced one day, as Nerino and this friend of his were conversing now about this thing and now about that, they engaged (as is the manner of sprightly youths) in a discourse anent the beauty of women, and on this subject the former took one view and the latter another. But Nerino, though he had never in

---

[1] Orig., *credonsi signare il fronte à se stessi cavano gli occhi.*

times past cast eyes upon any woman save his mother and his nurse, declared with some heat that in his reckoning there could not be found in all the world any lady who should be more beautiful, more graceful, and more exquisite than was his own mother. And when, by way of putting this speech of his to the test, they brought divers ladies to his notice, he still declared that in comparison to his mother they were little better than carrion.

Now Messer Raimondo had to wife a lady who was one of the fairest nature ever created, and when he listened to this chattering he settled his gorget and said: 'Signor Nerino, I happen to have seen a certain lady who is of such great loveliness that when you shall have beheld her I think it probable you will judge her to be not less but more beautiful than your mother.' To this speech Nerino made answer that he could not believe there could be any woman more lovely than his mother, but at the same time it would give him great pleasure to look upon this one. Whereupon Messer Raimondo said: 'Whenever it shall please you to behold her I will gladly point her out to you.' Nerino replied: 'I am much pleased at what you propose, and I shall ever be obliged to you.' Then Messer Raimondo said at once: 'Since it will give you pleasure to see her, take care to be present in the Church of the Duomo to-morrow morning, for there I promise you that you shall have sight of her.'

When he had returned to his house, Messer Raimondo said to his wife: 'To-morrow morning see that you rise betimes, and deck carefully your head, and make yourself seem as fair as you can, and put on the most sumptuous raiment you possess, for I have a mind that you should go to the Duomo at the hour of high mass to hear the office.' Genobbia (for this was the name of Messer Raimondo's wife), not being in the habit of going now hither now thither, but rather to pass all her time at home over her sewing and broidery work, was much astonished at these words; but, seeing that her husband's command fell in well with her own desire, she did all she was directed to do, and set herself so well in order and decked herself so featly that she looked more like a goddess than like a mortal woman. And when Genobbia, following the command which her husband had laid upon her, had entered into the holy fane, there came thither likewise Nerino, the son of the king, and when he had looked upon her he found that she was exceedingly fair. When the lady had gone her way, Messer Raimondo came upon the scene, and having gone up to Nerino spake thus : ' Now how does that lady who is just gone out of the church please you ? Does she seem to you to be one who ought to be compared with any other ? Say, is she not more beautiful than your mother ? ' ' Of a truth,' replied Nerino, ' she is fair, and nature could not possibly make aught that is fairer; but tell me of your courtesy of whom is she the wife, and where does she dwell ? ' But to this query Messer Raimondo did not answer so as to humour Nerino's wish, forasmuch as he had no mind to give him the clue he sought.   Then said Nerino, ' My good Messer Raimondo, though you may not be willing to tell me who she is and where she dwells, at least you might do me such good office as to let me see her once more.' ' This I will do willingly,' answered Messer Raimondo. ' To-morrow come here again into the church, and I will so bring it to pass that you shall see her as you have seen her to-day.'

When Messer Raimondo had gone back to his house, he said to his wife, ' Genobbia, see that you attire yourself to-morrow; for I wish that you should go to the mass in the Duomo, and if hitherto you have ever made yourself look beautiful or have arrayed yourself sumptuously, see that you do the same to-morrow.' When she heard this, Genobbia (as on the former occasion) was greatly astonished, but since the command of her husband pointed to this matter, she did everything even as he had ordered.   When the morrow came, Genobbia, sumptuously clothed and adorned more richly than was her wont, betook herself to the church, and in a very short time Nerino came likewise. He, when he saw how very fair she was, was inflamed by love of her more ardently than ever man had burned for woman before, and, when Messer Raimondo arrived, begged him to tell straightway what might be the name of this lady who seemed in his eyes to be so marvellously beautiful.   But Messer Raimondo, making excuse that he was greatly pressed for time to give to his own affairs, was in no humour to thus inform Nerino on the spot, and was rather disposed to leave the galliard to stew for a time in his own fat ; so he went his way in high spirits.   Whereupon Nerino, with his temper somewhat ruffled by the mean account in which Messer Raimondo seemed to hold him, spake thus to himself: ' Aha ! you are not willing that I should have an inkling as to who she is and where she lives, but I will know what I want to know in spite of you.'

After he had left the church, Nerino waited outside until such time as the fair dame should likewise issue forth, and then, having given her a modest obeisance with a smiling countenance, he went with her as far as her home. Now, as soon as Nerino had got to know clearly the house where she dwelt, he began to cast amorous eyes upon her, and never a day passed on which he would not pass up and down ten times in front of her window. Wherefore, having a great desire to hold converse with her, he set about considering what course he should follow in order to keep unsullied the honour of the lady, and at the same time to attain his own end. But, having pondered over the affair, and looked at it on every side without lighting upon any course which seemed to promise security, he at last, after a mighty amount of imagining, determined to make the acquaintance of an old woman who lived in a house opposite to that occupied by Genobbia. After having sent to her certain presents, and settled and confirmed the compact between them, he went secretly into the old woman's lodging, in which there was a certain window overlooking the hall of Genobbia's house, where he might stand and gaze at his good convenience at the lady as she went up and down about the house; at the same time, he had no wish to divulge himself, and thereby give her any pretext for withdrawing herself from his sight. Nerino, having spent one day after another in these amorous glances, at last found himself no longer able to resist the burning desire within him which consumed his very heart; so he made up his mind to write a letter and to throw it down into her lodging at a certain time when he should judge her husband to be away from home. And several times he wrote letters as he had planned and threw them down to her.

But Genobbia, without reading the billet she picked up, cast it into the fire, and it was burnt. After she had done this several times, on a certain day it came into her mind to break open one of the notes and see what might be written therein. When she had broken the seal and marked that the writer was no other than Nerino, the son of the King of Portugal, who declared thereby his fervent love of her, she was at first wellnigh confounded, but after a little, when she had called to mind the poor cheer she enjoyed in her husband's house, she plucked up heart and began to look kindly upon Nerino. At last, having come to an agreement with him, she found means to bring him into the house, when the youth laid before her the story of the ardent love he bore her, and of the torments he endured every day on her account, and in like manner the way by which his passion for her had been kindled. Wherefore the lady, who was alike lovely and kindly-hearted and complaisant, felt herself in no humour to reject his suit. And while the two thus foregathered, happy in the consciousness of mutual love and indulging in amorous discourse, lo and behold ! Messer Raimondo knocked suddenly at the door. When Genobbia heard this she bade Nerino go straightway and lie down on the bed, and to let down the curtains, and to remain there until such time as her husband should be once more gone out. The husband came in, and having taken divers trifles of which he had need, went away without giving heed to aught besides, and a little later Nerino followed him.

On the following day, when it happened that Nerino was walking up and down the piazza, Messer Raimondo by chance went that way, to whom Nerino make known by sign that he wanted to have a word with him. Wherefore, having approached him, he spake thus : ' Signor, have I not a good bit of news to tell you ?' ' And what may it be ?' replied Messer Raimondo. ' Do I not know,' said Nerino, ' the house where dwells that beautiful lady ? and have I not had some delightful intercourse with her ? But because her husband came home unexpectedly she hid me in the bed, and drew the curtains for fear that he should see me ; however, he soon went out again.' ' Is it possible ?' said Messer Raimondo. ' Possible !' answered Nerino, ' it is more than possible—it is a fact. Never in all my life have I seen so delightful, so sweet a lady as she. If by any chance, signor, you should meet her, I beg you to speak a good word on my behalf, and to entreat her to keep me in her good graces.' Messer Raimondo, having promised to do what the youth asked him, went his way with ill will in his heart. But before he left Nerino he said, ' And do you propose to go in search of your good fortune again ?' To this Nerino replied, ' Return ! what should one do in such case ? ' Then Messer Raimondo went back to his house, and was careful to let drop no word in his wife's presence, but to wait for the time when she and Nerino should again come together.

When the next day had come Nerino once more stole to a meeting with Genobbia, and while they were in the midst of their amorous delights and pleasant converse the husband came back to the house, but the lady quickly hid Nerino in a chest in front of which she heaped a lot of clothes from which she had been ripping the wadding to keep

them from destruction by insects. The husband, making believe to
search for certain things, turned the house upside down, and pried
even into the bed, but, finding nothing of the sort he looked for, went
about his business with his mind more at ease.

Very soon Nerino also departed, and afterwards, chancing to meet
Messer Raimondo, he thus addressed him: ' Signor doctor, what would
you say if you heard I had paid another visit to my charming lady, and
that envious fortune broke in upon our pleasure, seeing that the husband
again arrived and spoilt all our sport ? ' ' And what did you then ? '
said Messer Raimondo. ' She straightway opened a chest,' said Nerino,
' and put me therein, and in front of the chest she piled up a heap of
clothes which she was working at in order to preserve them from moth,
and after he had turned the bed upside down more than once without
finding aught, he went away.' What tortures Messer Raimondo
must have suffered when he listened to these words I leave to the
judgment of any who may know the humours of love.

Now Nerino had given to Genobbia a very fine and precious
diamond, within the golden setting of which was engraved his name
and his likeness. The very next day, when Messer Raimondo had gone
to see to his affairs, the lady once more let Nerino into the house, and
while they were taking their pleasure and talking pleasantly together,
behold ! the husband again came back to the house. But the crafty
Genobbia, as soon as she remarked his coming, immediately opened a
large wardrobe which stood in her chamber, and hid Nerino therein.
Almost immediately Messer Raimondo entered the chamber, pretending as before that he was in search of certain things he wanted, and
in quest thereof he turned the room upside down. But, finding
nothing either in the bed or in the chest, like a man out of his wits
he took fire and strewed it in the four corners of the chamber, with
the intention of burning the place and all that it contained.

Now the party walls and the wooden framing of the apartment
soon caught fire, whereupon Genobbia, turning to her husband, said:
' What is this you are doing, husband ? Surely you must be gone
mad.   Still, if you wish to burn up the room, burn it as you will, but
by my faith I will not have you burn this wardrobe, wherein are all
the papers relating to my dowry.' So, having summoned four strong
porters, she bade them carry the wardrobe out of the house and bear
it into the neighbouring house which belonged to the old woman.
Then she opened the wardrobe secretly when no one was by and

returned to her own house.   Messer Raimondo, now like one out of
his mind, still kept a sharp watch to see whether anybody who ought
not to have been there might be driven out of hiding by the con-
flagration, but he met with nothing save the smoke, which was becoming insufferable, and the fierce flames which were consuming the
house.   And by this time all the neighbours had gathered together
to put out the fire, and so well and heartily did they work that in
time it was extinguished.

On the following day, as Nerino was sallying forth towards the
fields in the valley, he met Messer Raimondo, and after giving him a
salute, said to him : ' Aha, my gentleman ! I have got a piece of news
to tell you which ought to please you mightily.'   ' And what may
this news be ? ' said Messer Raimondo.   ' I have just made my escape,'
said Nerino, ' from the most frightful peril that ever man came out of
without loss of his life.   I had gone to the house of my lovely mistress,
and while I was spending the time with her in all manner of delightful dallying her husband once more broke in upon our content, and
after he had turned the house upside down, lighted some fire, and this
he scattered about in the four corners of the room and burnt up all
the chattels there were about.'   ' And you,' said Messer Raimondo,
' where were you the while ? '   Then answered Nerino, ' I was hidden
in a wardrobe which she caused to be taken out of the house.'   And
when Messer Raimondo heard this, and clearly understood all which
Nerino told him to be the truth, he was like to die of grief and passion.
Nevertheless, he did not dare to let his secret be known, because he
was determined still to catch him in the act.   Wherefore he said to him,
' And are you bent upon going thither again, Signor Nerino ? ' to which
Nerino made answer, ' Seeing that I have come safely out of the fire,
what else is there for me to fear ? '   And, letting pass any further
remarks of this sort, Messer Raimondo begged Nerino that he would
do him the honour of dining with him on the morrow ; which civility
the young man willingly accepted.

When the next day had come, Messer Raimondo bade assemble
at his house all his own relations and his wife's as well, and prepared
for their entertainment a rich and magnificent repast—not in the
house which had been half consumed by fire, but in another.   He gave
directions to his wife, moreover, that she also should be present, not
to sit at table as a guest, but to keep herself out of sight, and see to
the ordering of aught which might be required for the banquet.   As

soon as all the kinsfolk had assembled, and the young Nerino as well, they were bidden take their places at the board, and as the feast went on Messer Raimondo tried his best with his charlatan science to make Nerino drunk, in order to be able to work his will upon him.   Having several times handed to the youth a glass of malvoisie wine, which he never failed to empty, Messer Raimondo said to him : ' Now, Signor Nerino, cannot you tell to these kinsfolk of mine some little jest which may make them laugh ? '   The luckless Nerino, who had no inkling that Genobbia was Messer Raimondo's wife, began to tell the story of his adventures, keeping back, however, the names of all concerned.

It chanced at this moment that one of the servants went into the room apart where Genobbia was, and said to her : ' Madonna, if only you were now hidden in some corner of the feasting-room, you would hear told the finest story you ever heard in your life.   I pray you go in quick.'   And, having stolen into a corner, she knew that the voice of the story-teller belonged to Nerino her lover, and that the tale he was giving to the company concerned himself and her as well.   Whereupon this prudent and sharp-witted dame took the diamond which Nerino had given her, and, having placed it in a cup filled with a very dainty drink, she said to a servant, ' Take this cup and give it to Signor Nerino, and tell him to drink it off forthwith, that he may tell his story the better.'   The servant took the cup and placed it on the table, whereupon Nerino gave sign that he wished to drink therefrom ; so the servant said to him, ' Take this cup, signor, so that you may tell your story the better.'

Nerino took the cup and forthwith drank all the wine therein, when, seeing and recognizing the diamond which lay at the bottom, he let it pass into his mouth.   Then making pretence of rinsing his teeth, he drew forth the ring and put it on his finger.   As soon as he was well assured that the fair lady about whom he was telling his story was the wife of Messer Raimondo, he had no mind to say more, and when Messer Raimondo and his kinsfolk began to urge him to bring the tale which he had begun to an end, he replied, ' And then and there the cock crowed and the day broke, so I awoke from my sleep and heard nothing more.'   Messer Raimondo's kinsmen, having listened to Nerino's story, and up to this time believed all he had said about the lady to be the truth, now imagined that both their host and the young man were drunk.

After several days had passed it happened that Nerino met Messer Raimondo, and feigning not to know that he was the husband of Genobbia, told him that within the space of two days he would take his departure, because his father had written to him to bid him without fail to return to his own country. Whereupon Messer Raimondo wished him good speed for his journey. Nerino, having come to a private understanding with Genobbia, carried her off with him and fled to Portugal, where they long lived a gay life together; but Messer Raimondo, when he went back to his house and found that his wife was gone, was stricken with despair, and died in the course of a few days.

Isabella's fable pleased the ladies and gentlemen equally well, and they rejoiced especially that Messer Raimondo himself proved to be the cause of his own misfortune, and that the thing which he had courted had really fallen upon him. And when the Signora marked that this discourse was come to an end, she gave the sign to Isabella to finish her task in due order, and she, in no wise neglectful of the Signora's command, gave the enigma which follows :

> In the middle of the night,
> Rises one with beard bedight.
> Though no astrologer he be,
> He marks the hours which pass and flee.
> He wears a crown, although no king;
> No priest, yet he the hour doth sing.
> Though spurred at heel he is no knight;
> No wife he calls his own by right,
> Yet children many round him dwell.
> Sharp wits you need this thing to tell.

Here the cleverly-devised enigma of Isabella came to an end, and although the various listeners went casting about in various directions, no one hit upon the exact truth except the somewhat haughty Lodovica, who, mindful of the slight which had of late been put upon her, rose to her feet and spake thus : " The enigma which our sister has set us to guess means nothing else than the cock, which is on the alert to crow while it is yet night; which wears a beard and has knowledge of the passage of time, although he is no astrologer. He bears a crest instead of a crown, and is no king; he sings the hours, yet is no priest. Besides this, he wears spurs on his heels; he has no wife, and brings up the children of others, that is to say, the young chickens."

All the listeners commended this solution of Isabella's skilful enigma, especially Capello, who said : ' Signora Isabella, Lodovica has given you back bread for your bannock,[1] seeing that a short time ago you very cleverly declared the meaning of her enigma and now she has mastered yours ; but for this reason you must not harbour malice one against another." Then Lodovica answered promptly, " Signor Bernardo, when the night time is come, I will pay you back yea for yea."[2]

But in order to keep the discourse within limits, the Signora imposed silence upon all, and, turning her face towards Lionora, whose turn it was to tell the last story of the night, directed her to begin, with due courtesy, her fable, and the damsel, with the best grace in the world, thus began.

THE FIFTH FABLE.

Flamminio Veraldo sets out from Ostia in search of Death, and, not finding it, meets Life instead ; this latter lets him see Fear and make trial of Death.

MANY are the men who with all care and diligence go searching narrowly for certain things, which, when they have gained them, they find of no value, and would gladly forego, fleeing therefrom with all speed, just as the devil flies from holy water. This was the case of Flamminio, who, when he went seeking Death, found Life, who made him see Fear and make trial of Death. All of which you will find clearly set forth in this fable.

In Ostia, an ancient city situated no great distance from Rome, there lived in former days, according to the common report, a young man of a nature rather weak and errant than stable and prudent, whose name was Flamminio Veraldo. He had heard it said over and over again that there was in all the world nothing more terrible and frightful than Death, the dark and inevitable one, seeing that he shows pity to none, having respect to no man, however poor or rich

---

[1] Orig., *pane per schiacciata.*   [2] Orig., *le renderò gnanf per gnaf.*

he may be. Wherefore, being filled with wonder at what he had heard, he determined by himself to find and to see with his own eyes what manner of thing this might be which men called Death. And having attired himself in coarse garments, and taken in hand a staff of strong cornel-wood well shod with iron, he set forth from Ostia. Flamminio, when he had travelled over many miles of road, came one day into a certain street, in the midst of which he espied, sitting in his stall, a cobbler making shoes and gaiters, and this cobbler, although there was lying about a great quantity of his finished work, kept on steadily at his task of making yet more.

Flamminio, going up to the cobbler, said to him, 'God be with you, good master!' and to this the cobbler replied, 'You are right welcome here, my son.' Then said Flamminio, 'What is this task you labour at?' 'I labour indeed,' replied the cobbler, 'and toil hard that I may not languish in want.[1] Nevertheless, I am in want, and I weary myself over making shoes.' 'Why do you thus,' said Flamminio, 'seeing that you have so many pairs made already? What is the good of making more?' 'I make them,' said the cobbler, 'to wear myself, to sell for my own sustenance and for the sustenance of my little household, and in order that when I become an old man I may be able to live on the money I have made by my handicraft.' 'And what will you do next?' asked Flamminio. 'After this,' said the cobbler, 'I shall die.' 'You will die!' cried Flamminio in reply. 'Yes,' said the cobbler. Then cried Flamminio, 'Oh, my good master! can you of your own knowledge tell me what may be this thing they call Death?' The cobbler answered, 'Of a truth I cannot.' 'What, have you never seen him?' said Flamminio. To this master cobbler made answer, 'I have never seen him, nor have I any wish to see him now, or to taste his quality. Moreover, all men say that he is the strangest and most terrible monster the world holds.' Then Flamminio said, 'At least you will be able of your knowledge to teach me and tell me where he abides, because day and night I wander over mountains and through valleys and swamps seeking him without ever hearing tidings as to where he may be found?' The cobbler answered, 'I know nothing as to where Death may dwell, nor where he is to be found, nor what he is made of; but if you go on with your journey somewhat farther, peradventure you will find him.'

[1] Orig., *stento per non stentare.*

E E

Whereupon Flamminio, having taken his leave, parted from the cobbler, and betook himself onwards to a spot where he came upon a dense and shadowy forest, and entered therein. In a certain place he saw a peasant, who, though he had already cut a vast pile of wood for burning, went on cutting more with all his might. And when they had exchanged greetings one with another, Flamminio said to him, 'My brother, what are you going to do with so vast a heap of wood as this?' And to this the peasant made answer, 'I am preparing it to kindle fire therewith in the winter that is coming, when we shall have snow and ice and villainous mist, so that I may be able to keep warm myself and my children, and to sell whatsoever may be to spare, and to buy with the profit thereof bread and wine and clothing, and all other things which may be necessary for our daily sustenance, and thus to pass our lives until Death comes to fetch us.' 'Now, by your courtesy,' said Flamminio, 'could you tell me where this same Death is to be found?' 'Of a surety I cannot,' the peasant replied, 'seeing that I have never once seen him, nor do I know where he abides. I am here in this wood all the day long taking heed to my own affairs. Very few wayfarers come into these parts, and I know none of those who pass by.' 'What then shall I do to find him?' demanded Flamminio; and to this the peasant made answer, 'As to myself, I know not at all what to say to you nor how to direct you. I can only bid you to travel yet farther onward, and then peradventure you may meet with him.'

Having taken leave of the peasant, Flamminio departed and walked and walked until he came to a certain place where dwelt a tailor, who had a vast store of clothes upon the pegs, and a warehouse filled with all kinds of the finest garments. Said Flamminio to him, 'God be with you, my good master!' and the tailor replied, 'And the same good wish to you.' 'What are you going to do with all this store of fair and sumptuous raiment, and all the noble garments I see here? Do they all belong to you?' Then the master tailor made answer, 'Certain of them are my own, some belong to the merchants, some to the gentlefolk, and some to various people who have dealings with me.' 'But what use can they find for so many?' asked Flamminio. 'They wear them in the different seasons of the year,' the tailor answered, and showing them all to Flamminio, he went on, 'These they wear in the summer and these in the winter, and these others in the seasons which come between, clothing themselves sometimes in one fashion and sometimes in another.' 'And in the end what do they do?' asked Flamminio. The tailor answered, 'They go on in this course until the day of their death.' Flamminio hearing the tailor speak of Death said, 'Oh, my good master! could you tell me where I may find this Death you tell of?' The tailor, speaking as if he were inflamed with anger and perturbed in spirit, said: 'My son, you go about asking questions which are indeed strange. I surely cannot tell you nor direct you where he may abide, for I never let my thoughts turn to him, and it is an occasion of great offence to me when anyone begins to talk of him. Wherefore I bid you either to discourse of some other matter or to go your way, for all such talk as this displeases me vastly.' And Flamminio, having taken leave of the tailor, departed on his journey.

It came to pass that Flamminio, after he had traversed many lands, came at last to a desert and solitary place, where he found a hermit with his beard all matted with dirt, and his body worn away by the passage of the years and by fasting, letting his mind concern itself only in contemplation. Whereupon, thinking that assuredly he had at last found Death, Flamminio thus addressed him: 'Of a truth, I am very glad to meet with you, holy father.' 'The sight of you is welcome to me, my son,' the hermit replied. 'My good father,' said Flamminio, 'what do you here in this rough and uninhabitable spot, cut off from all pleasure and from all human society?' 'I pass my time,' answered the hermit, 'in prayers and in fastings and in contemplation.' Then Flamminio inquired, 'And for what reason do you follow this life?' 'Why, my son,' exclaimed the hermit, 'I do all this to serve God, to mortify this wretched flesh of mine, to do penance for all the offences I have wrought in the sight of the eternal and immortal God and of the true son of Mary, and in the end to get salvation for my sinful soul, so that when the hour of my death shall come I may render it up pure of all stain, and in the awful day of judgment, by the grace of my redeemer and by no merit of my own, may make myself worthy of that happy and glorious home where I may taste the joys of eternal life, to which blessedness God lead us!' Then said Flamminio, 'Oh, my dear father! spare a few words to tell me—if it be not an offence to you—what manner of thing is this Death, and after what fashion is it made?' The holy father answered, 'Oh, my son! trouble not yourself to gain knowledge of this thing you

seek; for Death is a very terrible and a fearful being, and is called
by wise men the final end of all our sufferings, a misery to the happy,
a happiness to the miserable, and the term and limit of all worldly
things. It severs friend from friend; it separates the father from the
son, and the son from the father, the mother from the daughter, and
the daughter from the mother. It cuts the marriage bond, and finally
disunites the soul and the body, so that the body, severed from the
soul, loses all its power and becomes so putrid and of so evil a savour
that all men flee therefrom and abandon it as a thing abominable.'
'And have you never set eyes on him, my father?' asked Flamminio.
'Of a certainty I have never seen him,' answered the hermit. 'But
can you tell me what I should do in order to see him?' asked Flamminio. 'Ah, my son!' said the hermit, 'if you are indeed so keenly
set on finding him, you have only to keep going further and further
on; because man, the longer the way he has journeyed through this
world, the nearer he is to Death.' The young man having thanked
the holy father, and received his benediction, went his way.

Then Flamminio, continuing his journey, traversed a great number of deep valleys and craggy mountains and inhospitable forests,
seeing by the way many sorts of fearsome beasts, and questioning
each one of these whether he was the thing called Death, and always
getting in return the answer 'No.' At last, after he had passed
through many lands and seen many strange things, he came to a
mountain of no little magnitude, and having climbed over this, he
began to descend into a gloomy and very deep valley, closed in on all
sides by profound caverns. Here he saw a strange and monstrous
wild beast, which made all the valley re-echo with its roaring. 'Who
are you?' said Flamminio. 'Ho! is it possible that you may be
Death?' To which the wild beast made answer, 'I am not Death;
but pursue your way, and soon you will find him.'

Flamminio, when he heard the answer he had so long desired to
hear, felt his heart grow lighter. The wretched youth, now worn
out by fatigue and half dead by reason of the long weariness and the
heavy toil he had undergone, was almost sunk in despair, when he
found himself on the borders of a wide and spacious plain. Having
climbed to the summit of a little hill of no great height, delightful,
and covered with flowers, he looked round about him, now here, now
there, and espied the lofty walls of a magnificent city not far
from the spot where he stood. Whereupon he began to walk more

rapidly with nimble steps, and when the shadows of evening were falling he came to one of the city gates, which was adorned with the finest white marble.   And when he had entered therein, with the leave of the keeper of the gate, the first person he met was a very old woman, full of years, with a face like that of a corpse, and a body so meagre and thin that, through her leanness, it would have been easy to count one by one every bone in her body.   Her forehead was thickly marked with wrinkles, her eyes were squinting, watery, and red, as if they had been dyed in purple, her cheeks all puckered, her lips turned inside out, her hands rough and callous; her head was palsied, and she trembled in every limb; she was bent almost double in her gait, and she was clad in rough and dusky clothes. Over and above this she bore by her left side a keen-edged sword, and carried in her right hand a weighty cudgel, at the end of which was wrought a point of iron made in the shape of a triangle, and upon this staff she would now and then lean as if to rest herself.   On her shoulders also she carried a large wallet, in which she kept a great store of phials and pots and bottles all filled with divers sorts of liquors and unguents and plasters fitted for the remedying of various human ailments and accidents.   As soon as Flamminio's eye fell upon this toothless ugly old harridan he was seized with the thought that peradventure she might prove to be that Death to find whom he was going wandering about the world; so having approached her he said, 'Ah, my good mother, may God keep and preserve you!'   In a husky voice the old woman made answer to him, 'And may God keep and preserve you, my son!'   'Tell me, my mother,' Flamminio went on, 'whether perchance you may be the thing men call Death?' The old woman replied, 'No, I am not.   On the other hand, I am Life; and know, moreover, that I happen to have with me here in this wallet which I carry behind my back certain liquors and unguents by the working of which I am able with ease to purify and to cure the mortal body of man of all the heavy diseases which afflict him, and in the short space of a single hour to relieve him in like manner from the torture of any pain he may feel.'   Then said Flamminio, 'Ah, my good mother! can you not let me know where Death is to be found?'   'And who may you be,' asked the old woman, 'who make this demand of me with so great persistence?'   Flamminio answered, 'I am a youth who has already spent many days and months and years wandering about in search of Death, and never yet have I been able to find in any land a man who could tell me aught concerning him. Wherefore, if you should happen to possess this knowledge, I beseech you of your courtesy to let me share it, because I am possessed by so keen a desire to look upon him and to know what he is like, in order that I may be certain whether he really is the hideous and the dreadful thing which all men hold him to be.'

The old woman, when she heard the foolish request of the young man, spake thus to him: 'My son, when would it please you that I let you see Death, and judge how hideous he is, and when would you make trial of his terrors?' To this Flamminio replied: 'Ah, my mother! keep me no longer in suspense I beg you, but let me see him now, at this present moment.' Thereupon the old woman, to satisfy his desire, made him strip himself quite naked, and, while he was taking off his garments, she worked up together certain of her drugs useful in the cure of divers diseases, and when the thing was ready, she said to him: 'Bend yourself down here, my son.' And he, in obedience to her direction, bent down. 'Now bow your head and close your eyes;' and Flamminio did as she bade him. Scarcely had the old woman finished her speech than she took the sharp blade which she wore by her side and with one blow struck off his head from his shoulders. Then she quickly took up the head, and, having replaced it upon the bust, she smeared it well with the plaster which she had prepared, and thereby the wound was quickly healed. But how the thing which now happened was caused I cannot say, whether it arose through the over-quickness of the old hag in putting back the head upon the shoulders, or whether she herself brought it to pass through her own craft. The head when it was joined once more to the body was put on hind part forward. Wherefore Flamminio, when he looked down upon his shoulders, his loins, and his big buttocks standing out (all of which things he had never seen hitherto), fell into such a fit of terror and dismay that, not being able to think of any place where he might be suffered to hide himself, he cried out to the old woman in a trembling dolorous voice: 'Alas, alas, my good mother! bring me back once more to my old shape; bring me back, for the love of God, for by my faith I have never seen anything more frightful and more hideous than what I now behold. Alas! deliver me from this miserable state in which I now find myself fixed. Alas! alas! do not delay your help, my sweet good mother. Lend me your aid, for I am sure you can help me easily if you will.' The cunning old woman still kept silence feigning all the while to know nothing of the mischance that had been wrought, and letting the wretched fellow work himself into an agony and stew in his own fat;[1] but at last, after having kept him in this plight for the space of two hours, she agreed to work the remedy he sought. So, having made him bend himself down as before, she put her hand to her sharp-cutting sword and struck off his head from his shoulders. Then she took the head in her hand, and, having placed it upon the trunk and smeared it well with her ointment, brought Flamminio back to his former condition.

The youth, when he perceived that he had once more become his old self, put on his clothes; and now, having seen what a terrible thing, and by his own experience proved what a hideous and ugly thing Death was, he made his way back to Ostia by the shortest and the quickest way he knew without saying any more farewell words to the old woman, occupying himself for the future in reaching after Life and flying from Death, devoting himself more diligently to the consideration of those matters which he had hitherto neglected.

It now only remained that Lionora should propose her enigma, so she gave out the following one in merry wise :

> About a meadow fair and wide,
> Gay decked with flowers on every side,
> Three nymphs on task divine intent,
> Pass to and fro, and firmly bent
> To speed their work, nor night nor day
> Take pause, nor rest upon their way.
> One in her left the distaff plies,
> Between another's feet swift flies
> The spindle, and last one doth stand
> With keen-edged weapon in her hand,
> And cuts in twain the fragile strand.

This enigma was very easily understood by all the company, because it was clear that the fine and spacious meadow must be this world in which all men dwell. The three nymphs are the three sisters, Clotho, Lachesis, and Atropos, who by the fancy of the poets are held to represent the beginning, the middle, and the end of our lives. Clotho, who holds the rock, shows forth our birth; Lachesis,

---

[1] Orig., *cuocersi nel suo unto.*

who spins it, the season of our existence, and Atropos, who severs the thread just spun by Lachesis, inevitable Death.

Already the watchful cock, bird sacred to Mercury, had given signal by his crowing of the approaching dawn, when the Signora brought to an end the story-telling for the night, and all the guests departed to their own homes, pledged, however, to return on the following evening under whatever penalty the Signora might deem fitting to inflict.

The End of the Fourth Night.

Night the Fifth.

The Fables and Enigmas of Messer Giovanni Francesco Straparola da Caravaggio.

Night the Fifth.

THE sun, the glory of the smiling firmament, the measurer of our fleeting time, and the true eye of the universe, from whom likewise the horned moon and all the stars receive their radiance, had at last hidden his red and burning rays beneath the waters of the sea, and the chaste daughter of Latona, circled around by bright and beaming stars, was already lighting up the clustering shadows of the obscure night, and the shepherds, quitting the wide and open fields and the fresh herbage and the cool and limpid streams, had taken their way back with their flocks to their wonted folds, and, worn out and weary as they were, had sunk into deep slumber on the beds of soft and yielding rushes, when the fair and noble troop of companions, letting go thought of everything else, hastened to the place of meeting. And when it had been signified to the Signora that all had come, and that it was now time to recommence the story-telling, she, escorted in courteous and reverent wise by the other ladies, went joyful and smiling with soft and measured step to the hall of meeting. Then having graciously greeted the company of friends with gladsome face, she ordered them to bring out the vase of gold. In this were put the names of five ladies, and of these the first to come out was that of Eritrea, the second that of Alteria, the third that of Lauretta, the fourth that of Arianna, and the last that of Cateruzza. When this was done they all began to dance to the music of the flutes, and to pass from one to another pleasant and loving words. Immediately after the end of the dance, three damsels, by the leave of the Signora, began the following song.

SONG.

Madonna, when the springs of passion rise,
And through thy fair sweet bosom surge and swell;
And in those lucent sacred eyes,
Which tell me I may live, and eke my death may tell;
From those gracious looks and kind,
A gracious hope my longings find.
Now calm, and now spurred on by rage,
With hope and fear a fight I wage;
Eftsoons my hope the vantage gains,
And I am rid of all my pains,
And know no stroke of fate can lure,
Or drive me from my course secure.
Wherefore I bless the passing days;
Great nature, and the stars I praise,
That thy fair self my passion fired,
Thy service sweet my song inspired.

As soon as the three damsels had brought to an end their amorous canzonet, which seemed to break up the air around into sighs of passion, the Signora made a sign to Eritrea, who had been chosen for the first place this evening, that she should make a beginning of her story-telling. The damsel, seeing that she could in no wise excuse herself, put aside all bashfulness, and began to speak in turn that the order which had hitherto prevailed might not be disturbed.

THE FIRST FABLE.

Guerrino, only son of Filippomaria, King of Sicily, sets free from his father's prison a certain savage man. His mother, through fear of the king, drives her son into exile, and him the savage man, now humanized, delivers from many and measureless ills.

I HAVE heard by report, and likewise gathered from my own experience, most gracious and pleasure-loving ladies, that a kindly service done to another (although at the time the one served may seem in no sense grateful for the boon conferred) will more often than not come back to the doer thereof with abundant usury of benefit. Which thing happened to the son of a king who, having liberated from one of his father's prisons a wild man of the woods, was more than once rescued from a violent death by the captive he had freed. This you will easily understand from the fable which I intend to relate to you, and for the love I bear to all of you I will exhort you never to be backward in aiding others; because, even though you be not repaid by those in whose behalf you have wrought, God Himself, the rewarder of all, will assuredly never leave your good deed unrecompensed; nay, on the contrary, He will make you partakers with Him of His divine grace.

Sicily, my dear ladies (as must be well known to all of you), is an island very fertile and complete in itself, and in antiquity surpassing all the others of which we have knowledge, abounding in towns and villages which render it still more beautiful. In past times the lord of this island was a certain king named Filippomaria, a man wise and amiable and of rare virtue, who had to wife a courteous, winsome, and lovely lady, the mother of his only son, who was called Guerrino. The king took greater delight in following the chase than any other man in the country, and, for the reason that he was of a strong and robust habit of body, this diversion was well suited to him.

Now it happened one day that, as he was coming back from hunting in company with divers of his barons and huntsmen, he saw, coming out of a thick wood, a wild man, tall and big and so deformed and ugly that they all looked upon him with amazement. In strength

of body he seemed no whit inferior to any of them; wherefore the
king, having put himself in fighting trim, together with two of the
most valiant of his barons, attacked him boldly, and after a long and
doughty struggle overcame him and took him a prisoner with his
own hands.   Then, having bound him, they conveyed him back to
the palace, and selected for him a safe lodging, fitted for the purpose,
into which they cast him, and there under strong locks he was kept
by the king's command closely confined and guarded.   And seeing
that the king set high store upon his captive, he ordained that the
keys of the prison should be held in charge by the queen, and never
a day passed when he would not for pastime go to visit him.

Before many days had gone by the king once more put himself
in array for the chase, and, having furnished himself with all the
various things which are necessary thereto, he set forth with a gallant
company of courtiers, but before he left he gave into the queen's care
the keys of the prison.   And during the time that the king was
absent on his hunting a great longing came over Guerrino, who was
at that season a young lad, to see the wild man of the woods; so
having betaken himself all alone, carrying his bow, in which he
delighted greatly, to the prison grating, the creature saw him and
straightway began to converse with him in decent orderly fashion.
And while they talked thus, the wild man, who was caressing the
boy, dexterously snatched out of his hand the arrow, which was richly
ornamented.   Whereupon the boy began to weep, and could not
keep back his tears, crying out that the savage ought to give him
back his arrow.   But the wild man said to him : 'If you will open
the door and let me go free from this prison I will give you back your
arrow, but if you refuse I will not let you have it.'   The boy answered,
'How would you that I should open the door for you and set you
free, seeing that I have not the means therefor.'   Then said the wild
man, 'If indeed you were in the mood to release me and to let me
out of this narrow cell, I would soon teach you the way in which it
might be done.'   'But how?' replied Guerrino; 'tell me the way.'
To which the wild man made answer : 'Go to the chamber of the
queen your mother, and when you see that she is taking her midday
sleep, put your hand softly under the pillow upon which she is resting, and take therefrom the keys of the prison in such wise that she
shall not notice the theft, and bring them here and open my prison
door.   When you shall have done this I will give you back your

arrow forthwith, and peradventure at some future time I may be able
to make you a return for your kindness.'

Guerrino, wishing beyond everything to get back his gilded dart,
did everything that the wild man had told him, and found the keys
exactly as he had said, and with these in his hand he returned to the
prison, and said to him : ' Behold ! here are the keys ; but if I let you
out of this place you must go so far from hence that not even the
scent of you may be known, for if my father, who is a great huntsman,
should find you and capture you again, he would of a surety kill you
out of hand.'   ' Let not that trouble you, my child,' said the captive,
' for as soon as ever you shall open the prison and see me a free man,
I will give you back your arrow and will get me away into such distant
parts that neither your father nor any other man shall ever find me.'
Guerrino, who had all the strength of a man, worked away at the
door, and finally threw open the prison, when the wild man, having
given back to him his arrow and thanked him heartily, went his way.

Now this wild man had been formerly a very handsome youth,
who, through despair at his inability to win the favour of the lady he
ardently loved, let go all dreams of love and urbane pursuits, and took
up his dwelling amongst beasts of the forest, abiding always in the
gloomy woods and bosky thickets, eating grass and drinking water
after the fashion of a brute.   On this account the wretched man had
become covered with a great fell of hair; his skin was hard, his beard
thick and tangled and very long, and, through eating herbs and grass,
his beard, his hairy covering, and the hair of his head had become so
green that they were quite monstrous to behold.

As soon as ever the queen awoke from her slumbers she thrust
her hand under her pillow to seek for the keys she had put there,
and, when she found they were gone, she was terrified amain, and
having turned the bed upside down without meeting with any trace
of them, she ran straightway like one bereft of wit to the prison, which
was standing open.   When on searching further she found no sign
of the wild man, she was so sore stricken with grief and fear that she
was like to die, and, having returned to the palace, she made diligent
search in every corner thereof, questioning the while now this courtier
and now that as to who the presumptuous and insolent varlet was who
had been brazen enough to lay hands upon the keys of the prison
without her knowledge.   To this questioning they one and all declared
that they knew nought of the matter which thus disturbed her.   And

when Guerrino met his mother, and remarked that she was almost beside herself in a fit of passion, he said to her : ' Mother, see that you cast no blame on any of these in respect to the opening of the prison door, because if punishment is due to any thereanent it is due to me, for I, and I alone, unlocked it.'   The queen, when she heard these words, was plunged in deeper sorrow than ever, fearing lest the king, when he should come back from his hunting, might kill his son through sheer anger at the fault he had committed, seeing that he had given into her charge the keys, to guard them as preciously as her own person.   Wherefore the queen in her desire to escape the consequences of a venial mistake fell into another error far more weighty, for without the shortest delay she summoned two of her most trusty servants, and her son as well, and, having given to them a great quantity of jewels and much money and divers fine horses, sent him forth to seek his fortune, at the same time begging the servants most earnestly to take the greatest care of Guerrino.

A very short time after the son had departed from the presence of his mother, the king came back to the palace from following the chase, and as soon as he had alighted from his horse he betook himself straightway to the prison to go and see the wild man, and when he found the door wide open and the captive gone, and no trace of him left behind, he was forthwith inflamed with such violent anger that he determined in his mind to cause to be slain without fail the person who had wrought such a flagrant misdeed.   And, having sought out the queen, who was sitting overcome with grief in her chamber, he commanded her to tell him what might be the name of the impudent, rash, and presumptuous varlet who had been bold enough of heart to open the doors of the prison and thereby give opportunity to the wild man of the woods to make his escape. Whereupon the queen, in a meek and trembling voice, made answer to him : ' O sire! be not troubled on account of this thing, for Guerrino our son (as he himself has made confession to me) admits that he has done this.'   And then she told to the king everything that Guerrino. had said to her, and he, when he heard her story, was greatly incensed with rage.   Next she told him that, on account of the fear she felt lest he should slay his son, she had sent the youth away into a far distant country, accompanied by two of their most faithful servants, and carrying with him rich store of jewels and of money sufficient to serve their needs.   The king, when he listened to this speech of the queen, felt one sorrow heaping itself upon another, and he came within an ace of falling to the ground or of losing his wits, and, if it had not been for the courtiers who fell upon him and held him back, he would assuredly have slain his unhappy queen on the spot.

Now when the poor king had in some measure recovered his composure and calmed the fit of unbridled rage which had possessed him, he said to the queen: 'Alas, my wife! what fancy was this of yours which induced you to send away into some unknown land our son, the fruit of our mutual love? Is it possible that you imagined I should hold this wild man of greater value than one who was my own flesh and blood?' And without awaiting any reply to these remarks of his, he bade a great troop of soldiers mount their horses forthwith, and, after having divided themselves into four companies, to make a close search and endeavour to find the prince. But all their inquest was in vain, seeing that Guerrino and his attendants had made their journey secretly, and had let no one know who they might be.

Guerrino, after he had ridden far and traversed divers valleys and mountains and rivers, making a halt now in one spot and now in another, attained at last his sixteenth year, and so fair a youth was he by this time that he resembled nothing so much as a fresh morning rose. But after a short time had passed, the servants who accompanied him were seized with the devilish thought of killing him, and then taking the store of jewels and money and parting it amongst themselves. This wicked plot, however, came to nought, because by the working of divine justice they were not able to agree amongst themselves. For by good fortune it happened that, one day while they were devising this wickedness, there rode by a very fair and graceful youth, mounted upon a superb steed, and accoutred with the utmost magnificence. This youth bowed and graciously saluted Guerrino, and thus addressed him: 'Most gracious sir, if it should not prove distasteful to you, I would fain make my journey in your company.' And to this Guerrino replied: 'Your courtesy in making your request will not permit me to refuse it and the pleasure of your company. Therefore I give you cordial thanks, and I beg you as a special favour that you will accompany us on our road. We are strangers in this country and know but little of its highways, and you may be able of your kindness to direct our paths therein. Moreover, as we ride on together we can discuss the various chances which have befallen us, and thus our journey will be less irksome.'

Now this young man was no other than the wild man whom Guerrino had set free from the prison of King Filippomaria his father. This youth, after wandering through various countries and strange lands, met one day by chance a very lovely and benignant fairy, who was at that time suffering from a certain distemper. She, when she looked upon him and saw how misshapen and hideous he was, laughed so violently at the sight of his ugliness that she caused to burst an imposthume which had formed in the vicinity of her heart—an ailment which might well have caused her death by suffocation. And at that very moment she was delivered from all pain and trouble of this infirmity, as if she had never been afflicted therewith in the past, and restored to health. Wherefore the good fairy, in recompense for so great a favour done to her, said to him, not wishing to appear ungrateful to him: 'O thou creature, who art now so deformed and filthy, since thou hast been the means of restoring to me my health which I so greatly desired, go thy ways, and be thou changed from what thou art into the fairest, the wisest, and the most graceful youth that may anywhere be found. And, besides this, I make you the sharer with me of all the power and authority conferred upon me by nature, whereby you will be able to do and to undo whatsoever you will according to your desire.' And having presented to him a noble horse endowed with magic powers, she gave him leave to go whithersoever he would.

Thus as Guerrino journeyed along with the young man, knowing nothing as to who he might be, but well known of him the while, they came at last to a mighty and strong city called Irlanda, over which at that time ruled King Zifroi. This King Zifroi was the father of two daughters, graceful to look upon, of modest manners, and in beauty surpassing Venus herself, one of them named Potentiana and the other Eleuteria. They were held so dear by the king their father that he could see by no other eyes than theirs. As soon as Guerrino entered the city of Irlanda with the unknown youth and with his train of servants, he hired a lodging of a certain householder who was the wittiest fellow in the whole of Irlanda, and who treated his guests with cheer of the best. And on the day following, the unknown youth made believe that he must needs depart and travel into another country, and went to take leave of Guerrino, thanking him in hearty wise for the boon of his company and good usage, but Guerrino, who had conceived the strongest love and friendship for him, would on no account let him go, and showed him such strong evidence of his good feeling that in the end the young man agreed to tarry with him.

In the country round about Irlanda there lived at this time two very fearful and savage animals, one of which was a wild horse, and the other a mare of like nature, and so ferocious and cruel were these beasts that they not only ravaged and devastated all the fair cultivated fields, but likewise killed all the animals and the men and women dwelling therein. And through the ruin wrought by these beasts the country had come to such piteous condition that no one was found willing to abide there, so that the peasants abandoned their farms and the homes which were dear to them and betook themselves to find dwelling-places in another land. And there was nowhere to be found any man strong and bold enough to face them, much less to fight with them and slay them. Wherefore the king, seeing that the whole country was being made desolate of all victuals, and of cattle, and of human creatures, and not knowing how to devise any remedy for this wretched pass, gave way to dolorous lamentations, and cursed the hard and evil fortune which had befallen him. The two servants of Guerrino, who during the journey had not been able to carry out their wicked intent through want of concord between themselves, and on account of the arrival of the unknown youth, now deliberated how they might compass Guerrino's death and remain possessors of the money and jewels, and said one to the other : 'Let us now see and take counsel together how we may easiest take the life of our master.' But not being able to find any means thereto which seemed fitting, seeing that they would stand in peril of losing their own lives by the law if they should kill him, they decided to speak privily with their host and to tell him that Guerrino was a youth of great prowess and valour; furthermore, that he had often boasted in their presence that he would be ready to slay this wild horse without incurring any danger to himself. Thus they reasoned with themselves : 'Now this saying may easily come to the ears of the king, who, being so keenly set on the destruction of these two animals and on safeguarding the welfare of his country, will straightway command them to bring Guerrino before him, and will then inquire of the youth in what manner he means to accomplish this feat. Then Guerrino, knowing nothing what to say or to do, will at once be put to death by the king, and we shall remain sole

masters of the jewels and the money.' And they forthwith set to
work to put this wicked plan of theirs into action.

The host, when he listened to this speech, rejoiced amain, and was
as glad as any man in all the world, and without losing a moment of
time he ran swiftly to the palace, and having knelt down before the
king and made due reverence, he said to him secretly, ' Gracious king,
I have come to tell you that there is at present sojourning in my hostel
a fair and gallant knight errant, who is called by name Guerrino.
Now whilst I was confabulating about divers matters with his servants
they told me, amongst other things, how their master was a man of
great prowess and well skilled in the use and practice of arms, and that
in this our time one might search in vain to find another who could
be compared with him. Moreover, they had many and many a time
heard him boast that of his strength and valour he could without
difficulty overcome and slay the wild horse which is working such dire
loss and damage to your kingdom.'

When King Zifroi heard these words he immediately gave command that Guerrino should be brought before him. Whereupon the
innkeeper, obedient to the word of the king, returned at once to his
inn and said to Guerrino that he was to betake himself alone into the
presence of the king, who greatly desired to speak with him. When
Guerrino heard this he went straightway to the palace and presented
himself to the king, and after saluting him with becoming reverence
begged to be told for what reason he had been honoured with the royal
commands. To this Zifroi the king made answer : ' Guerrino, the
reason which has induced me to send for you is that I have heard you
are a knight of great valour, and one excelling all the other knights
now alive in the world. They tell me, too, that you have many and
many a time declared that you are strong and valorous enough to
overcome and slay the wild horse which is working such cruel ruin
and devastation to this my kingdom, without risk of hurt to yourself
or to others. If you can pluck up courage enough to make trial of an
emprise so full of honour as this, and prove yourself a conqueror, I
promise you by this head of mine to bestow upon you a gift which
will make you a happy man for the rest of your days.'

Guerrino, when he heard this proposition of the king, so grave
and weighty, was mightily amazed, and at once denied that he had
ever spoken such words as had been attributed to him. The king,
who was greatly disconcerted at this answer of Guerrino, thus addressed

him : 'Guerrino, it is my will that you should without delay undertake this task, and be sure if you refuse and fail to comply with my
wishes I will take away your life.'   The king, having thus spoken,
dismissed from his presence Guerrino, who returned to his inn overwhelmed with deep sorrow, which he did not dare to disclose to
anyone.   Whereupon the unknown youth, marking that Guerrino,
contrary to his wont, was plunged in melancholy, inquired the reason
why he was so sad and full of grief.   Then Guerrino, on account of
the brotherly love subsisting between them, and finding himself unable to refuse this just and kindly request, told him word for word
everything that had happened to him.   As soon as the unknown
youth heard this, he said, ' Be of good cheer, and put aside all doubts
and fears, for I will point out to you a way by which you will save
your life, and be a conqueror in your enterprise, and fulfil the wishes
of the king.   Return, therefore, to the king, and beg of him to grant
you the services of a skilful blacksmith.   Then order this smith to
make for you four horseshoes, which must be thicker and broader by
the breadth of two fingers than the ordinary measure of horseshoes,
well roughed, and each one to be fitted behind with two spikes of a
finger's length and sharpened to a point.   And when these shoes are
prepared, you must have my horse, which is enchanted, shod therewith, and then you need have no further fear of anything.'
     Guerrino, after he had heard these words, returned to the presence
of the king, and told him everything as the young man had directed
him.   The king then caused to be brought before him a well-skilled
marshal smith, to whom he gave orders that he should carry out whatever work Guerrino might require of him.   When they had gone to
the smith's forge, Guerrino instructed him how to make the four horseshoes according to the words of the young stranger, but when the
smith understood in what fashion he was required to make these shoes,
he mocked at Guerrino, and treated him like a madman, for this way
of making shoes was quite strange and unknown to him.   When
Guerrino saw that the marshal smith was inclined to mock him, and
unwilling to serve him as he had been ordered, he went once more to
the king, and complained that the smith would not carry out his directions.   Wherefore the king bade them bring the marshal before him,
and gave him express command that, under pain of his highest displeasure, he should at once carry out the duties which had been imposed upon him, or, failing this, he himself should forthwith make

ready to carry out the perilous task which had been assigned to Guerrino. The smith, thus hard pressed by the orders of the king, made the horseshoes in the way described by Guerrino, and shod the horse therewith.

When the horse was thus shod and well-accoutred with everything that was necessary for the enterprise, the young stranger addressed Guerrino in these words : ' Now mount quickly this my horse, and go in peace, and as soon as you shall hear the neighing of the wild horse dismount at once, and, having taken off from him his saddle and his bridle, let him range at will. You yourself climb up into a high tree, and there await the issue of the enterprise.' Guerrino, having been fully instructed by his dear companion in all that he ought to do, took his leave, and departed with a light heart.

Already the glorious news had been spread abroad through all the parts of Irlanda how a valiant and handsome young knight had undertaken to subjugate and capture the wild horse and to present him to the king, and for this reason everyone in the city, men and women alike, all flew to their windows to see him go by on his perilous errand. When they marked how handsome and young and gallant he was, their hearts were moved to pity on his account, and they said one to another, ' Ah, the poor youth! with what a willing spirit he goes to his death. Of a surety it is a piteous thing that so valiant a youth should thus wretchedly perish.' And they could none of them keep back their tears on account of the compassion they felt.

But Guerrino, full of manly boldness, went on his way blithely, and when he had come to the spot where the wild horse was wont to abide, and heard the sound of his neigh, he got down from his own horse, and having taken the saddle and bridle therefrom he let him go free, and himself climbed up into the branches of a great oak, and there awaited the fierce and bloody contest.

Scarcely had Guerrino climbed up into the tree when the wild horse appeared and forthwith attacked the fairy horse, and then the two beasts engaged in the fiercest struggle that the world had ever seen, for they rushed at one another as if they had been two unchained lions, and they foamed at the mouth as if they had been bristly wild-boars pursued by savage and eager hounds. Then, after they had fought for some time with the greatest fury, the fairy horse dealt the wild horse two kicks full on the jaw, which was put out of joint thereby; wherefore the wild horse was at once disabled, and could no longer either fight or defend himself. When Guerrino saw this he rejoiced greatly, and having come down from the oak, he took a halter which he had brought with him and secured the wild horse therewith, and led him with his dislocated jaw back to the city, where he was welcomed by all the people with the greatest joy. According to his promise he presented the horse to the king, who, together with all the inhabitants of the city, held high festival, and rejoiced amain over the gallant deed wrought by Guerrino.

But the servants of Guerrino were greatly overcome with grief and confusion, inasmuch as their evil designs had miscarried; wherefore, inflamed with rage and hatred, they once more let it come to the hearing of King Zifroi that Guerrino had vaunted that he could with the greatest ease kill the wild mare also whenever it might please him. When the king heard this he laid exactly the same commands on Guerrino as he had done in the matter of the horse, and because the youth refused to undertake this task, which appeared to him impossible, the king threatened to have him hung up by one foot as a rebel against his crown. After Guerrino had returned to his inn, he told everything to his unknown companion, who smilingly said: 'My good brother, fret not yourself because of this, but go and find the marshal smith, and command him to make for you four more horseshoes, as big again as the last, and see that they are duly furnished with good sharp spikes. Then you must follow exactly the same course as you took with the horse, and you will return here covered with greater honour than ever.' When therefore he had commanded to be made the sharply-spiked horseshoes, and had caused the valiant fairy horse to be shod therewith, he set forth on his gallant enterprise.

As soon as Guerrino had come to the spot where the wild mare was wont to graze, and heard her neighing, he did everything exactly in the same manner as before, and when he had set free the fairy horse, the mare came towards it and attacked it with such fierce and terrible biting that it could with difficulty defend itself against such an attack. But it bore the assault valiantly, and at last succeeded in planting so sharp and dexterous a kick on the mare that she was lamed in her right leg, whereupon Guerrino came down from the high tree into which he had climbed, and having captured her, bound her securely. Then he mounted his own horse and rode back to the palace, where he presented the wild mare to the king, amidst the rejoicings and acclamations of all the people. And everyone, attracted by wonder-

ment and curiosity, ran to see this wild beast, which, on account of
the grave injuries she had received in the fight, soon died. And by
these means the country was freed from the great plague which had
for so long a time vexed it.

Now when Guerrino had returned to his hostel, and had betaken
himself to repose somewhat on account of the weariness which had
come over him, he found that he was unable to get any sleep by
reason of a strange noise which he heard somewhere in the chamber.
Wherefore, having risen from his couch, he perceived that there was
something, I know not what, beating about inside a pot of honey,
and not able to get out. So Guerrino opened the honey-pot, and
saw within a large hornet, which was struggling with its wings without being able to free itself from the honey around it. Moved by
pity, he took hold of the insect and let it go free.

Now Zifroi the king had as yet given to Guerrino no reward for
the two valiant deeds which he had wrought, but he was conscious
in his heart that he would be acting in a very base fashion were he
to leave such great valour without a rich guerdon, so he caused
Guerrino to be called into his presence, and thus addressed him:
'Guerrino, by your noble deeds the whole of my kingdom is now
free from the scourge, therefore I intend to reward you for the great
benefits you have wrought in our behalf; but as I can conceive of no
other gift which would be worthy and sufficient for your merits, I
have determined to give you one of my two daughters to wife. But
you must know that of these two sisters one is called Potentiana, and
she has hair braided in such marvellous wise that it shines like golden
coils. The other is called Eleuteria, and her tresses are of such
texture that they flash brightly like the finest silver. Now if you
can guess—the maidens being closely veiled the while—which is she
of the golden tresses, I will give her to you as your wife, together
with a mighty dowry of money; but if you fail in this, I will have
your head struck off your shoulders.'

Guerrino, when he heard this cruel ordeal which was proposed by
Zifroi the king, was mightily amazed, and turning to him spake
thus: 'O gracious sovereign! Is this a worthy guerdon for all the
perils and fatigues I have undergone? Is this a reward for the strength
I have spent on your behalf? Is this the gratitude you give me for
having delivered your country from the scourge by which it was of
late laid desolate? Alas! I did not merit this return, which of a truth

is not a deed worthy of such a mighty king as yourself. But since this is your pleasure and I am helpless in your hands, you must do with me what pleases you best.' 'Now go,' said Zifroi, 'and tarry no longer in my presence. I give you till to-morrow to come to a decision.'

When Guerrino went out of the king's presence full of sadness, he sought his dear companion, and repeated to him everything that the king had said. The unknown youth when he heard this seemed but little troubled thereanent, and said: 'Guerrino, be of good cheer, and do not despair, for I will deliver you from this great danger. Remember how a few days ago you set free the hornet which you found with its wings entangled in the honey. Now this same hornet will be the means of saving you, for to-morrow, after the dinner at the palace, when you are put to the test, it will fly three times buzzing and humming round the head of her with the golden hair, and she with her white hands will drive it away. And you, when you shall have marked her do this action three times, may know for certain that this is she who is to be your wife.' 'Ah me!' cried Guerrino to his companion, 'when will the time come when I shall be able to make you some repayment for all the kind offices you have done me? Certes, were I to live for a thousand years, I should never have it in my power to recompense you the very smallest portion thereof. But that one, who is the rewarder of all, will in this matter make up for me in that respect in which I am wanting.' To this speech of Guerrino his companion made answer: 'Guerrino, my brother, there is in sooth no need for you to trouble yourself about making any return to me for the services I may have wrought you, but assuredly it is now full time that I should reveal to you, and that you should know clearly who I am. For in the same fashion as you delivered me from death, I on my part have desired to render to you the recompense you deserve so highly at my hands. Know, then, that I am the wild man of the woods whom you, with such loving compassion, set free from the prison-house of the king your father, and that I am called by name Rubinetto.' And then he went on to tell Guerrino by what means the fairy had brought him back into his former state of a fair young man. Guerrino, when he heard these words, stood like one bemused, and out of the great tenderness and pity he had in his heart he embraced Rubinetto, weeping the while, and kissed him, and claimed him as his own brother.

And forasmuch as the day was now approaching for Guerrino to solve the question to be set to him by King Zifroi, the two repaired to the palace, whereupon the king gave order that his two beloved daughters, Potentiana and Eleuteria, should be brought into the presence of Guerrino covered from head to foot with white veils, and this was straightway done. When the two daughters had come in so much alike in seeming that it was impossible to tell the one from the other, the king said : 'Now which of these two, Guerrino, do you will that I should give you to wife?' But Guerrino stood still in a state of doubt and hesitation, and answered nothing, but the king, who was mightily curious to see how the matter would end, pressed him amain to speak, crying out that time was flying, and that it behoved him to give his answer at once. To this Guerrino made answer: 'Most sacred majesty, time forsooth may be flying, but the end is not yet come to this day, which is the limit you have given me for my decision.' And all those standing by affirmed that Guerrino only claimed his right.

When, therefore, the king and Guerrino and all the others had stood for a long time in expectation, behold! there suddenly appeared a hornet, which at once began to fly and buzz round the head and the fair face of Potentiana of the golden hair. And she, as if she were afeared of the thing, raised her hand to drive it away, and when she had done this three times the hornet flew away out of sight. But even after this sign Guerrino remained uncertain for a short time, although he had full faith in the words of Rubinetto, his well-beloved companion. Then said the king, 'How now, Guerrino, what do you say? The time has now come when you must put an end to this delay, and make up your mind.' And Guerrino, having looked well first at one and then at the other of the maidens, put his hand on the head of Potentiana, who had been pointed out to him by the hornet, and said, 'Gracious king, this one is your daughter of the golden tresses.' And when the maiden had raised her veil it was clearly proved that it was indeed she, greatly to the joy of all those who were present, and to the satisfaction of the people of the city. And Zifroi the king gave her to Guerrino as his wife, and they did not depart thence until Rubinetto had wedded the other sister. After this Guerrino declared himself to be the son of Filippomaria, King of Sicily, hearing which Zifroi was greatly rejoiced, and caused the marriages to be celebrated with the greatest pomp and magnificence.

When this news came to the father and the mother of Guerrino they felt the greatest joy and contentment, seeing that they had by this time given up their son as lost. When he returned to Sicily with his dear wife and his well-loved brother and sister-in-law, they all received a gracious and loving welcome from his father and mother, and they lived a long time in peace and happiness, and he left behind him fair children as the heirs to his kingdom.

This touching story told by Eritrea won the highest praise of all the hearers, and she, when she saw that all were silent, proposed her enigma in the following words:

> A cruel beast of nature dread
> From out a tiny germ is bred.
> In hate all beings else it holds,
> And each one trembles who beholds
> Its form of fear. Death all around
> It spreads, and oft itself is found
> The victim of its fatal rage,
> And war on all the world will wage.
> Beneath its breath the trees decay,
> The living plants will fade away.
> A beast more cruel, fierce, and fell,
> Ne'er rose from out the pit of hell.

When the enigma set to the worshipful company by the clever damsel had been considered and highly praised by everyone, some found one solution therefor and some another, but not one of them gave the one which rightly explained its meaning. Wherefore Eritrea, seeing that her riddle had not been understood, said, " It seems to me that the cruel animal I have described cannot be anything else than the basilisk, which hates all other living beasts in the world, and slays them with its sharp and piercing glances. And if peradventure it should chance to see its own form mirrored anywhere, it straightway dies." When Eritrea had come to the end of the interpretation of her enigma, the Signor Evangelist,[1] who sat by her side, said to her smiling: " Of a truth you yourself are this basilisk, signora, for with your beautiful eyes you bring soft death to all those who gaze upon you." But Eritrea, with her cheeks suffused with the lovely tint of nature, answered nought. Alteria sat near by, and, as soon as she perceived that the enigma was now completed, having been highly praised

---

[1] Pietro Bembo.

by all, she called to mind that it was now her turn to tell a story
according to the Signora's pleasure, so she began in the following wise
a fable which proved in the end to be fully as mirthful as it was
commendable.

THE SECOND FABLE.

*Adamantina, the daughter of Bagolana Sabonese, by the working of a
certain doll becomes the wife of Drusiano, King of Bohemia.*

S O powerful, so commanding, so subtle is the wit of man
that without doubt it may be held to overtop and to
exceed every other human force to be found in the world ;
wherefore it has been said, not without just cause, that
the wise man is the governor of the stars.   This saying recalls to my
memory a fable, by the telling of which I hope to make quite clear
to you how a young girl, of mean estate and very poor, was succoured
by fortune, and in the end became the wife of a mighty king.
Although my fable will be very short, it may, if I mistake not, be
found to be none the less pleasing and diverting on that account.   I
beg you therefore to lend me your ears attentively, and listen to me,
as hitherto you have listened to our very worthy associates, who, of
a surety, have merited from you praise rather than blame.

In the country of Bohemia, dear ladies, there lived not a long time
ago a little old woman known by the name of Bagolana Savonese,
miserably poor in her way of life, and the mother of two daughters,
one of whom was called Cassandra and the other Adamantina.   Now
this woman, though she had scarce anything to call her own, was
anxious to set her affairs in order, so that she might die in peace, and
as the whole of the wealth that she had to dispose of in her house and
out of it consisted of a small coffer filled with tow, she made her will
and gave this coffer and what it contained to her two daughters, begging them at the same time to live peacefully together after she should
be dead.

These two sisters, though they were very poor in any of the
endowments of fortune, were by no means wanting in mental gifts,
so that in all virtues and in righteous behaviour they were no whit
inferior to other women.   After the old woman was dead and her

body had been buried, Cassandra, who was the elder sister of the two, took a pound of the tow and sat down and began to spin the same with great care, and, as soon as she had spun it, she gave the thread she had made to Adamantina, her younger sister, bidding her to take it out into the piazza and to sell it, and with the proceeds of the sale to purchase some bread wherewith they might keep themselves alive. Thereupon Adamantina took the thread, and, having put it under her arm, she went her way into the piazza to sell her wares, according to the commandment of her sister Cassandra; but, as chance would have it, what she did ran entirely counter to her own wishes and to those of her sister, for as she was walking in the piazza she happened to meet there an old woman who was carrying in her apron the most beautiful and most perfectly made doll that had ever been seen. So much indeed was Adamantina's fancy taken by the doll that, after she had looked at it and feasted her eyes upon it, her thoughts were more occupied in considering how she might become the owner thereof, than how she should dispose of her yarn. Therefore Adamantina, letting her thoughts run on in this wise, and not knowing how to get possession of the doll by anything she might say or do, made up her mind at last to tempt fortune and to see whether she could not obtain the doll through exchange. So having gone up to the old woman she spake thus: 'Good mother, if it seem a fair thing to you, I will gladly give you this thread of mine in barter for your doll.' The old woman, when she saw that this fine handsome young girl was so eager to have the doll for her own, was not disposed to baulk her fancy; so, having taken the thread, she handed the doll over to Adamantina.

As soon as the girl could call the doll her own, she went back to her home as joyous and content as anyone in all the world, and her sister Cassandra, when she saw her, at once inquired of her whether she had sold the yarn. To this Adamantina replied that she had sold it. 'But where is the bread which you have bought with the price you got for the thread?' inquired Cassandra. Then Adamantina opened wide the apron she was wearing and showed Cassandra the doll which she had got by barter of her own ware. Cassandra, who was sorely hungry and eager for the bread, when she saw the doll was filled with such violent anger and indignation that she seized Adamantina by the hair of her head, and belaboured her so grievously with cuffs and blows that the unfortunate girl could scarcely move.

Adamantina took the blows with patience, and, without making any attempt to defend herself, she went away and hid herself in another room, taking her doll with her.

When the evening had come Adamantina, according to the habit of young girls, sat down by the fireside, and, having taken some oil out of the lamp, she anointed therewith the doll's stomach and loins. Then she wrapped the doll carefully in some bits of tattered cloth, and placed it in her own bed, and a very short time afterwards she went to bed herself and lay down beside the doll. Scarcely had Adamantina fallen into her first sleep when the doll began to cry out : ' The stool, mother, the stool.' Whereupon Adamantina, wakening from her sleep, said : ' What is the matter with you, my daughter ? ' and to this the doll replied in the same words as before. Then Adamantina said : ' Wait a little, my daughter ; ' and she straightway arose and ministered to the doll as if it had been a young child, and to her amazement she found that the doll filled the stool with a great quantity of coins of all sorts.

As soon as Adamantina saw what had happened she straightway awakened her sister Cassandra and showed her the money which had come to her in this strange fashion. Cassandra, when she marked what a great sum of money was there, stood as one stricken with wonder, and rendered hearty thanks to God for sending them such welcome succour in their want and misery, and, turning to Adamantina, she begged pardon of her for the blows which she had so cruelly and unjustly given to her, and she took the doll and caressed it tenderly and kissed it, holding it closely in her arms. And when the next day had come, the two sisters took of the money and purchased therewith bread and wine and oil and wood, and all other sorts of provisions which are suitable to a well-ordered house, taking care every evening to anoint the stomach of the doll with oil, and to wrap it in a piece of the finest linen, and the doll on its part never failed to supply them with money in abundance whenever they had need thereof.

It chanced on a certain day that one of their neighbours, having gone into the house of the two sisters, remarked that their home was well furnished with all the necessaries of life in great abundance, and on this account began to wonder how it was that they could have become rich in so short a time, remembering, moreover, how miserably poor they had been hitherto, and knowing full well that no one could say otherwise than that they were honest and upright in all their ways. Wherefore the neighbour, having given the matter due consideration, determined to find out the source from which they might have gathered such gain; so having betaken herself once more to the house of the two sisters, she thus addressed them : 'My daughters, I beg you to tell me by what means you have been able to furnish your house so plentifully, seeing that but yesterday you were in sore poverty.' To this question Cassandra, the elder sister, made reply : 'Good neighbour, we have done all this by the means of a single pound of flaxen yarn, which we gave in exchange for a doll, and this doll gives us money in abundance, and supplies us with everything we need.' The neighbour, when she heard these words, was greatly disturbed in her mind, and was so filled with envy of the good fortune which had befallen the girls that she determined to steal the doll. As soon as she returned to her house, she told her husband how the two sisters had a certain doll which every night was accustomed to give them great store of gold and silver, and that she had made up her mind to steal the doll from them come what might.

Now although the husband made mock of his wife's words at first, she went on telling her story with such a show of reason that in the end she convinced him that it was nought but the truth. But he said to his wife : 'And how do you mean to steal it?' To this the good woman made answer : 'To-night you must feign to be drunk, and, having caught up your sword, you must run after me threatening to take my life, but at the same time only striking the wall. And I, pretending to be in great terror of you, will run out of the house into the street, and the two sisters, who are kindly and compassionate by nature, will assuredly open their door to me, and take me in and shelter me. I will stay there for the night, and will do the best I can for the furtherance of my plan.'

And when the evening had come, the husband of this good dame took a rusty old sword of his, and, laying about with it now against this wall and now against that, ran after his wife, who, screaming and crying with a loud voice, fled out of the house. The two sisters, when they heard this hurlyburly, ran to look out into the street to see what might be the cause thereof, whereupon they recognized the voice of their neighbour, who was screaming lustily. They at once rushed away from the window, and ran down to the door giving on to the street, and having opened this they pulled her into the house. The good woman, when she had been questioned by them for what reason her husband had pursued and assaulted her with such anger, thus made reply: 'This evening he came home so dazed with wine-bibbing that he wots not anything that he does. And only for the reason that I reproved him on account of his drunkenness, he seized his sword and ran after me threatening to kill me; but as I am more nimble and swift of foot than he, I was only too ready to get out of his way, so as to keep him from working some scandalous deed, and here I am in your charge.' When they heard these words both the sisters said: 'You did well, my mother, and you must assuredly bide this night with us, lest you should fall into some fresh danger of your life, and in the meantime your husband's drunken humour will dissipate itself.' And when they had prepared the supper they all sat down together.

Adamantina, when she went to bed, anointed the doll according to her wont, and afterwards at the same hour of the night the doll cried out as before, and Adamantina, when she had attended to its wants, found that a large quantity of money had come from the doll in the same marvellous wise as before. The good woman who had sought refuge with the sisters was mightily astonished at what she saw, and every hour which must pass until she could steal the doll, and work this miracle for her own benefit, seemed a thousand years.

When the morning had come the good woman rose secretly from her bed, leaving the two sisters still sleeping, and stole the doll from Adamantina's side without letting the girl know aught of the theft. Then having aroused the girls she begged leave of them to return to her home, affirming that by this time her husband would doubtlessly have got rid of the fumes of the wine with which he had so inordinately filled himself. Therefore, when she had returned to her home, she said to her husband, with a joyful face: 'My husband, we have at last alighted upon our good fortune, for see, here is the doll I told you about, which can work such wonders.' And one hour seemed a thousand years till the night should come, and she should be able to work the charm that would make her a rich woman. And when the night had fallen the woman took the doll, and, having lighted a good fire in her chamber, she anointed with oil the stomach and loins of the doll, and wrapped it carefully in child's clouts. Then, having taken off her own clothes, she got into bed and placed it by her side.

After the first sleep of the night was over the doll woke up and cried out: 'The stool, madonna, the stool!' (it did not call her mother, inasmuch as it did not know who she was), and the good woman, who was anxiously awaiting the result which was to follow, rose from her bed and attended to the doll as if it had been a young child; but this time it happened that, in lieu of coins of gold and silver, the doll filled the chamber with so offensive a smell that the good woman was fain to get as far away from it as she could. The husband, when he perceived what had happened, said to her: 'See, fool that you are, what a pretty trick this doll has played you, and I myself am just as big a fool for having lent an ear to such crazy trash.' But the wife, waxing angry with her husband on account of these reproaches, affirmed with many an oath that she had seen with her own eyes the vast quantity of money that the doll had given to the two sisters. However, seeing that she was mightily anxious to make a fresh experiment on the following night, the husband, who was in no humour to face again the discomfort he had lately felt, began to abuse her roundly, and launched against her the most opprobrious speeches that ever man applied to woman. Not content with this, he seized the doll in his hand, and having opened the window, he hurled it out into the street, letting it fall upon a heap of sweepings which lay below. Soon after he had done this, it happened that some peasants who tilled the ground outside the city loaded on their cart this heap of refuse, and without knowing what they did loaded up the doll likewise, and when they had filled their cart they returned to the country, and spread the load of sweepings over their fields in order to enrich the soil.

Not many days after this, it chanced that Drusiano the king, who had gone out into the country to seek diversion in the chase, was seized with a sharp pain of his intestines, and forthwith sought relief of the same by the remedy of nature, but not having upon him wherewith to accommodate himself afterwards, he called to him one of his servants and charged him to go search for something which might serve his ends. Whereupon the servant went towards the manure heap which the peasants aforesaid had collected, to see whether he might be able to find anything which would be suitable for the purpose, and, looking now on this side and now on that, his eye fell upon the doll, and having picked it up, he bore it at once to the king, who, without any fear or suspicion, took hold of it and proceeded to apply it to the

use for which he wanted it.   But the next moment the king broke
out into loud cries and bellowings of pain, for the doll had seized upon
his hinder parts with its teeth, and held on thereto with so tight a
grip that he screamed out with agony at the top of his voice.   And
when those of his train heard these terrible cries, they forthwith all
ran towards the king to lend him their aid.   Seeing him lying on the
ground more dead than alive, they were hugely astonished to find
that he was suffering pain on account of the doll which had fastened
on to him, and they began at once with their united strength to try
to disengage it from his hinder parts; but all their strivings were in
vain, for the more violently they tugged to get the thing away, the
greater torment it inflicted on the poor king, and there was not one
of them who could disturb its hold, much less make it let go.   And
now and again the doll would claw him with its sharp fingers so
grievously that he seemed to see all the stars of the firmament,
although it was yet high noon.

When the unfortunate king had returned to his palace with the
doll still hanging on to him, and was still unable to find any means of
getting rid of his plague, he caused to be put forth a proclamation
declaring that any man, no matter what his condition might be, who
should have the wit and courage to remove the doll should be rewarded by a gift of one third part of the king's dominions, and if it
should chance that any maiden might be found able to perform this
work he would take her for his beloved wife.   And in addition to this
King Drusiano swore by his crown, and bound himself by the most
solemn oaths to keep every promise he had made in the proclamation
above named.   As soon as the king's proclamation was made public,
a vast crowd of people repaired to the palace in the hope of obtaining
the promised reward, but to not one of them was granted the good
fortune of being able to rid the king of his trouble; on the contrary,
as soon as anyone chanced to come near the king the doll tormented
him more grievously than ever, so the wretched Drusiano, thus cruelly
vexed and tortured, and unable to light upon any remedy for his
strange and incomprehensible affliction, lay there almost as if he were
a dead man.

Cassandra and Adamantina, who in the meantime had shed many
tears over the loss of their doll, as soon as they heard the terms of
the proclamation which had been issued, went straightway to the
palace and presented themselves before the king.   Then Cassandra,

who was the elder of the two, began at once to fondle and caress
the doll with signs of the greatest affection, but thereupon, so far from
loosening its hold, it only vexed the poor king yet more sorely with
its teeth and claws.   Then Adamantina, who stood somewhat apart
from the others, now came forward and said : 'Gracious king! I
beg you that you will now suffer me to try my fortune in ridding
you of this ill,' and, having gone close to the doll, she spake thus :
' Ah, my child ! leave my lord the king in peace now, and do not torment him any longer.'   And with these words she took hold of it
by its clothes, and began to fondle and caress it.   The doll, as soon
as it recognized its own little mother, who had been in the habit of
tending and caring for it, at once let go its hold on the king's
person and sprang into Adamantina's arms.   And when Drusiano
perceived what was done, he was utterly astonished and amazed, and
forthwith lay down to get some repose, for during many and many
nights and days he had not been able to find either rest or peace on
account of the sharp agony he had undergone.

When King Drusiano was at length healed of the ills that had
befallen him on account of the biting of the doll, in order that he
might not fail in the fulfilment of the promise he had made, he
caused Adamantina to be brought into his presence, and, seeing that
she was a fair and graceful young maiden, he married her in the presence of all his people.   A short time afterwards he honourably
bestowed her elder sister Cassandra in marriage with sumptuous
feastings and triumphs, and they all lived long together in peace and
happiness.

The doll, when it saw how both of the sisters had been so honourably and richly married, and how everything had come to a happy
issue, suddenly disappeared, and whither it went and what became of
it no man ever knew.   But in my opinion it merely disappeared
after the common fashion of phantoms.

The fable told by Alteria, which here came to an end, gave great
pleasure to all the company, and the laughter was loud and long as
they recalled to mind the beneficent ways and habits of the doll, and
in what fashion the thing hung with its teeth and its claws upon the
hinder parts of the king.   And when the laughter had somewhat
abated, the Signora at once gave the word to Alteria to follow the
customary rule and propound her enigma, which the damsel gave in
the following words, smiling pleasantly the while :

Just a span in length is he,
And plump in form in due degree.
Full of eagerness and pride,
And ready aye with men to bide.
Very fair his seeming shows ;
Capote red he wears and hose;
Bells also.   A thing of pleasure
To those who love him in due measure.

As soon as Alteria had spoken the last word of her gracefully
turned and difficult enigma, the Signora, who by this time had put off
her kindly mood and was casting angry looks upon the damsel, cried
out that it was most unseemly to speak such immodest words to the
ears of honest women in her presence, and that for the future she
must be careful not to trespass in like manner.   Whereupon Alteria,
blushing somewhat, rose from her seat, and having turned her bright
face towards the Signora, spake thus : " Signora, of a truth the
enigma which I have just proposed is not in any way immodest as
you seem to believe, and this I shall make quite clear to you by
giving you the real interpretation thereof, which I will straightway
make known to you and to the rest of my gracious hearers.   For be
it understood my enigma signifies nothing else except the falcon,
which is a bird at once tractable and bold, and comes readily to the
falconer's call.   It wears on its feet jesses and bells, and it will give
great pleasure and diversion to anyone who goes out fowling therewith."   When the real interpretation of this clever riddle, which
had been set down by the Signora as being unseemly, had been given,
all the listeners praised it heartily, and the Signora, having by this
time laid aside every sinister imagining she had harboured concerning
Alteria's riddle, turned her face towards Lauretta and made a sign to
her that she should approach her, and the damsel at once came
in obedience to the command.   And because Lauretta stood next in
turn to follow with her fable, the Signora thus addressed her: " It is
my wish that you refrain for a while from telling us your story, and
that you should instead listen to that which the others may say.   It is
not because I hold you in light esteem that I speak thus to you, or
rate your powers less than those of your companions, but in order
that we may be entertained this evening in a fashion that is beyond
our wont."   To this Lauretta made reply : " Signora, any word of
yours is to me as a command," and having made a profound obeisance
to the Signora she went back to her place.

Then the Signora, turning an earnest gaze upon Molino's face, made a sign to him thus with her hand to bid him come to her, whereupon he got up quickly from his seat and went most respectfully towards her. To him she spake in these words: "Signor Antonio, this last evening of the week is for us a special time, a season of privilege for anyone to say whatsoever he may wish to say, so for my own pleasure and for the pleasure of this honourable company, I would that you yourself should relate to us a fable in your best and happiest vein and manner, and I further beg you that you will tell us this story in the speech of Bergamo. And if—as I hope you will—you grant us this favour, we shall all of us be held by a lasting obligation to you." Molino, when he rightly understood the Signora's speech, stood at first as one confounded, but when he realized that he had sailed up to a point he could not weather, he said: "Signora, it is for you to command and for us to obey, but I would warn you not to expect from me aught that shall give you any great pleasure, seeing that the illustrious damsels I see around me have brought the art of story-telling to such a high pitch of excellence that there is little or no chance for one like me to contribute aught to our diversion. Nevertheless, such as I am, I will do my best to give you satisfaction, not, indeed, so great as you wish, or as I would, but according to the measure of my humble powers." And having thus spoken, Molino went back to his seat and began his story in the following words.

THE THIRD FABLE.

Bertholdo of Valsabbia has three sons, all of them hunchbacks and much alike in seeming. One of them, called Zambo, goes out into the world to seek his fortune, and arrives at Rome, where he is killed and thrown into the Tiber, together with his two brothers.[1]

IT is indeed hard, sweet ladies and gracious Signora! hard, indeed, I say it is, to kick against the pricks, for the kick of an ass is a cruel thing; but still more cruel is the kick of a horse, and for this reason, since fortune has willed it that I should undertake to tell a tale, I had best

---

[1] Told in the dialect of Bergamo.

obey; for patience beatifies us, but obstinacy damns us, and, should we prove obstinate, we go straight to the devil. So if it should chance that I tell you something which may prove in no wise to your taste, do not give the blame to me, but to the Signora over yonder who has thus willed it.

It often happens that a man goes a-seeking that which he had better leave alone, and in consequence not seldom lights upon certain things which he never looked to find, and in the end will be left with his hand full of flies.[1] Thus, indeed, it happened some time ago to Zambo, the son of Bertholdo of Valsabbia, who sought to dupe two of his brothers, but by his brothers was himself duped. True it is that in the end they all three died miserably, as you will hear if you will lend me your ears, and with your minds and your understandings listen to the story which I am now about to relate.

I must tell you, therefore, that Bertholdo of Valsabbia, in the province of Bergamo, had three sons, all three hunchbacks, and all resembling each other so closely that it was impossible to tell the one from the other; they might, indeed, have been likened to three shrivelled pumpkins.[2] One of these sons was called Zambo, another Bertaz, and the third Santì; and Zambo, who was the eldest, had not yet attained his sixteenth year. It came one day to Zambo's ears that Bertholdo his father, by reason of the great dearth there was in the parts round about and in all the rest of the land besides, wished to sell for the sake of his family the small property which was his patrimony (in sooth, there were few or none to be found in that country who had any belongings of their own); wherefore Zambo, addressing himself to Bertaz and Santì, his younger brothers, spoke to them as an elder brother in the following words: ' It would surely be a wiser plan, my dear brothers, that our father should retain the little bit of property which we happen to have, so that after his death we may have something whereby to gain a sustenance, and that you should go out into the world and try to earn something upon which we may keep up our house. I, in the meantime, will remain at home with the old man, taking good care of him, and thus we shall have no need to waste our substance, and by such management may be able to tide over the season of scarcity.'

Bertaz and Santì, the younger brothers, who were no less crafty

---

[1] Orig., *e ixi romà co li ma pieni de moschi.*

[2] Orig., *con sarevef à di tre penduletti sgonfi de dre.*

and cunning than Zambo, at once made answer to their brother:
'Zambo, dear brother that you are, you spring a surprise upon us
somewhat suddenly, and question us in such wise that we scarcely
know how to answer you.   Give us thinking time for this one night;
then we will consider the matter, and to-morrow will let you have
our reply.'

The two brothers, Bertaz and Santì, had been brought forth at
one birth, and between these two there was a greater sympathy than
between either of them and Zambo.   And if Zambo were to be
reckoned a rascal of twenty-two carats, Bertaz and Santì were rascals
of twenty-six; for it not seldom happens that, where nature fails,
ingenuity and malice supply the want.

When the following morning had come, Bertaz, by agreement
with Santì his brother, went to find Zambo, and opened discourse
with him in these words: 'Zambo, my dear brother, we have well
thought over and considered the case in which we stand, and, seeing
that you are (as you will not deny) the elder brother, we think it
would be more seemly for you to go first into the world, and that we
who are younger should stop here to look after our father.   And we
would counsel you that if, in the meantime, you should come across
any good fortune for yourself and for us, you should write to us
here, and we would come at once to join you.'   Zambo, who had
hoped to get the better of Bertaz and Santì, was greatly disconcerted
when he heard this answer, and, muttering to himself, he said:
'These two are more cunning and malicious loons than I had
imagined.'   For he had hoped to be rid of his two brothers, and
himself be left master of all their property, trusting that they might
both of them die of hunger by reason of the dearth prevailing in the
land; moreover, their father was not long for this world, and had
already one foot in the grave.   But the issue of this affair proved to
be vastly different from anything Zambo had expected.   When,
therefore, Zambo heard the answer given to him by Bertaz and
Santì, he made a small bundle of the few rags he possessed, and,
having filled a pouch with some bread and cheese and a small flask
of wine, he put on his feet a pair of shoes of red pigskin, and departed thence and went towards Brescia.   But not finding anything
to suit him there, he went on to Verona, where he came across a
master cap-maker, who asked him whether he knew how to make
caps, to which question he answered no; and, seeing that there was

nothing for him to do there, he left Verona, and, having passed
through Vicenza, he came to Padua, where certain doctors saw him
and asked him whether he knew how to take care of mules, and he
answered them no, but that he could till the land and tend vines; but,
as he could not come to any understanding with them, he went on his
way to Venice.

Zambo had wandered about the city for a long time without
lighting on any employ to his taste, and, seeing that he had about
him neither a coin, nor anything to eat, he felt that he was indeed
in evil case. But after he had walked a long distance, he was
brought by God's pleasure to the port, but because he was penniless
no one would assist him. Wherefore the poor fellow knew not which
way he should turn, but having remarked that the ragged wastrels
who turned the machines for drawing boats ashore gained a few pence
by this labour, he took up this calling himself. But Fortune, who
always persecutes the poor, the slothful, and the wretched, willed that
one day when he was working one of these machines the leather strap
should break. This in untwining caught a spar, which hit him in the
chest and felled him to the ground, where for a time he lay as one
lifeless. Indeed, had it not been for the timely aid given to him by some
kind-hearted fellows, who haled him into their boat by his legs and
arms and rowed him back to Venice, he assuredly would have died.

When Zambo had recovered from the ill effects of this mischance
he went in search of someone who might give him employment, and
as he passed by a grocer's shop he was remarked by the master thereof,
who was pounding in a mortar almonds wherewith to make marzapan.
Whereupon the grocer asked him whether he was minded to come
and serve in the shop, and Zambo replied that he was; so, having
entered, he was at once set to work by the grocer at dressing certain
comfits, and instructed how to separate the black from the white,
working the while beside another apprentice. This fellow and Zambo
(greedy gluttons, forsooth), in the course of their task of comfit
dressing, set to work in such a manner that they stripped off and
used the outer rind of the sweet almonds and ate the kernels themselves. The grocer, when he saw what was going on, took a stick in
his hand and gave each of them a sound beating, saying: 'If you
are set on plunder, you thievish knaves, I would that you pilfered
your own stores and not mine,' and having thus spoken he belaboured
them still more and bade them go to the devil.

Zambo, smarting from the blows dealt him by the grocer, took his departure and went to St. Mark's Place, and as he passed by the spot where herbs and vegetables are set out for sale, he met by good luck a herbalist from Chiozza, Vivia Vianel by name, who straight-way demanded of him whether he would be willing to enter his service, where he would get good food and good treatment as well. Zambo, who at this time wore the armorial bearings of Siena[1] on his back, and was longing for a good meal, replied that he was ; so, when Vianel had sold his few last bunches of herbs, they took a boat and returned to Chiozza, where Zambo was at once set to work in the garden and bidden to tend the vines.

Now Zambo, after he had gone up and down in Chiozza for a certain time, became acquainted with divers of his master's friends, and when the season for the first ripe figs had come, Vivia took the three finest he could pluck from his garden, and, having put them on a platter, sent them as a present to a friend of his in Chiozza whose name was Peder. He called Zambo and gave him the three figs, and said to him : ' Zambo, take these three figs and carry them to my friend Ser Peder, and ask him to accept them for love of me.' Zambo in obedience to Vivia's command replied : 'With pleasure, my master,' and taking the figs he merrily went his way. But it chanced by ill luck that as Zambo was going along the street a greedy humour took possession of him, and having looked at the figs over and over again he thus addressed gluttony : ' What shall I do ? shall I eat or shall I refrain?' To this gluttony replied : 'A starving man observes no law ; wherefore eat.' And for the reason that Zambo was greedy by nature and very hungry to boot, he listened to these counsels of gluttony, and having taken in his hands one of the figs, he began to rend the skin from the neck thereof. Then he took a bite here and a bite there, saying the while, ' It is good ; it is not good ; ' and so he went on till he had consumed it all in tasting, and nought but the skin remained.

When Zambo had eaten the fig he began to wonder whether, perchance, he might not have transgressed somewhat, but for the reason that gluttony still urged him on, he did not stand long in balancing chances, but took the second fig in his hand and treated it as he had treated the first. After the greedy fellow had made an end of the second fig he was again assailed by fears, and hardly knew

[1] *i.e.*, a famished wolf.

whether, on account of his fault, he should go on or turn back; but after a short term of indecision he took courage and determined to go on. As soon as he had come to Ser Peder's door he knocked thereat, and as he was well known there the door was quickly opened. Having entered he went to find Ser Peder, who was walking up and down, and when he saw him the good man thus addressed him: 'What has Zambo come to tell me? What good news does he bring?' 'Good morrow, good morrow,' answered Zambo; 'my master gave me three figs to bring to you, but of these three I have eaten two.' 'But how could you do such a thing as this?' said Ser Peder. 'I did it in this fashion,' said Zambo, and with these words he took the last fig and ate it deliberately, and so it fell out that all three of the figs found their way into Zambo's belly. When Ser Peder saw this saucy jest he said to Zambo: 'My son, tell your master that I thank him, but that in future he need not trouble himself to send me presents of this sort.' Zambo answered, 'No, no, Messer Peder, say not so, for I shall never weary of such errands,' and with these words he left Messer Peder and went home.

When the report of Zambo's smart trick came to Vivia's ears, and when he learned furthermore how finely lazy he was and a glutton as well, guzzling when he was hungry till he was ready to burst, and how he would never work save when he was driven thereto, the good man chased the hunchback out of his house. So Zambo, poor devil, when he found himself driven out of his employ, knew not whither to turn; thus after a little he determined to go to Rome in the hope that he might there find better fortune than he had hitherto come across, and this plan of his he duly carried out.

Zambo, when he had arrived in Rome, went about seeking here and there a master, and at last met a certain merchant who was called Messer Ambros dal Mul, who kept a great shop full of cloth goods. With him Zambo took service, and was set to mind the shop, and seeing that he had suffered much in the past, he made up his mind to learn the trade and to live a decent life for the future. Though he was deformed and ugly, he was nevertheless very shrewd, and in a short time he made himself so useful in the shop that his master seemed to take no more trouble himself about buying or selling, but trusted everything to him and made use of him for service of all kinds. Now it chanced that one day Messer Ambros had occasion to go to the fair of Recanati with a stock of cloth, but perceiving that

Zambo had made himself so competent in the business and had proved himself worthy of trust, he determined to send Zambo to the fair, and bide at home himself and mind the shop.

After Zambo's departure it happened by ill fortune that Messer Ambros was seized with so grave and insidious an illness that after the lapse of a few days he died. When his wife, who was called Madonna Felicetta, found that she was a widow, she wellnigh died herself, of grief[1] for the loss of her husband, and of anxiety on account of the breaking up of her business. As soon as Zambo heard of the sad news of his master's death, he returned straightway and bore himself as a godly youth should, and diligently went about the affairs of the shop. Madonna Felicetta, as time went on, remarked that Zambo behaved himself well and uprightly, and was diligent over the business. She considered, likewise, that a year had now rolled away since the death of Messer Ambros her husband, and, as she feared to lose Zambo some day, together with divers of the customers of her shop, she took counsel with some of her gossips whether she should marry or not, and in case she should resolve to marry, whether it would be well for her to take for a husband Zambo the factor of her business, who had been for a long time in the service of her first husband, and had gathered much experience in the conduct of her affairs. These worthy gossips deeming her proposition a wise one, counselled her to marry Zambo; and between the word and the deed but little time[2] intervened, for the nuptials were celebrated at once, and Madonna Felicetta became the wife of Ser Zambo and Ser Zambo the husband of Madonna Felicetta.

When Ser Zambo perceived himself raised to this high estate, how he had a wife of his own and a fine shop well stocked with all manner of cloth goods, he wrote to his father, telling him he was now in Rome, and of the great stroke of luck which had befallen him. The father, who since the day of Zambo's departure had heard no tidings of his son, nor had ever received a written word from him, now gave up the ghost from sheer joy, but Bertaz and Santì were mightily pleased and consoled with the news.

One day it chanced that Madonna Felicetta found herself in need of a new pair of stockings, because the ones she wore were rent and torn, wherefore she said to Ser Zambo her husband that he must have

---

[1] Orig., *anch ella no tira le calzi.*
[2] Orig., *e dal dichg al fahg se fe le nozzi.*

made for her another pair. To this Zambo replied that he had other
business to do, and that if her stockings were torn, she had better go
and mend them and patch them and put new heels thereto. Madonna
Felicetta, who had been greatly pampered by her late husband, replied
that it had never been her wont to go shod in hose which had been
mended and heeled, and that she must have a new pair. Then
answered Ser Zambo that in his country customs were different, and
that she must do without. Thus the bout of wrangling began, and,
flying from one angry word to another, it came to pass in the end
that Ser Zambo lifted his hand and cuffed her over the head so heavily
that she fell to the ground.[1] Madonna Felicetta, planning the while
how she might give back these blows of Ser Zambo, was little disposed
to come to terms with him or to pacify him in any way, so she began
to hurl foul words at him. Ser Zambo, feeling that his honour was
impugned thereby, belaboured her so soundly with his fists that the
poor woman was constrained to hold her peace.

When the summer had passed, and the cold weather had set in,
Madonna Felicetta asked Ser Zambo to let her have a silken lining
wherewith to repair her pelisse, which was in very bad condition, and
in order that he might be assured that she spoke the truth she brought
it to him to see; but Ser Zambo did not trouble to cast his eye over
it, but simply said that she must mend it and wear it as it was, for
that in his country people were not used to so much pomp. Madonna
Felicetta, when she heard these words, was mightily wroth, and affirmed
that she must have granted to her what she asked at any cost. Ser
Zambo, however, answered that she must hold her peace and be
careful not to arouse his anger, otherwise it would be the worse for
her. But Madonna Felicetta went on insisting that she must have it,
and they one and the other worked themselves up into such a fury
that they were well nigh blinded with rage. Whereupon Ser Zambo,
according to his wont, began to thump her with his stick, and gave
her as shrewd a jacketing of blows as she could bear, and she lay half
dead.[2] When Madonna Felicetta saw how hugely Zambo's humour
towards herself had changed, she began to blaspheme and to curse the
day and the hour when she had first spoken to him, nor did she forget
those who had advised her to take him for a husband. ' Is this the way

---

[1] Orig., *una mostazzada si fatta in sol mostaz, che la fe andà d'inturem.*

[2] Orig., *e fag una pellizza de tanti bastonadi, quanti la ne pos mai portà, e la lassà
quasi per morta.*

you treat me,' she cried, 'you poltroon, you ungrateful rascal, hangman, Goth, and villainous scoundrel ? Is this the reward you return to me for the many benefits you have received ? for, from the base hireling you formerly were, have I not made you the master not only of my wealth but of my person as well ? And yet you deal with me in this wise Hold your peace, traitor, for I will make you pay smartly for this.' Ser Zambo, hearing how his wife waxed more and more wroth, and poured out her abuse of him more copiously than ever, made farther shrewd play upon her back with his cudgel to give her a finishing touch, whereupon Madonna Felicetta was reduced to such a state of fear, that when she heard the sound of Zambo's voice or footstep, she trembled like a leaf in the wind, and became all wet with terror.

When the winter had passed and the summer was coming on, it chanced that Ser Zambo had need to go to Bologna on account of business, and to collect certain sums of money due to him. As this journey would occupy some days, he said to Madonna Felicetta : 'Wife, I would have you know that I have two brothers, who are both hunchbacks as I am myself, and so closely do we all resemble one another that if anyone should see us all three together he would never know which was which. Now I bid you watch well lest they come here and attempt to lodge with us. See that you do not let them come over the threshold on any account, for they are wicked, deceitful, and crafty knaves, and would assuredly play you some evil trick. Then they would go to the devil and leave you with your hands full of flies.[1] If I should learn that you have harboured them in this house I will make you the most wretched woman in the world.' And having said these words he departed.

A few days after Zambo's departure the brothers Bertaz and Santì arrived, and went about asking for Ser Zambo's shop, which was pointed out to them. When the two rascals saw the fine shop, furnished richly with all manner of cloth goods, they were astounded, and marvelled amain how it was that he could have gathered together all this wealth in so short a time. And, lost in wonderment, they went to the shop and said they desired to have speech with Ser Zambo, but were told that he was gone into the country ; if, however, they had need of aught they could ask for it. Whereupon Bertaz said they much wished to speak with him, but as he was not at home they

---

[1] Orig., *che ti remagnis con le ma pieni de meschi.*

would speak with his wife, so they bade the servant call Madonna
Felicetta, and when she came into the shop she knew at once that the
men before her were her brothers-in-law.   Bertaz, when he saw her,
straightway inquired of her, 'Madonna, are you the wife of Zambo?'
And she made answer that she was.   Then said Bertaz: 'Madonna,
shake hands, for we are the brothers of your husband, and therefore
your brothers-in-law.'   Madonna Felicetta, who well remembered the
words of Ser Zambo as well as the belabouring he had given her, refused to touch their hands, but they went on plying her with so many
affectionate words and gestures that in the end she shook hands with
them.   As soon as she had thus greeted them, Bertaz cried out:
'Oh, my dear sister-in-law! give us somewhat to eat, for we are half
famished.'   But this she refused to do.   The rogues, however, knew
so well how to use the trick of flattery, and begged so persistently,
that Madonna Felicetta was moved to pity, and took them into the
house and gave them food and drink in plenty, and even allowed them
to sleep in a certain corner.   Scarcely had three days passed since Bertaz
and Santi had come to Madonna Felicetta's house when Ser Zambo returned.   His wife, as soon as she heard of this, was almost beside herself
with terror, and she hardly knew what to do so as to keep the brothers
out of Ser Zambo's sight, and as she could hit upon no better plan she
made them go into the kitchen, where was a trough in which they were
accustomed to scald pigs, and in this she bade them conceal themselves.

When Ser Zambo entered the house and marked how dishevelled
and worried his wife seemed to be, he was mightily upset in his mind
and said: 'Why do you look so frightened?   What ails you?   I
suppose there is no gallant hidden anywhere in the house?'   But she
replied in a faint voice that there was nought the matter with her.
Ser Zambo, who was regarding her sharply the while, said: 'Certes,
there is something the matter with you.   Are those brothers of mine
by any chance in the house?'   But she answered boldly that they
were not; whereupon he began to give her a taste of the stick, according to his custom.   Bertaz and Santi, who were under the pig-
trough, could hear all the hurlyburly, and, so terrified were they,
that they wet their breeches like children in a fright, and did not
venture to move.   Ser Zambo, when he at last put down his stick,
began to search the house in every corner to see whether he could
find anyone hidden, but finding nought he calmed himself somewhat
and went about the ordering of certain of his affairs, and so long was

he occupied thereanent (thus keeping his luckless brothers in their hiding-place) that Bertaz and Santi, either through fear, or through the great heat, or on account of the foul stench of the pig-trough, straightway gave up the ghost.

When the hour had come at which Ser Zambo was wont to repair to the piazza, there to transact business with the other merchants, he went out of the house, and as soon as he had taken his departure Madonna Felicetta went to the pig-trough to devise some scheme for getting rid of her brothers-in-law, so that Ser Zambo might have no suspicion that she had given them shelter. But when she uncovered the trough she found them lying there both stark dead, and looking exactly like two pigs. The poor woman, when she saw what had happened, fell into a terrible taking of grief and despair, and, in order that her husband might be kept altogether in ignorance of what had occurred, she spent all her force in trying to throw them out of the house, so that the mishap might be hidden from Ser Zambo, and from all the rest of the city as well.

I have heard people say that in Rome there is a certain custom according to which, should the dead body of any stranger or pilgrim be found in the public streets or in any man's house, it is straightway taken up by certain scavengers [1] appointed for this purpose and carried by them outside the walls of the city and then cast into the Tiber, so that of such unfortunates nothing more is ever heard or seen. Now Madonna Felicetta, having gone to look out of the window to see whether by chance any friends of hers might be passing by who would lend aid in getting rid of the two dead bodies, by good luck espied one of these corpse-bearers, and called to him to come in, telling him that she had a corpse in the house, and that she wanted him to take it away at once and cast it into the Tiber, according to the custom of the place. Already Madonna Felicetta had pulled out one of the corpses from under the cover of the trough, and had left it lying on the floor near thereto; so, when the corpse-bearer had come upstairs, she helped him to load the dead body on his shoulders, and bade him come back to the house after he had thrown it into the river, when she would pay him for his services. Whereupon the corpse-bearer went outside the city wall and threw the body into the Tiber, and, having done his work, he returned to Madonna Felicetta

---

[1] Orig., *picegamort.*

and asked her to give him a florin, which was the customary guerdon.
But while the corpse-bearer was engaged in carrying off the first body,
Madonna Felicetta, who was a crafty dame, drew out from the trough
the other body and disposed it at the foot of the trough in exactly the
same place where the first had lain, and when the corpse-bearer came
back to Madonna Felicetta for his payment, she said to him : 'Did
you indeed carry the corpse I gave you to the Tiber?' And to this
the fellow replied, 'I did, madonna.' 'Did you throw it into the
river?' said the dame ; and he answered : 'Did I throw it in? indeed
I did, and in my best manner.' At this speech Madonna Felicetta
said : 'How could you have thrown it in, as you say you have?
Just look and see whether it be not still here.' And when the corpse-
bearer saw the second dead body, he really thought it must be the one
he had carried away, and was covered with dismay and confusion ;
and, cursing and swearing the while, he hoisted it upon his shoulders,
and, having carried it off, he cast it into the Tiber, and stood for a
while to watch it as it floated down the stream.[1] And whilst he was
once more returning to Madonna Felicetta's house to receive his payment, it chanced that he met Ser Zambo, who was on his way home,
and when the corpse-bearer espied the man who bore so strong a
likeness to the two other hunchbacks whom he had carried to the
Tiber, he flew into such a violent fit of rage that he seemed, as it
were, to spit forth fire and flames on all sides and gave a free rein to
his passion. For in truth he deemed the fellow before him to be no
other than the one whom he had already twice cast into the river, and
that he must be some evil spirit who was returning to his own place ;
so he stole softly behind Ser Zambo and dealt him a grievous blow on
the head with an iron winch which he carried in his hand, saying :
'Ah! you cowardly, villainous loon, do you think that I want to spend
the rest of my days in haling you to the river?' and as he thus railed
he mishandled him so violently that poor Zambo, on account of the
cudgelling he got, was soon a dead man and went to talk to Pilate.[2]

When the corpse-bearer had got upon his shoulders the third
corpse, which was still warm, he bore it away and threw it into the
Tiber after the two others, and thus Zambo and Bertaz and Santi
miserably ended their lives. Madonna Felicetta, when she heard the
news of this, was greatly delighted thereat, and felt no small content

---

[1] Orig., *anda a segonda.*   [2] Orig., *se n'anda a parla a Pilat.*

that she was freed from all her hardships and might again enjoy her former liberty.

Molino's fable here came to an end. It had pleased the ladies so mightily that they could not forbear from laughing thereat and talking it over. And although the Signora more than once bade them be silent, she found it no easy matter to put an end to their merry laughter. At last, in order to bring the company once more into a sedater mood, she commanded Molino to set them to guess an enigma in the same dialect, and he, ever ready to obey her, gave his riddle in the following words:

> Out of their prison grave so dark
> Arise the bones of dead men stark,
> And 'twixt the hours of tierce and sext,
> By signs will tell to mortals vext
> What chance's smiles or frowns of fate
> May bless or ban till time grows late.
> Savage and deep the misers curse,
> Marking the signs of chance averse;
> But he, untouched by lust of gold,
> Unmoved will fortune's freaks behold.
> Next one with beard of flesh upsprings,
> And beak of bone, and warning sings
> To bid the watchers bury deep
> Their bodies in a downy sleep,
> And lie, poor fools by care unstirred,
> On welcome boon of foolish bird.

Though Molino's fable forsooth pleased the company much, this ingenious but somewhat gruesome enigma diverted them yet more; but forasmuch as no one had gathered any inkling of its meaning, the ladies with one voice begged him earnestly that he should give the solution thereof in the same dialect he had used in his narration. Molino, when he perceived that this was the general wish of the company, in order that he might not appear to be niggard of his gifts, solved the enigma in the following terms: " My enigma, dear ladies, signifies the game of hazard, and the bones of the dead which leave their graves are the dice which fall out of the dice-box, and when they mark tray, deuce, and ace, these are the points which show good luck, and will not such points as these put spirit into the play and money into the purse of the man who often wins the throw thereby? Does the loser ever like to go away a loser, and does not all this come by the change and variations of fortune? The avaricious

player who always seeks to win will now and again curse and swear
so fiercely that I cannot think why the earth does not open and
swallow him up.   And, at such times as the game goes on all through
the night, the cock, who has a beard of flesh and a beak of bone, will
get up and crow 'Cock-a-doodle-do,' thus letting the gamesters know
that it is past midnight and they ought to repair to their beds of goose
down.   When they lie in these is it not like sinking into a deep grave?
Are you all content with this my explanation?"

The explanation of this subtle enigma was received by the whole
company with great laughter; so hearty was it in sooth that they
could scarce forbear from rolling about on their seats.   And after the
Signora had commanded everyone to keep silent, she turned towards
Molino and said : " Signor Antonio, as the fair orb of Dian outshines
all other stars, so the fable just told to us by you, together with your
enigma, bears off the palm from all others which we have hitherto
heard."   Molino answered : " The praise you give me, Signora, cannot
surely be due on account of my skill; it comes rather from the great
courtesy which always abides in you.   But if it should happen that the
Trevisan were willing to tell you a story in the dialect of his country,
I am sure you would listen to this with still greater pleasure."   The
Signora, who desired greatly to hear a story told in this fashion, said :
" Signor Benedetto, do you hear what our Molino says?   Certainly
you would do him a great wrong were you to make false these words
of his.   Put, therefore, your hand in your pouch and draw therefrom
some peasant story to enliven us all."   The Trevisan, to whom it
appeared unseemly that he should occupy the place of Arianna, whose
turn came next, at first excused himself, but seeing that he could not
weather [1] this point, began his fable in the following words.

[1] Orig., *schiffare tal scoglio.*

THE FOURTH FABLE.

Marsilio Vercelese, being enamoured of Thia, the wife of Cechato Rabboso, is taken by her into her house during her husband's absence. He having come back unexpected, is cozened by Thia, who feigns to work a spell, during which Marsilio silently takes to flight.[1]

IN good sooth, what more would you have, my lady mistress and fair damsels all? Has not Messer Antonio acquitted himself well? Has he not told you an excellent story? But, by the blood of a dog, I will do my best to match him, and to gather the best credit I may.

We villagers have always heard tell, that amongst gentlemen of the world, one man will manage his affairs in this way, and another in that. But I, who am an ignorant loon, and who know nothing of letters, tell you what I have always heard said by our elders, namely, that he who dances badly raises the loudest laugh;[2] so if you will have patience, I will do my best to amuse you. But do not think that I say these words because I wish to escape the trouble of telling you a tale, for I am not in the least fearful on this score. And, over and beyond this, I would have you understand that the story which Messer Antonio has told you, with so good a grace that it would be hard to beat, has fired me with so much courage that now, when I see I am indeed launched on my task, it seems to me a thousand years until I shall be able to begin. Perhaps indeed this fable of mine will be no less pleasing and laughable than Messer Antonio's, especially as I purpose to tell you of the ingenuity of a peasant woman who played a trick upon her fool of a husband; wherefore, if you will listen to me and give me your kind attention, I will tell it to you as well as I can.

Above the domain of Piove de Sacco, which is, as I need hardly tell you, a territory of Padua, seeing that this must be well known to all of you, is situated a village called Salmazza, wherein there lived, a very long time since, a peasant called Cechato Rabboso, who, although he was a fellow with a big head and body, was nevertheless

---

[1] Told in the dialect of Treviso.   [2] Orig., *chi mal balla, ben solazza.*

a poor fool and over-trustful of his own powers.   This Cechato
Rabboso had to wife the daughter of a farmer called Gagiardi, who
lived in a village called Campelongo, and she was a wily, crafty, and
mischievous young woman, called by the name of Thia.   Besides
being so shrewd, she was in her person a stout wench and handsome
of face, so that it was commonly said there was not another peasant
woman for miles round who could be compared with her.   And
because she was so sprightly and nimble at country dances, the young
gallants who saw her would not seldom lose their hearts to her straightway.   Now it happened that a certain young man, who was himself
handsome and of a sturdy figure, a prosperous citizen of Padua, by
name Marsilio Vercelese, became enamoured of this Thia, and so
ardently was he consumed by the flame of his love that whenever she
went to a village dance this youth would be sure to follow her thither,
and for the greater part of the time he would dance with her, devoting
himself entirely to her and never dancing with any other woman.
But although this young gallant was so fiercely enamoured of her, he
kept his love a secret as well as he could, so as not to let it be known
to anybody, nor to become a matter of common gossip to all the
neighbours round about.

Marsilio, knowing quite well that Cechato, Thia's husband, was a
poor man, supporting his house by the work of his hands, and from
the early morning till late at night labouring hard, now at this,
now at that work, began to prowl about Thia's house, and, by constantly plying her with soft glances, he soon found an opportunity
of addressing her.   Now, although Marsilio had determined in his
mind to disclose the love which he bore her, still he doubted whether
she might not be angered and refuse to see him again in case he should
declare his passion, for it did not seem to him that she looked upon
him so kindly as he deserved, seeing how great was the love he had
for her.   And, besides this, he was afraid of being discovered by some
malicious person who would caution Cechato her husband, who on
this account might very likely do him some evil turn; for Cechato,
although he was such a numskull, was sharp enough to be jealous.

Marsilio, therefore, spent his days in assiduously haunting the
house where Thia lived, and he would gaze at her so long and so in-
tently that at last she could not fail to be aware that he was enamoured
of her.   But, for certain reasons best known to herself, she forbore to
look favourably upon him, or show that she was in any way inclined

to return his passion, and although she was in her secret mind quite willing to meet his wishes, she feigned to be indifferent to him, and turned her back upon him.

One day it chanced that Thia was sitting all alone on a wooden bench placed near the outer door of the house, and holding under her arm the distaff on which some flax was wound—she was, indeed, busy doing some spinning for her landlady—when Marsilio, who had taken a little heart of grace, came forward and said to her: 'God be with you, my friend Thia!' And Thia answered: 'Welcome, young gentleman!' 'How is it that you do not know,' said Marsilio, 'that I am consumed of love for you, and am like to die, and you on your part make no account of it, and care not in the least about my cruel sufferings?' To this Thia answered: 'How should I know whether you love me or not?' Said Marsilio: 'If you never knew it before, I will now let you know that such is my case, for I am consumed with all the grief and passion that a man can feel.' And Thia answered him: 'Well, of a surety you have let me know it now.' Then Marsilio said, 'And you? Ah, tell me the truth, by the faith you have! Do you love me too?' Thia, with a smile, answered, 'Perhaps I love you a little.' Then said Marsilio, 'Heaven help you, tell me how much?' 'I love you very much,' answered Thia. Then Marsilio cried, 'Alas, Thia! if you really loved me as much as you say, you would show it to me by some sign, but I cannot believe that you love me at all.' Thia answered, 'Well, and what sign would you have me give you?' 'Oh, Thia!' said Marsilio, 'you know very well what is in my mind without my telling you.' 'No, I cannot possibly know it unless you tell me,' said Thia. Then Marsilio replied, 'I will tell you if you will listen to me, and not be angered.' Thia then answered, 'Say on, sir, for I promise you on my soul that, if it is a good thing and not against my honour, I will not be angered with you.' Then Marsilio said, 'Then, my love, when will you give me the chance of holding you in my arms in lover's fashion?' 'I now see clearly enough,' said Thia, 'that you are only deceiving me, and making a mock of me. How can I be fitted for you, who are a gentleman and a citizen of Padua, whilst I am a peasant of the village? You are rich, and I am poor; you are a signor, and I am a working woman; you can have fine ladies to your taste, and I am of low condition. You are wont to walk gaily with your embroidered surcoat, and your bright-coloured hose, all worked with wool and silk, and I, as you see, have nought but a dimity petticoat, old, torn, and mended. I have nothing better when I go to dances than this old garment and this linen head-cloth. You eat wheaten loaves, and I rye-bread and beans and polenta, and even then I have often not enough to satisfy my hunger. I have no pelisse for the cold winter, poor wretch that I am! nor do I know which way to turn to get one, for I have neither money nor goods to sell that will enable me to buy the few necessaries that I want. We have not enough corn to eat to keep us alive till Easter, and I know not what we shall do during the great dearth. And besides all this, there are the forced dues that we have to pay to Padua every day. Oh, we poor peasants! what pleasure have we in life? We toil hard to till the earth and to sow our wheat, which you fine folk consume, whilst we poor people have to make the best shift we can with rye-bread. We tend the vines and make the wine, of which you drink the best, and we have to be satisfied with wine lees or water.'

In answer to Thia's speech Marsilio said: ' Do not distress yourself on account of this, for if you will grant me the favour I desire I will see that you want for nothing that can give you delight.' Thia replied : ' Ah! this is what you cavaliers always say until we have done your pleasure; then you go away and we never see any more of you, and, fools as we are, are left in the lurch, deceived and duped and shamed in the world's esteem. You, meantime, go your ways, bragging of your good fortune and washing out your mouths, as far as concerns us and all that belongs to us,[1] treating us as if we were carrion only fit to be cast out on the dunghill. I know full well the tricks you worthy citizens of Padua can play.' Then said Marsilio : ' Enough, now let us have done with words for good and all. I ask you once more whether you will grant me the favour I desire ?' ' Go away, for the love of God, I pray you,' cried Thia, ' before my husband comes back, for nightfall is drawing near and he will certainly be here in a few minutes. Come back some time to-morrow, and we will talk as long as you will, for in sooth I love you well.' But Marsilio, who was indeed passionately in love with her, was loath to leave off this pleasant conversation, and still remained by her side; so she said once more, ' Go away immediately, I beg you, and do not stay here any longer.' When Marsilio saw that Thia was thus strongly moved, he cried out, ' God be with you, Thia, my sweet soul! I recommend

---

[1] Orig., *V'ande laldando, e lavando la bocca di fatti nuostri.*

my heart to you, for it is surely in your keeping.' ' May God go with you, dearest hope of my life!' said Thia, 'I commend you to His care.' ' By His good help,' said Marsilio, 'we will meet again to-morrow.' ' Very well, let it be so,' said Thia; and with these words Marsilio took his leave.

When the morrow had come Marsilio, to whom the time until he should once more repair to Thia's house seemed a thousand years, went thither forthwith and found her busy in the garden digging and mulching round about certain vines which grew therein, and as soon as they saw one another they exchanged greetings and began to talk lovingly together. And when this conversation had gone on for some time Thia said to Marsilio: ' Dear heart of mine, to-morrow morning early Cechato my husband will have occasion to go to the mill, and he will not return hither until the next day; wherefore, if it should be your pleasure, you may come here late in the evening. I will be on the watch for you; only be sure that you come without fail, and do not deceive me.' When Marsilio heard this good news, there was no man in all the world so happy as he was; he jumped and danced about for very gladness, and took leave of Thia, half out of his wits for joy.

As soon as Cechato had come home, the crafty Thia went up to him and said, ' Cechato, my good man, you must needs go to the mill straightway, for we have nothing more in the house to eat.' ' Very well, very well, I will see about it,' answered Cechato. 'I tell you that you must go to-morrow, whatever happens,' said Thia. ' Very well, then,' replied Cechato, ' to-morrow morning before I go I will borrow a cart with two oxen from the people for whom I work, then I will come back to load it, and go off to the mill at once.'

In the meantime Thia went to prepare the corn and to put it into sacks, so that on the morrow Cechato should have nothing to do but to load his cart therewith, and to go on his way singing. On the following morning Cechato took the corn which his wife had put into sacks the night before, and loaded it on the cart and went on his way towards the mill. And seeing that it was now the season of short days and long nights, and that the roads were broken up and in bad condition, and that the weather was foul with rain and ice and intense cold, poor Cechato found himself obliged to remain that night at the mill, and this in sooth fell in most opportunely with the plans that Thia and Marsilio had devised for their own satisfaction.

As soon as the dark night had fallen, Marsilio, according to the agreement he had made with Thia, took a pair of fine well-cooked capons and some white bread and wine unspoilt by any drop of water therein, all of which he had carefully prepared before he left his home, and stole secretly across the fields to Thia's house. Then, having opened the door, he found her sitting by the fireside winding thread. After greeting one another they spread the table and both sat down to eat, and after they had made an excellent meal off Marsilio's good cheer, they went to lie down in the bed; thus, whilst that poor fool of a Cechato was having his corn ground at the mill, in his bed at home Marsilio was sifting flour.

When the time of sunrise was near, and the day was beginning to break, the two lovers awoke and rose from their bed, fearing lest Cechato might return and find them there together; but while they were still amorously talking, Cechato drew near to the house, whistling aloud the while, and calling upon Thia, saying: 'Oh, my Thia! make up a good fire, I pray you, for I am more than half dead with cold.' Thia, who was a clever, artful minx, was somewhat frightened when she heard her husband's voice, and feared amain lest some evil should befall Marsilio, and injury and shame be put upon herself; so she quickly opened the door, managing the while to allow Marsilio to hide himself behind it; then with a merry face she ran to meet her husband, and began to embrace him. And after Cechato had come into the courtyard, he cried out once more to his wife: 'Make a fire at once, good Thia, for I am wellnigh frozen to death. By the blood of St. Quintin, I was almost starved to death by cold last night up at that mill; so cold was it, indeed, that I was not able to sleep a wink, or even to close an eye.' Whereupon Thia went without delay to the wood-house, and having taken therefrom a good armful of billets she lighted a fire whereat Cechato might warm himself, herself occupying craftily that spot by the hearth from whence Marsilio might perchance be seen by Cechato.

Then Thia, chatting with her husband of this and of that, said: 'Ah! Cechato, my good man, I have a fine bit of news to give you.' 'What has happened?' inquired Cechato. To this Thia replied, 'Whilst you were away at the mill a poor old man came to the house begging alms of me for the love of God, and as a recompense for some bread I gave him to eat and a small cup of wine, he taught me an incantation wherewith to throw a spell over that greedy kite which often comes hereabouts, and never in my life have I heard anything more beautiful than his words, which I have learnt well by heart.' 'What is this thing you are telling me?' said Cechato; 'is it really the truth?' Thia replied, 'It is true, by my faith, and I can tell you that I set great store by it.' 'Then tell it to me at once,' said Cechato, 'and do not hold me longer in suspense.' Whereupon Thia said to her husband, 'You must lie down flat on the ground stretched out your full length, just as if you were dead (which thing may God avert!), and having done this you must turn your head and your shoulders towards the door, and your knees and feet towards the stove, and then I must spread a white cloth over your face, and put our corn measure over your head.'

'But I am quite sure,' said Cechato, 'that my head will never go into our corn measure.' 'I am sure it will,' replied Thia; 'just look here!' And with these words she took the measure, which happened to be close at hand, and put it over his head, saying, 'Nothing in God's world could be a better fit than this. And now you must keep yourself quite still, neither moving a limb nor saying a word, otherwise we shall be able to do nothing. Then I will take our tamis sieve in my hand, and will begin to jump and dance around you, and whilst I am thus dancing I will speak the incantation which the old man taught me. And in this fashion the spell may be well and truly worked. But again I tell you that you must on no account stir a finger until I shall have repeated the incantation thrice, for it must be said three times over you in order that it may have any effect. After this we shall see whether the kite gives us any more trouble, or comes to steal our chicken.' To this Cechato replied: 'Would to God that what you say might be true, so that we might have a little rest and breathing space. You know well enough how hard we find it to bring up any chicken at all, on account of that fiend of a kite which devours every one we hatch. Never have we been able to rear enough chicken to sell, and with the money gained thereby to pay our landlord and the tax-gatherer, and to buy oil and salt and any other stores we may want for housekeeping.'

'Let us begin quickly then,' said Thia, 'for in this fashion we shall be able to do ourselves a good turn. Now, Cechato, lie down quickly.' And Cechato straightway laid himself down on the floor. 'Now stretch yourself out well to your full length,' said Thia. And Cechato at once did his best to stretch himself out as far as ever he could. 'That is right,' said Thia, and hereupon she took a cloth of thick white linen and shrouded his face therewith. Next she took the corn measure and rammed it down on his head, and then caught up the tamis sieve and began to dance and skip around him and to repeat in the following wise the incantation which she said had been taught her by the old beggar:

> Thievish bird, I charge you well,
> Hearken to my mystic spell.
> While I dance and wave my sieve,
> All my tender chicks shall live.
> Not a bird from all my hatch,
> Thievish rascal, shall you snatch.
> Wolf nor rat his prey shall seek,
> Nor bird with sharp and crooked beak.
> Thieves who stand behind the door,
> Hearken, fly, and come no more.
> If my speech you cannot read,
> Surely you are fools indeed.

When Thia had come to the end of her mummery she still went on dancing round Cechato, keeping her eyes fixed upon the outer door the while, and making signs to Marsilio, who was there concealed, that he had better run away at once. But Marsilio, who was neither nimble-minded nor quick to catch her meaning, failed to comprehend what might be the purport of the gestures she was making or what she meant by going through these rites of exorcism; so he kept still in his hiding-place and did not budge an inch. Meantime Cechato, being now half stifled and mightily weary of lying stretched out on the floor, was anxious to get up, and spake thus to Thia: 'Well, is it all over now?' But Thia, who had not been able to induce Marsilio to move from his place behind the door, answered Cechato in these words: 'Stay where you are, for heaven's sake, and move not at your peril. Did I not tell you that I should have to repeat the incantation three times? I hope you may not have wrecked everything, as it is, by wanting to get up.' 'No, no, surely not,' said Cechato. And Thia made him lie down stretched out as he was before, and began to chant her incantation anew.

Now by this time Marsilio had at last come to understand how matters really stood, and what was the meaning of Thia's mummery, so he seized the opportunity to slip out from his hiding-place, and to run away as fast as his legs could carry him. Thia, when she saw

Marsilio take to his heels and run out of the courtyard, finished her
form of exorcism against the kite, and when she had brought it to
an end she suffered her cuckoldly fool of a husband to get up from
the ground.   Then with Thia's help he began forthwith to unload
the flour which he had brought back from the mill.   Now Thia
when she went with Cechato outside into the courtyard to help
unload the flour, saw Marsilio in the distance hurrying away at
the top of his speed, whereupon she began to shout after him in
a lusty voice: 'Ah, ah! what a wicked bird! Ah, ah! begone, get
away!   For, by my faith, I will send you packing with your tail
between your legs if ever you show yourself here again.   Away
then, I tell you!   Is not he a greedy wretch?   Do you not see that
the wicked beast was bent on coming back?   Heaven give him a
bad year!'

And in this fashion it happened, that every time the kite came
and flew down into the courtyard to carry away a chick or two,
he would first have a bout with the hen herself,[1] who would afterwards set to work with her conjuration as before.   Then he would
take to flight with his tail down, but all the while the fowls be-
longing to Cechato and Thia suffered no damage at all from his
harrying.

This fable, given by the Trevisan, was found to be so mirthful
and amusing that the ladies, and the gentlemen as well, almost split
their sides with laughter; so well did he mock the rustic speech that
there was no one of the company who would not have judged him to
be a peasant of Treviso.   And when the merriment had abated
somewhat, the Signora turned her fair face towards the Trevisan and
spake to him thus: "In truth, Signor Benedetto, you have this
evening diverted us in such featly wise that with one voice we
declare your fable may deservedly be held to be the equal of Molino's
in merit.   But to fill up the measure of my content and that of this
honourable company, I entreat you—an it displease you not—that
you will set forth to us an enigma which shall be as graceful in form
as amusing in matter."   The Trevisan, when he saw how the Signora
was inclined, was unwilling to disappoint her; so, standing up, with a
clear voice and with no hesitation of any sort, he began his riddle in
the following words:

---

[1]   Orig., *in prima el se spellatava con la chiozza.*

Sir Yoke goes up and down the field,
To every tug is forced to yield.
One on the left, one on the right
Plods on, and next there comes a wight,
A cunning rascal who with power
Beats one who goes on carriers four.
Now if an answer you can give,
Good friends, we will for ever live.

When the Trevisan, with the true manner and bearing of a peasant, had finished his enigma, which was comprehended by few or none of the company, he thus gave the interpretation thereof in peasant dialect in order that its meaning might be made clear to them all: "I must not keep this gentle company waiting any longer. Tell me, do you understand the meaning of my enigma? If you do not know, I will tell you. Sir Yoke goes to and fro, that is to say, the yoke, to which the oxen are attached, goes up and down the fields and roads, and is dragged hither and thither by them. Those who fare, the one on this side and the other on that side of it, are the oxen. He who beats one who stands on four, means that the ploughman who walks behind lashes the bull, who has four legs, with his leathern whip. And to end my explanation, I tell you once more that the answer to my riddle is the yoke, and I hope you will all understand it."

Everyone was greatly interested over this riddle dealing with country life, and, laughing heartily thereat, they praised it highly. But the Trevisan, remembering that only one more story remained to be told this night, to wit, that of the charming Cateruzza, turned with a smiling face towards the Signora and spake thus: "Signora, it is not for the reason that I wish to disturb the settled order of this our entertainment, or to dictate to your highness, my mistress and sovereign lady, but merely to satisfy the desire of this devoted company, that I beg your excellency to make us the sharers of some fair fancies of your own, by telling us, for our delight and recreation, a story with your wonted grace. And if I peradventure have been more presumptuous (which God forbid) in making this request than is suitable to my humble estate, I beg you will forgive me, seeing that the love I bear towards this gracious assembly has been the chief cause why I have been led to prefer it."

The Signora, when she heard the courteous petition of the Trevisan, at first cast her eyes down upon the ground; not, however, for any fear or shame that she felt, but because she deemed that, for divers reasons, it was more seemly for her to listen than to discourse. But after a time, with a gracious and smiling look, as if her humour were a merry one, she turned her bright face towards the Trevisan and said : " Signor Benedetto, what though your request is a pleasant and seemly one, it appears to me that you are somewhat too insistent a beggar, forasmuch as the duty of story-telling pertains rather to these young damsels round about than to me ; therefore you must hold me excused if I decline to give way at once to your demand, and bid Cateruzza, who has been chosen by lot to tell the fifth story of this evening, to favour you with her discourse." The merry listeners, who were mightily eager to hear the Signora tell her story, forthwith all rose to their feet and began to support the request of the Trevisan, begging her most earnestly that she would in this matter favour them with her courtesy and kindness, and not stand too severely by the exalted dignity of her position, for time and place will allow anyone, however high in rank, to speak freely whatever thing may be pleasing. The Signora, when she heard the gentle loving terms of this petition, in order that she might not seem ungracious in her bearing, smilingly replied : " Since this is the wish of all of you, and your pleasure withal, that I should conclude this evening with some little story of my own, I will gladly grant your wish." And without further demur she blithely began to tell her fable.

THE FIFTH FABLE.

Madonna Modesta, wife of Messer Tristano Zanchetto, in her young days gathers together a great number of shoes, offerings made by her various lovers. Having grown old, she disposes of the same to divers servants, varlets, and other folk of mean estate.

IT commonly happens that ill-gotten wealth, and indeed all riches which have been acquired by evil ways, are scattered abroad and dissipated in brief space of time, for by the divine will it has been decreed that, quickly as such riches come, quickly they shall depart. This, indeed, proved to be the case with a certain woman of Pistoia, who, had she been honest and wise in the same degree as she was dissolute and foolish, would never have given occasion for the story which I am now about to tell to you. And although perhaps this fable of mine is one hardly suitable for your ears, forasmuch as it comes to an end in a picture of shame and dishonour, which obscures and tarnishes the fame of those who live honest lives, nevertheless I will not hesitate to relate it to you, for at the right time and place it may serve (I speak here to those to whom it may apply) as a useful incentive for all to pursue the ways of uprightness and well-doing, and to eschew all wicked courses and lewd inclinations.

I must first tell this worshipful company that, not far from these our days, there lived in Pistoia, an ancient city of Tuscany, a young woman called by name Madonna Modesta, but this name, on account of her reprehensible manner of life and the shameful courses she followed, was one in no wise befitting her. In person, indeed, this woman was very lovely and graceful, though she was of mean condition. She had a husband called Tristano Zanchetto[1] (a name as well suited to him as his wife's was unfitting to her), a good-tempered fellow, given to merry company, and thinking of little else save of his business of buying and selling, whereby he gained a good living for himself. Madonna Modesta, who was by nature of a lecherous temper, and inclined for nought else but amorous sport, when she saw that her husband was given up heart and soul to commerce, and careful only about the matters appertaining thereto, took it into her head that she too would embark in merchandise and set up a new trade, concerning which her husband, Messer Tristano, should know nothing.

Wherefore every day she was wont to go out upon the balcony for her amusement, now on one side, now on the other, and throw glances at any gallant who might be passing in the street, and when her eye might chance to fall upon anyone whose appearance pleased her, she would strive by divers suggestive signs and gestures to arouse his curiosity and desire, and to lure him to her. And in the course of time it proved that Madonna Modesta had no mean skill in the art of traffic; indeed, so diligent was she in the display of her merchandise, and so carefully did she attend to the needs of her customers, that there was to be found in all the city no one, rich or poor, noble or plebeian, who was not anxious to take and taste of her goods. When, therefore,

---

[1] *Zanchetto, zannetto,* a buffoon, a zany.

Madonna Modesta had attained a position of great notoriety in her calling, and had gathered together much wealth thereby, she made up her mind to exact only a very small guerdon from anyone who might come to her as a claimant for her favours. That is to say, she made it her custom to demand from her lovers no greater reward than a pair of shoes, stipulating, however, that each one should give shoes of a sort such as he might in an ordinary way wear himself. Thus, if the lover who had been with her happened to be a noble, she would expect from him a pair of velvet shoes; if a burgher, she would ask for a pair of shoes made of fine cloth; if a mechanic, a pair made of leather. So great a concourse of clients flocked to this good woman's place of business that it was rarely or never empty, and seeing that she was young and beautiful and of fine figure, seeing likewise that the price which she demanded for her favours was such a modest one, all the men of Pistoia freely repaired to her house and took their pleasure therein. At the time of which I am writing, Madonna Modesta had already filled a very large storehouse with shoes, the wealth she had gathered together in her tender amorous calling, and so mighty was the tale of shoes of every sort and quality, that if any man here in Venice had searched diligently every shop in the city he would not have found a third part of the number of shoes which Madonna Modesta had heaped up in her storehouse.

It happened one day that Messer Tristano her husband had need to use this same storehouse for the stowing away of certain chattels and merchandise which by chance had been consigned to him at the same time from divers parts of the world; so, having called Madonna Modesta his beloved wife, he asked her to hand over to him the keys of the warehouse. And she, like the crafty jade that she was, presented them to him without excuse of any sort; and the husband, when he opened the storehouse, which he expected would be empty, found it quite full of shoes (as has already been told) of divers qualities. When he saw this he was mightily astonished thereat, and could in no wise understand whence had come this great quantity of shoes of all sorts; so, having called his wife, he put a question to her as to where these shoes with which his warehouse was filled had come from. To this the astute Madonna Modesta answered in these words: 'What think you of this, good Messer Tristano my husband? Did you in sooth set yourself down as the only merchant in this city? Certes, if you did, you were hugely mistaken, for be sure that

we women likewise know somewhat concerning the art of traffic;
and, although you may be a great merchant, accustomed to concern
yourself with many and weighty ventures, I content myself with
commerce on a smaller scale. Wherefore I have stored my merchandise in this warehouse, and put it safely under lock and key
in order that it may be kept secure. So I beg you to keep your care
and watchfulness for the benefit of your own goods and your own
traffic, and I will do the same with regard to mine.' Messer Tristano,
who knew nothing more than what his wife told him, and asked no
further questions, was gratified amain with the exceeding ingenuity
and great foresight of his clever and far-seeing wife, and besought
her to prosecute with diligence the enterprise she had undertaken.
Madonna Modesta therefore continued in secret to carry on her
amorous trade, and, as in the exercise thereof she prospered mightily,
she gathered together so vast a store of shoes that she could have
easily supplied the wants not only of Pistoia, but of any other great
city as well.

Thus whilst Madonna Modesta remained young and full of grace
and beauty her trade showed no sign of falling off. But in the
process of years cruel Time, the master of all things and all men,
who fixes ever a beginning, a middle, and an end for all, so dealt with
Madonna Modesta, who had been heretofore fresh and plump and
lovely, that he changed the semblance of her face, and of her hair[1]
likewise—leaving her desire unsubdued the while—and traced many
wrinkles upon her forehead, and disfigured her countenance. Her
eyes became rheumy and her breasts all dry and empty as shrivelled
bladders, and whenever she happened to smile the skin of her face
became so puckered that anyone who looked at her was fain to laugh
and hold her in ridicule. And when the time came that Madonna
Modesta was grown old and grey-headed, and lovers no longer sought
her to pay court to her as formerly, she found that she added no more
shoes to her store, and she lamented bitterly in her heart thereanent.
From the first years of her youth until the present hour she had
given herself over entirely to the vice of luxury, the destructive enemy
of the body and of the purse as well, and she had likewise become
more accustomed to dainty living and libidinous life than any other

---

[1] Orig., *e mutò le usate penne*. The use of *penne* or *piume* for *capelli* is not
uncommon. Thus in Dante, "Che riavesse le maschile penne" (*Inferno*, xx.);
"Movendo quell' oneste piume" (*Purgatorio*, i.).

woman in the world, therefore she could find no method or means by which she might withdraw herself from these noxious ways.   And although in her body, from day to day, the vital fluid, through which all plants and living things take root and grow, failed more and more, nevertheless the desire of satisfying her wicked and unrestrained appetite was as violent as ever.   Therefore Madonna Modesta, seeing that she was entirely bereft of youthful beauty, and was no longer one to be flattered and caressed by handsome young gallants as in former days, made up her mind to order her plans anew.   For the furtherance of these she once more went out upon the balcony, and began to ogle and to spread her lures to catch any varlets or porters or peasants or chimney-sweepers or idle fellows of any sort, who might be passing by, and any of these whom she might attract she would entice into her house for her own purposes, and with them take such pleasure as she had hitherto been wont to take.   And as in times past she had always demanded from each one of her lovers a pair of shoes of a quality according with the donor's condition as the reward for her favours granted, now, on the other hand, she found herself obliged to give a pair of shoes from her stock to anyone who would come to her.   Madonna Modesta had now sunk into such a shameful state that all the lowest ruffians of Pistoia would betake themselves to her dwelling, some to have their pleasure of her, others to make mock of her and to befool her, and others to receive the disgraceful guerdon which she was wont to give.

In this manner of life pursued by Madonna Modesta, it came to pass that the storehouse, which had once been crammed full of shoes, became wellnigh void.   Messer Tristano one day, having a mind to go by stealth and see how his wife was prospering in her commerce, and whether her store of merchandise was increasing, took the key of the warehouse without his wife's knowledge and opened the door, only to find, when he looked in, that nearly all the shoes were gone.   Wherefore Messer Tristano was beyond measure amazed, for he could not understand how his wife could have disposed of the many pairs of shoes he had formerly seen there.   On this account he began to fancy that by this time his wife must, as it were, be made of gold by reason of her prosperous traffic, and he felt himself mightily consoled at the thought; for he deemed that he might hereafter be a sharer in her wealth.   So he straightway called her to him and thus addressed her : ' Modesta, I have always rated you as a wise and prudent woman, but this day I chanced to open your storehouse, wishing to see how your commerce was thriving, and deeming that by this time your stock of shoes must have greatly increased, but I found, instead of any increase, that your wares had nearly all disappeared. At first I was mightily astonished thereat, but afterwards it came into my mind that you must have trafficked them away and received therefor a great sum of money, whereupon I was greatly reassured, and if this notion of mine should prove to be correct I shall hold that you have traded at great profit.'

Madonna Modesta, when her husband had finished his speech, heaved a deep sigh and thus made answer to him : ' Messer Tristano, my husband, do not be amazed at what you have lately seen, for I must tell you that all those shoes you saw some long time ago in my warehouse, have walked away in the same fashion in which they came to me. And over and above this let me tell you that those things which are ill got will, for the most part, ill go in a very brief space of time. Therefore I bid you once more not to wonder or be surprised at what you have seen.' Messer Tristano, who did not in any way fathom the meaning of his wife's words, fell into a great state of fright and confusion, fearing hugely lest a similar mischance might befall the goods and merchandise he himself had collected. However, he forbore to discuss the matter with her farther, but bestirred himself anxiously to see that his own merchandise might not vanish as his wife's had vanished.

Madonna Modesta finding herself now slighted by men of all sorts and conditions, and entirely beggared of all the shoes she had gained in the course of her lecherous youth, fell into a grave malady, and in a very brief space of time died miserably of consumption. And in this manner Madonna Modesta, who took so little heed for the future, made a shameful end of her life and also of the possessions she had gathered together, leaving nothing behind her to serve as an example to the rest of the world, but rather a disgraceful memory.

When the Signora had ended her short fable all the company began to laugh aloud, and heaped abundant blame upon Madonna Modesta, who lived moderately enough in all things save only in the matter of lecherous indulgence. And again they could not help laughing when they recalled to mind the story of the shoes which were so easily got and so easily spent. But because it was on Cateruzza's account that the Trevisan had urged the Signora to tell this fable, the latter now began to spur on the damsel with words which, though gently spoken, had a sting therein, and afterwards, as a penalty for having failed to tell her fable, expressly commanded Cateruzza to propound an enigma which should not be irrelevant to the subject of the fable they had just heard. Whereupon Cateruzza, when she heard the command of the Signora, rose from her seat, and turning herself towards her spake thus: "Dear Signora, the biting rebukes which you have just addressed to me are not in any way displeasing to me; on the contrary, I gladly take them home to myself with my whole heart. But the task of making my enigma agree in some measure with the fable you have just told us is no light one, seeing that I am entirely unprepared. Since, however, it pleases you to punish in this fashion my fault, if indeed it be a fault, I, as an obedient girl and your most complaisant handmaiden, will begin at once.

> My lady seats her in a chair,
> And raises then her skirt with care;
> And as I know she waits for me,
> I bring her what she fain would see.
> Then soft I lift her dainty leg,
> Whereon she cries, 'Hold, hold, I beg!
> It is too strait, and eke too small;
> Be gentle, or you'll ruin all.'
> And so to give her smallest pain,
> I try once more, and eke again."

The enigma told by Cateruzza provoked as great laughter as the ingenious fable which the Signora had recently given; but, for the reason that certain of the listeners put thereupon a somewhat lewd interpretation, she set herself at once to make the honesty of her intent clear to them in as civil terms as she could use: "Noble ladies, the real subject of my enigma is nothing greater or less than a tight shoe; for when the lady has sat down, the shoemaker, with the shoe in his hand, raises her foot, whereupon she tells him to put the shoe on gently, as it is too tight, and causes her much pain. Then he takes it off and puts it on again and again till it fits her well, and she is content therewith."

When the explication of Cateruzza's enigma had been brought to an end and highly praised by the whole company, the Signora, seeing that the hour was now late, gave order that under pain of her displeasure no one should leave the place, and, having bidden them

summon into her presence the trusty steward of the household, she
directed him to set out the tables in the great hall.   And while the
feast was in course of preparation she proposed that the ladies and
gentlemen should divert themselves with the dance, and, after the
dancing was finished, they sang two songs.   Then the Signora rose to
her feet and went into the supper room, having the Signor Ambassador
on one hand and Messer Pietro Bembo on the other, the rest of the
company following in their due order.   And when they had all washed
their hands, each one sat down according to his rank at the table,
which was richly spread with rare and delicate dishes and new wines.
When this merry feast had come to end amidst the loving discourse
of the guests, each one being in blither mood than ever, they rose
from the board and forthwith began to sing and dance in a circle.
But forasmuch as the rosy light of dawn was now beginning to appear,
the Signora bade the servants to kindle the torches and go in attendance on the Signor Ambassador as far as the steps, having first begged
him and all the others to return to the meeting-place at the appointed
hour.

The End of the Fifth Night.

Lightning Source UK Ltd.
Milton Keynes UK
UKHW030952061021
391759UK00006B/305